The Gospel of
JOHN MARRANT

Religious Cultures of African and African Diaspora People

SERIES EDITORS:
Jacob K. Olupona, Harvard University   Dianne M. Stewart, Emory University
and Terrence L. Johnson, Georgetown University

The book series examines the religious, cultural, and political expressions of African, African American, and African Caribbean traditions. Through transnational, cross-cultural, and multidisciplinary approaches to the study of religion, the series investigates the epistemic boundaries of continental and diasporic religious practices and thought and explores the diverse and distinct ways African-derived religions inform culture and politics. The series aims to establish a forum for imagining the centrality of Black religions in the formation of the "New World."

The Gospel of
JOHN MARRANT

*Conjuring Christianity
in the Black Atlantic*

ALPHONSO F. SAVILLE IV

Duke University Press
Durham and London
2024

Project Editor: Livia Tenzer
Designed by Courtney Leigh Richardson
Typeset in Garamond Premier Pro by Westchester Publishing Services

Library of Congress Cataloging-in-Publication Data
Names: Saville, Alphonso F., IV (Alphonso Ferdinand), [date] author.
Title: The gospel of John Marrant : conjuring Christianity in the Black
Atlantic / Alphonso F. Saville, IV.
Other titles: Religious cultures of African and African diaspora people.
Description: Durham : Duke University Press, 2024. | Series: Religious cultures
of African and African diaspora people | Includes bibliographical references
and index.
Identifiers: LCCN 2023052348 (print)
LCCN 2023052349 (ebook)
ISBN 9781478030447 (paperback)
ISBN 9781478026211 (hardcover)
ISBN 9781478059424 (ebook)
Subjects: LCSH: Marrant, John, 1755–1791. | Bible—Black interpretations. |
African American clergy. | African Americans—Religion. | Christianity—
African influences. | Religion and culture—United States. | Magic—Religious
aspects—Christianity—History of doctrines. | BISAC: SOCIAL SCIENCE /
Ethnic Studies / American / African American & Black Studies | HISTORY /
African American & Black
Classification: LCC BR563.B53 S28 2024 (print) | LCC BR563.B53 (ebook) |
DDC 287.092 [B]—dc23/eng/20240416
LC record available at https://lccn.loc.gov/2023052348
LC ebook record available at https://lccn.loc.gov/2023052349

COVER ART: John Marrant. Yarmouth: D. Boulter, 1795.

For Buddy and Pat

Contents

Acknowledgments

The completion of this book would not have been possible without the support and guidance of intellectual and spiritual communities of colleagues, family, and friends. I am grateful to God for the gift of life. I am grateful to the divine community of ancestors that has attended and sustained me during the long process of research and writing. I hope that this effort honors the Saville and Heard legacies from which I am proudly descended.

I have been fortunate to receive generous support from a number of institutional partners. Financial support from the Mellon Foundation, the Luce Foundation, Dartmouth College, Georgetown University, and the Crossroads Project, under the auspices of the Center for Culture, Society, and Religion at Princeton University, has enabled not only the completion of this manuscript but also growth and professional development critical to my career as a scholar and public intellectual. I am especially grateful to Derrick White, Dia Draper, Michael Chaney, and Gretchen Gerzina for feedback and support during the early stages of research at Dartmouth. At Georgetown, I received generous support from Darryl Chisholm, Joe Ferrara and the Office of the President, and Carol Sargeant and the Office of Scholarly Publications. At Princeton, Judith Weisenfeld, Seth Perry, Wallace Best, and members of the Religion in America program provided valuable feedback on various drafts of the manuscript; I am greatly indebted to you all. I received much needed support from church communities as well. I would like to extend my most sincere thanks to the Reverend Dr. Asa Lee and Pastor James Victor of Mount Olive Baptist Church in Arlington, Virginia, and to Pastor Eugene Johnson of Mount Olive Baptist Church in Centreville, Virginia, for extending opportunities to explore topics related to this research with their respective congregations.

Additionally, I would like to thank the community of mentors and colleagues at Emory University who have provided critical feedback, words of encouragement, and valuable insight over the course of this project. Members of the faculty at Emory—Dianne Stewart, Gary Laderman, Theophus Smith, Mark Sanders, and Tracey Hucks—provided invaluable feedback that helped the project take shape from an early stage. I am also grateful to my colleagues in the Graduate Division of Religion—Alexis Wells-Oghoghomeh, Melva Sampson, Shively Smith, Jamil Drake, Mark Andrews, Diana Louis, Asha French, and Meredith Tobias-Coleman—for countless conversations, words of encouragement, and general collegiality. Your support was more valuable than you know.

Finally, I wish to express my most sincere appreciation to my family for their unwavering support throughout this long and often difficult process. To my parents, Alphonso and Patricia Saville, thank you for constant support. From my earliest days at Snowden Elementary until now, you have been there to remind me that I can accomplish whatever I can conceive—thank you. To my aunts Julie Saville and Nan Alice Saville Fifier, I am so appreciative of every sacrifice that you made to invest in my future. Thank you for the models of academic, creative, and professional excellence over the course of your respective careers in academia. I hope this work makes you proud.

To my daughter, Angela (who published her first story before I could finish mine), I am so proud of you and amazed by all of your early accomplishments. I look forward to reading, hearing, and seeing your work in the near future. To Jasmin, my wife, my partner in life, my friend, you have been my biggest supporter since we met. You have believed in this project, and in me, when I did not. My gratitude goes beyond words. I love you. Thank you.

Introduction

In roughly 1770, John Marrant rose from the dead. As he explained in his autobiographical narrative of 1785, he returned to his family in Charleston, South Carolina, following a nearly two-year absence in which he joined and evangelized several Native American communities in the Georgia and South Carolina low country. Several years before the earliest Black congregations—Silver Bluff Baptist (1775) in South Carolina and First African Baptist (1777) in Savannah—were organized by George Leile and George Galphin, respectively, Marrant's vision for his ministry was coming into clearer view. Like Moses, who returned from the wilderness of Midian to lead Israel to freedom after a forty-year absence, he quickly organized a small congregation of enslaved people on the Jenkins plantation in Combahee, South Carolina, and led them to the wilderness for religious instruction. His account of his brush arbor Bible study is one of the earliest depictions of what Albert Raboteau called the "invisible institution" in American literature.[1]

By the last decade of the eighteenth century, Marrant stood at the helm of one of the earliest postslavery Black Christian communities in American history. Prior to the formation of the Bethel African Methodist Episcopal Church (1794) in Philadelphia by Richard Allen, Marrant pastored Black Loyalists in Nova Scotia in the Huntingdon Connexion, a Calvinist branch of Methodism founded by Selina Hastings outside London. Marrant's account of his ministry in Nova Scotia reveals important details about the early formation of Black autonomous Christian communities. *The Gospel of John Marrant* studies the life and writings of North America's first Black ordained minister and the religious worlds he reflected and created through his texts.[2]

Given his widespread travels and fascinating career as an author and minister, it is surprising that John Marrant has not been more widely studied by scholars of American religion. The religious texts he produced allow scholars to see the multiple and diverse religious cultures that contributed to the formation of African American Christianity in the latter half of the eighteenth century. Born in New York in 1755, Marrant encountered multiple religious communities throughout the North American Atlantic Seaboard. At age four, he moved to St. Augustine, Florida, where he lived within the sphere of Afro-Catholic religious influence. Years later in Savannah, he observed an influx of Africana religious cultures, as the Georgia colony saw unprecedented growth in slave importations during the years of Marrant's residency. As an adolescent in Charleston, he witnessed the preaching of renowned Methodist minister George Whitefield and took part in the rituals of American revivalism. Later, he resided with a community of Cherokee for two years in Georgia and returned to Carolina as an exhorter to enslaved persons in Charleston and surrounding plantations. At the siege of Charleston during the American War of Independence, he was impressed into British military service and remained at sea seven years before his discharge. Following the war, he was ordained in the Huntingdon Methodist Connexion, in Bath, England. That same year he journeyed to Nova Scotia as an itinerant preacher to a community of Black Loyalists in Birchtown. After three years there, he went to Boston, where he was quickly acquainted with the prominent abolitionist and Masonic leader Prince Hall. Hall installed Marrant as chaplain of the African Lodge of Free and Accepted Masons in Boston, making him the first person appointed to that position. He returned to London in 1790 and, after a short illness, died the following year. The story of his brief but adventurous life enables readers to witness the transformation of African American Christianity from the backwoods religion of enslaved people in South Carolina to the institutional face of the abolitionist movement in the years of the early republic.

Marrant's Texts

Marrant's gospel message is announced in his two autobiographical texts, *A Narrative of the Lord's Wonderful Dealings with John Marrant, a Black (Now Going to Preach the Gospel in Nova Scotia)*, an account of his early life before the War of Independence, and *A Journal of the Rev. John Marrant from August the 18th, 1785, to the 16th of March, 1790*, a travel book that recounts his ministry to Black Loyalists in Nova Scotia. The *Journal* also includes *A Sermon Preached on the 24th Day of June 1789*, which Marrant delivered in Boston at the Masonic festival of Saint John the Baptist.[3] *The Gospel of John Marrant: Conjuring Christianity in the Black Atlantic* closely analyzes Marrant's texts to demonstrate how West and West Central African religious and cultural themes, symbols, and cosmologies informed biblical interpretation, ritual culture, and communal formation in early Black North American Christian communities. My analysis of Marrant's use of biblical narrative forms alongside African, African diaspora, and Native American beliefs and practices offers new perspectives on eighteenth-century Black religious sensibilities in transatlantic worlds of encounter and transformation. Marrant's texts illuminate the multiplicity of spiritual sensibilities, identities, and cultural sources inhabiting the ritual and social worlds of African diaspora peoples in the colonial period.

The present study analyzes *A Narrative of the Lord's Wonderful Dealings with John Marrant*, Marrant's first autobiographical text. *Narrative* was first published in 1785 following Marrant's ordination at Spa Fields Chapel in Bath, England, and went through several editions of publication well into the nineteenth century, extending the span of its public life beyond that of its author. Marrant narrates his early childhood in New York and St. Augustine and his adolescence in Savannah and Charleston, his captivity among Creek Indians, and impressment in the British navy and subsequent discharge in England—all leading to his ordination in May 1785. *Narrative* not only recounts Marrant's early life but also provides important first-person commentary on Black social life in colonial America. It gives eyewitness accounts of early Black Christian ritual culture, Black and Native American cultural exchange, and the use of religion as a curative tool against racial violence.

This study examines the fourth edition of Marrant's *Narrative*, which he arranged, authorized, and published himself in August 1785. That edition includes a description of an enslaved community's violent confrontation with a slave owner and overseer and also places Native American plantation raids within the context of colonial displacement. None of the other versions of *Narrative* includes these mysterious passages, which are analyzed in detail in chapter 3. The fourth edition is reprinted in Joanna Brooks and John Saillant's *"Face Zion Forward"* (2002), the only complete collection of Marrant's works.[4] A physical copy of the text is located at the Harry Ransom Humanities Research Center at the University of Texas at Austin.

This study also analyzes *A Journal of the Rev. John Marrant*, Marrant's second autobiographical text, which depicts his ministry in Nova Scotia and describes early formations of institutional Black Christianity. *Journal*, published by Marrant in 1790 on his return to London just one year before he died, is the most extensive account published by a Black minister prior to the Civil War. The original publication included a copy of Marrant's eulogy of Mr. John Lock, his friend and a fellow resident of Nova Scotia. The text was republished for the first time since its original printing in Brooks and Saillant's volume. A physical copy of *Journal* is held at Pennsylvania State University.

Conjuring Christianity

Marrant's autobiographical accounts also help uncover the role of conjure in the formation of early African American Christianity. In his seminal work *Conjuring Culture: Biblical Formations of Black America* (1994), the religious studies scholar Theophus Smith argues for the centrality of conjure in Black spirituality and culture. During the colonial period and the years of the early republic, Africana religious culture was vital to the social formation of early Black North Americans. Conjure, on the one hand, describes the Black folk magic tradition in which practitioners utilize complex invocations of powers and processes intended to heal and harm others. It is this feature, notes Smith, that distinguishes African American conjure traditions from European counterparts that tend to associate conjure more narrowly with witchcraft and occultism. In addition to folklore practices, conjure also encompasses ritual performance intended to transform material realities of history. I examine the religious writings of John Marrant to demonstrate how early Black Christians utilized the Bible as a conjure book. In the religious imagination of early Black Christians, the Bible prescribed "ritually patterned behaviors and performative uses of language and symbols" to convey "a pharmacopeic or healing/harming intent." Additionally, early Black Christians redeployed the narrative tropes of "biblical figures" to render "biblical configurations of cultural experience."[5] In many Black Christian communities, conjure was the operative framework through which practitioners related to the unseen powers of the spirit world. Marrant's writings demonstrate how conjuring Christian communities utilized the Bible as the source of ritual and oral prescriptions intended to transform and remedy systemic and interpersonal oppression produced by racial slavery and social proscription.

Conjure also helps to unlock hidden meanings embedded in Marrant's texts conveyed via allusions to biblical narratives, symbols, and scriptures. As Brooks and Saillant note in their introduction to their complete collection of his works, Marrant's texts are "more than a missionary's autobiography." "Behind the traditional genre," they note, "lurks a hidden transcript" encoded in "numerous biblical citations" throughout the texts. Marrant's allusion, rather than direct reference, to biblical texts aimed to "disguise the specifically black content of his preaching from the Huntingdon Connexion and other potentially hostile or dangerous readers."[6] The message revealed in the hidden transcript of his texts discloses a religious outlook that esteems social action integral to religious devotion for Black communities of faith. Additionally, it uncovers the centrality of Africana ritual traditions in the religious repertoire of early Black North American Christian communities. My analysis utilizes conjure to decode the "hidden transcript" lurking beneath the surface of Marrant's texts and to analyze his use of conjure, or the "specifically black content" of his preaching, which he sought to disguise.

The centrality of conjure in Marrant's texts is most observable in the West and West Central African oral cultures that precede the formation of African American literature. The oral legacies of African cosmology narratives and African American folktales are the narrative precursors to the Black Atlantic literary tradition founded and developed by Marrant and his contemporaries. Both oral and literary traditions of Black storytelling evince spiritual strategies and methods that resist injustice and counter racism. The Black storytelling tradition is a repository of spirituality that offers unique insight into not only the virtues of Black collective consciousness but also the vices of the dominant culture's social world. Oral legacy is indispensable to understanding Black literature.[7] In Black oral traditions, spirituality is embodied within the structures, symbols, and forms that determine the rules for interpretation.

Although the Bible was the primary source on which Marrant's autobiographical texts were based, his redeployment of biblical symbols and structures evinces an Africana cultural strategy for communicating religious meaning. Like many early Black American spiritual narratives, his texts maintain a fundamental plot structure based on stories from the Bible. Within this mythic narrative pattern, an idyllic beginning is disrupted by tragedy; protagonists undergo spiritual transformation (often in a wilderness setting); this is followed by divine intervention and deliverance to a land of promise that completes the arc of tranquility from the story's beginning. This pattern, along with corresponding symbols that signal spiritual transformation, is consistently observed throughout the Old and New Testaments, as well as in early Black American literature. John Marrant relies on this same narrative pattern and includes many of the symbols that signify the various stages of development in the biblical saga in his own self-portrayal. However, his understanding of the Bible's stories draws on the interpretive principles of African storytelling rather than the doctrines of Euro-American Protestantism.

Black narrators like Marrant mimicked the Bible's storytelling structures in their narratives and adapted details like settings and characters to their own historical contexts. In the nineteenth-century genre of slave narratives, mythological patterns were realized in four chronological phases. In the first phase, the enslaved protagonist experiences a "descent from perfection" that brings the realization of "what it means to be a slave." In the second phase, the protagonist learns and considers alternatives to enslavement and ultimately formulates the resolve to be free. "The resolution to quit slavery," notes the literary scholar Frances Smith Foster, "is, in effect, a climax to a conversion experience." In the third phase, the protagonist narrates their escape—allegorizing the struggle to overcome evil. Though the journey may be encumbered with perils and dangers, "the outcome is never in doubt," since "the narrative, after all, was written by a freeman." In the fourth phase, freedom is attained, signifying a new beginning and "the jubilation period of ancient ritual."[8]

The imitation of the Bible's narrative patterns and symbols in early Black narratives demonstrates the mimetic principle of conjure within Black Atlantic religious consciousness. Within the cultural framework of West African conjure, mimesis played an integral role in the efficacy of ritual performance. Mimesis consists in first discerning and then performing a series of patterned operations based on an inferred relationship between one or more things. Perceived similarities based on appearance, function, or prior experience determined how practitioners devised "effective means of turning to human advantage the perceived similarity or habitual proximity of the two objects."[9] The mimetic performance of the Bible's narrative structures and symbols helped early Black Christians establish Africana rituals and practices that enabled the development of collective identities and cohesive communities. While early Black American authors utilized biblical imagery and symbolism, the rules that governed the meanings assigned to biblical tropes reflected West and West Central African epistemologies. Early Black Christians perceived similarities between the Bible's stories, symbols, and narrative structures and broad, expansive notions of Africana religion that were critical to the formation of Black racial identity. Consequently, the meanings assigned to the Bible's stories—and, by extension, to Black Christianity—diverge sharply from those of Euro-American Christians. I argue that Africana religious rituals and cosmologies, more than the doctrines of mainstream American Protestantism, gave rise to the development of Black Christianity during the early republic. Conjuring Christianity refers to a process by which early Black Christians utilized biblical storytelling to establish (and in many cases disguise) rituals, practices, and meanings associated with and derived from traditional Africana religious cultures.

The autobiographical narratives published by Marrant and his contemporaries also reveal moral and ethical norms that enabled the formation of Black Christian communities. Within the Africana oral cultures that preceded eighteenth-century African American formal literature, storytelling was a didactic tool that safeguarded rituals and customs of the African past in the collective memory of Black New World communities. Historical memory was preserved in folklore and family legends passed on from one generation to the next. For early Black North Americans, these family narratives often recalled days on the African continent, stories of capture and transport across the Atlantic Ocean to the New World, and stories of the American Revolutionary War. Increasingly, however, the focus of their stories reflected less of their previous lives in Africa and more of their New World circumstances. The embellished anecdotes shared among enslaved and free Blacks recounted the realities of their lived experience: religious meetings and festive celebrations, whippings and punishments, and stories of those who resisted by escaping or directly confronting the limitations of enslavement.[10]

Additionally, the stories included codes for moral behavior. Some espoused overtly religious virtues such as humility and Sabbath observance. The majority, however, focused on everyday human relationships. The importance of family ties, children's responsibility to parents, obligations to friendship, courting and marriage, and the necessity of parental love and care were frequently touched on in the oral narratives that early Black Americans exchanged with one another. Collectively, these stories helped to solidify kinship groups, fortify communal identities, and preserve cultural memories in the collective consciousness of African diaspora religious communities, all important to sustaining the inner resolve necessary to resist myths of Black inferiority.[11] I analyze how John Marrant conjures biblical narrative forms to depict the centrality of Africana communal values such as intergenerational wellness and the relationship between social and bodily illness.

Conjure also renders ritual aspects of Masonic oratory within African American Freemasonry more intelligible. As Theophus Smith explains, three variants of the Greek word *pharmakon* form the theoretical basis for understanding conjure rituals in Black religion. The first variant, *pharmakos*, refers to the conjure client or victim; the second variant, *pharmakon*, refers to curative and toxic conjure prescriptions; and the third variant, *pharmakeus*, refers to the conjure practitioner. Smith notes that variants are not always distinct and can coincide in the same person or object. "It is notable, in this regard," writes Smith, "that the pharmakos (victim) and pharmakeus (practitioner) may coincide in the same person in those cases where the practitioner is also a target of malign phenomena requiring conjurational transformation. Notable as well is the coincidence of the pharmakos (victim) as an embodied pharmakon (tonic/toxin)."[12] John Marrant's *Sermon* exhibits how the three variants of Black conjurational performance are deployed as rituals of race. As one of the earliest public orators in the history of African American Freemasonry, Marrant conjures a vision for a new social order as a practitioner (*pharmakeus*) of Masonic rhetorical ritual. Because he is a member of a victimized social group, he is also a client (*pharmakos*) seeking the transformation brought about by conjurational performance. *Sermon* itself prescribes the foundational principles and teachings of the Craft as the tonic (*pharmakon*) that cures American society by revising the perception of Black humanity. Marrant's Masonic oratory is a ritual of race that demonstrates how conjurational performance is operative in the religious consciousness of early African American Freemasons.

This study of John Marrant's life and writings aims to complicate oversimplified understandings of Black religion and rhetoric in colonial America. It examines the underlying meanings of this public Christian performance by employing conjure theory to make salient the radical dimensions of Marrant's political rhetoric and organizing efforts. These aspects of Marrant's ministry stem from his reevaluation of Christian orthodoxy in light of the immediate needs of his Black fellows, his efforts to institutionalize Black culture in transnational religious organizations, and his recognition of African-descended people's divinely ordered, collective purpose and identity in the transatlantic world. Black evangelicalism, or the appropriation of Christian identity, was not simple acquiescence to the norms and values of the dominant society. Rather, Marrant and other Black evangelicals fashioned a religious outlook uniquely suited for their particular experience. The needs of the African American community, more so than the orthodox doctrines of European and American Protestantism, determined the practices of Marrant's Christian communities. Thus, Black evangelicalism in the eighteenth-century African diaspora was not mere Christianity; instead, it represented a pragmatic, multicultural and spiritually diverse endeavor primarily intended to reformulate Black humanity via religious institutions that functioned autonomously.[13] Marrant and other spokespersons within this tradition established distinct, authoritative perspectives on issues related to collective identity, religious liberty, and political sovereignty within expansive New World discourses. Throughout the Atlantic world, African-descended people employed Christian rhetoric and symbols to articulate a vision of collective identity and destiny, and a desire for self-determination that countered notions of Black inferiority.[14] In the process, spokespersons like Marrant helped shape a unique religious voice that challenged prevailing notions regarding the presumed irreconcilability of Christian identity and Black humanity.

Chapter Outlines

Chapter 1 explores John Marrant's early childhood and reconstructs the religious and cultural worlds he encountered in New York, St. Augustine, and Savannah. I analyze the formation of brotherhood societies in colonial New York. Afro-Iberian fraternal societies fostered unity, collective identity, and aid to community members in need. The New York colonial cultural environment also included Pinkster celebrations, a spring religious festival that combined African and Dutch Protestant cultural elements. In St. Augustine, African, European, and Native American cultural sources existed within complex networks of exchange between Spanish settlers and African slaves that enabled the formation of new societies. Afro-Catholic communities such as Fort Mose, an all-Black settlement two miles north of St. Augustine, existed alongside maroon communities formed by escaped African slaves who joined with Seminole and other Native American groups. In Savannah, vibrant Africana religious culture could be attributed to an influx of enslaved laborers in Yamacraw, a multiracial neighborhood on the west side of town and home to a substantial free Black community of market women, seamen, and fugitive slaves. In each locale, Africana ritual traditions and cultural norms enabled Black communities to establish New World collective identities. Marrant's formation in these contexts of vibrant Africana religious culture shaped his adoption of Christianity and the development of his ministry in his adolescent and adulthood years.

Chapter 2 analyzes Marrant's depiction of his call and initiation into prophetic ministry in *Narrative*. His portrayal of his call to ministry in the Georgia and South Carolina low country mimics phases of West African–based initiation rites that marked the transition from adolescence to adulthood. Phases of West and West Central African initiatory rituals—call, wilderness seclusion, instruction from tutors or guides, physical impression, and communal reintegration, or covenant—represent a general model of initiation and provide the organizational structure for Marrant's autobiographical tale.[15] Structural elements of Marrant's call story are also reproduced in the autobiographical narratives of Olaudah Equiano and Ukawsaw Gronniosaw, contemporary Black Atlantic writers whose texts help illuminate the religious and literary world of ideas in which Marrant's consciousness took shape. Gronniosaw's *A Narrative of the Most Remarkable Particulars* was published in 1772 just after slavery was legally ended in England. The publication of his story, which detailed his birth and early life in Africa before he was lured into transatlantic slavery, had been made possible by the patronage of Selina Hastings, the Countess of Huntingdon. Her support enabled Black Atlantic authors like Phillis Wheatley and Marrant to find their voice in a British environment more receptive to Black writers than in North America. Hastings supported the publication of Equiano's *Interesting Narrative* in 1789, and through her support, Equiano emerged as one of the leading voices in the Atlantic world's fledgling abolitionist movement at the dawn of the nineteenth century. Each of these Black Atlantic writers deploys religious vocabulary and biblical symbolism to catalyze social change for Black communities. Throughout Marrant's *Narrative*, he adapts the stories of numerous biblical figures to dramatize the process by which he comes to understand his prophetic identity. By narrating his call to ministry according to the pattern of African initiation, Marrant reveals that ritual and structural, rather than theological, modes of analysis informed his understanding of biblical Christianity.

Chapter 3 focuses on Marrant's depiction of his confrontation with slave owners on the Jenkins plantation described at the book's opening. Near the conclusion of *Narrative*, Marrant conjures the Exodus story to denounce American slavery. His redeployment of that story utilizes symbols—blood and wilderness—to depict a narrative pattern of retaliation. The retaliation narrative, which appears only in the fourth edition of *Narrative*, represents his most dramatic example of biblical conjure. This symbolic pattern of retaliation is also identified in the respective narratives of Nat Turner and Frederick Douglass. In each case, the author's use of the symbols of wilderness and blood signify ritualized prophetic initiation and subsequent direct confrontation with oppressive rulers. Taken together, these symbols, read within narrative structures derived from traditional Africana storytelling cultures, reveal retribution tales for injuries suffered at the hands of enslavers.

While this study utilizes conjure to interpret Marrant's texts, it is important to note that Marrant likely would have eschewed conjure as a religious practice. Eurocentric associations of conjure solely with witchcraft led many Black Christians to distance themselves from any depiction as conjurors. Both Nat Turner and Frederick Douglass explicitly expressed their disdain and distrust for the practice of conjure. Turner notes that the influence he exerted over the minds of fellow slaves was owed to his possession of spiritual and intellectual gifts, and not "by conjuring and such like tricks," adding that he "always spoke of such things with contempt."[16] Similarly, Douglass reluctantly accepted a protective herb from Sandy Jenkins, an older adviser who insisted the root contained properties that could protect its carrier from racial violence. Despite both narrators' stated distrust of conjure, the autobiographical depictions utilize biblical figures to allegorize supernatural retaliation according to the narrative patterns of Bible stories and African retaliation narratives.

Chapter 4 analyzes Marrant's ministry in Nova Scotia as an ordained minister of the Huntingdon Connexion, an offshoot branch of the Methodist Church founded by the Countess of Huntingdon, Selina Hastings. The Huntingdon Connexion emerged in the tumultuous eighteenth century amid the upheaval of religious institutions and ideologies, when doctrines regarding creation and the nature of God were hotly debated throughout England. Hastings had been persuaded to adopt George Whitefield's Calvinistic approach to Christianity, and in the latter half of the century, she began to build her society through networks of individual ministers and chapels that were dependent on her patronage. For many Black settlers in Nova Scotia, the formation of Christian congregations aided their quest for religious and political autonomy. Black Christian congregations led by the Methodist ministers Boston King and David Wilkerson, alongside the Baptist preacher David George, deployed Africana rituals to establish autonomy, combat hardship and material lack, and challenge racial hierarchies. In *Journal*, Marrant's appropriation of biblical symbols and narrative structures to his own autobiographical context discloses how Africana ritual cultures and ways of knowing enabled the formation of autonomous Black Christian communities.

Chapter 5 analyzes Marrant's generative impact on ritual oration and notions of Black social organization within African American Freemasonry. In Boston, Marrant was appointed to the chaplaincy at the African Lodge of Free and Accepted Masons by Prince Hall, the leading founder of the African Lodge. The chapter examines Marrant's generative role in the early history of African American Freemasonry and argues for a more expansive understanding of the temporal and geographic origins of the tradition. The expansive temporal and geographic reach of European Freemasonry throughout the Atlantic world underscores that multiple individual and cultural sources can be credited with generative contributions to the origins of African American Freemasonry. Ritual similarities and multiple points of correspondence—including extreme secrecy and ritual progressions by degrees—point to West African initiation societies as institutional predecessors to African American Freemasonry. I also analyze Marrant's *Sermon* at the Saint John the Baptist celebration in 1789, his most enduring contribution to the legacy of African American Freemasonry. *Sermon* was addended to Marrant's *Journal* and introduced Black Freemasonry to transatlantic print culture. In *Sermon*, Marrant conjures biblical genealogies to mythologize Black racial ethnogenesis and establishes the foundations of an enduring template for African American male identity formation. *Sermon* inaugurates a tradition of Masonic oration succeeded by grand masters and lodge leaders in subsequent years. In the chapter's final section, I provide an overview of the lives and contributions of Prince Hall, David Walker, and Lewis Hayden—important Masonic leaders who expanded oratorical and rhetorical foundations laid by Marrant.

John Marrant's navigation of transatlantic geographies, cultures, and institutions reflects the voluntary and forced movements that characterized the experience of many African-descended people in the eighteenth-century transatlantic world. The circulation of bodies and ideas throughout Africa, the Caribbean, South America, North America, and Europe necessitates the consideration of transnational phenomena for scholars of eighteenth-century Black religion. However, much of the religious studies scholarship isolates African-descended people in the British North American colonies from the broader Africana world. By employing a transnational lens to the study of John Marrant's life, *The Gospel of John Marrant* complicates simplistic portrayals of Black Atlantic religion by giving critical attention to the role of African-inspired religious cultures in the development of Black religion in North America. Additionally, the utilization of conjure to interpret Marrant's texts proposes to elucidate hitherto understudied dimensions of his religious consciousness. As a result, *The Gospel of John Marrant* yields new conceptual categories and interpretive possibilities for phenomena within Black Atlantic religious experience.

1. "No Continuing City"

Colonial Black Religion during Marrant's Early Life

⫙

Apart from their proper context, stories can be difficult to interpret. The art of storytelling demands that storytellers provide context so that the unfolding of events can be understood. Critical details like the time and place in which stories happen greatly determine meaning. The historical and cultural settings in which they occur help explain the relationships between characters and the motivations that influence their actions.

John Marrant was born in New York in the late spring of 1755. He does not provide significant details about his background. His recollection of early childhood is scant—a mere four sentences—but the importance of this intro-ductory material should not be overlooked. Marrant's early childhood has not factored into scholarly analyses of his texts or religious outlook; nevertheless, the vibrant Africana religious cultures he encountered during his childhood in

New York, St. Augustine, Savannah, and Charleston established patterns of ritual performance and hermeneutical orientations that informed his practice of ministry. It is worth noting that each of these colonial urban centers had substantial native African populations. While Marrant's encounter with Methodist minister George Whitefield has factored centrally in shaping understandings of his religious identity, the impact of his residency in colonial urban centers with dense populations of African-born slaves and free Blacks must also be considered. His father passed away when John was "little more than four years of age," and by the time John was five, he had moved to North America's oldest European city, St. Augustine. But after just eighteen months in Florida, the family moved again—this time to Savannah, where they remained for several years. There, Marrant attended school and learned to read and write. When he turned eleven, they "left Georgia, and went to Charles Town." "The Lord spoke to me in my early days, by these removes, if I could have understood him," Marrant recounted, "and said, 'Here we have no continuing city.'"[1]

This brief account of Marrant's early years provides a framework for understanding the rest of his life's story. For his first eleven years, instability, rootlessness, and wandering—themes that would recur throughout his writings and inform his ministry—categorized his, and the wider Black community's, existence. His continual movement between the urban centers of the eastern Atlantic coast allegorized Black people's historical experience in colonial North America. Themes relating to voluntary and involuntary movement would continue to signify important meanings in the religious lives of Black Americans of the colonial period. Rather than mere chance or happenstance, for Marrant, "these removes" conveyed religious meaning—"Here we have no continuing city." In his partial quotation of Hebrews 13:14, "here" signifies the geographic rootlessness and political exclusion that contextualized the collective experience in colonial America.[2] However, the omitted portion of the verse—"but we seek one to come"—assigns purpose to Black people's otherwise meaningless wandering. In Marrant's view, their involuntary and chaotic movement signaled divine purpose—they were pilgrims in search of a city that was to come. Marrant's ministry would aim to establish a "continuing city" in which Black communities could thrive in religious and political autonomy. In this way, he utilizes silence to conjure meaning from scripture.[3]

The silences in Marrant's texts regarding his early childhood also convey important meanings that enable readers to better understand his subsequent religious development. He states in the opening sentence of his autobiographical *Narrative*, "I, John Marrant, born June 15, 1755, in New York, in North-America."[4] In the next four sentences, he quickly summarizes more than a decade of his early life, a span in which he lived with family members in New York, St. Augustine, Savannah, and Charleston. This chapter explores the silences in John Marrant's texts regarding his early childhood and reconstructs the religious and cultural worlds he encountered in New York, St. Augustine, and Savannah. In each of these early colonial urban centers, free and enslaved Black communities nurtured rich Africana religious cultures that spawned worlds of symbols, cosmologies, institutions, and rituals from which Marrant drew to shape his religious ideology. Within many of these communities, patterns of religious formation informed strategies of political organization and collective resistance to enslavement. In New York, Afro-Iberian fraternal societies developed to foster group unity, shape collective identity, and provide systematized aid to community members in need. Group members helped organize Pinkster celebrations, a spring religious festival that combined African and Dutch Protestant cultural elements. In St. Augustine, the Marrants drew on African, European, and Native American cultural sources that helped create new societies. Complex networks of relationships between Spanish settlers and escaped African slaves enabled the formation of Afro-Catholic communities at Fort Mose, an all-Black settlement two miles north of St. Augustine; while many of the earliest African slaves formed maroon communities with Seminole and other Native American groups. Savannah's vibrant Africana religious culture could be attributed to an influx of enslaved laborers in the decades prior to the Marrant family's arrival. By the time they arrived in Savannah, Yamacraw, a multiracial neighborhood on the west side of town, was home to a substantial free Black community that included seamen, fugitive slaves, and free Black women who created market settings similar to their counterparts in West African and Caribbean ports. In each locale, Black communities utilized opportunities for public gathering to establish collective identity through cultural traditions and ritual norms. Marrant's formation in the vibrant Africana cultural urban centers of colonial America would greatly impact his adoption of Christianity and the subsequent development of his pastoral ministry in his adolescent and adult years.

Africana Religions in Colonial New York

When John Marrant was only four years old, his father was laid to eternal rest. The details surrounding the elder Marrant's passing, along with those of his final resting place, are unknown. Most of New York's colonial Black population were buried in the Negro Burial Ground—a cemetery that had been designated for free Blacks, slaves, criminals, and paupers near downtown Manhattan. From

1712 to 1795, the Negro Burial Ground provided colonial New York's Black population with a "semi-autonomous social space" to venerate their dead and perform religious rites associated with West African practices and beliefs. Black mourners adorned the graves of loved ones with pieces of white pottery and smoking pipes. According to widely held West African beliefs, white was the symbolic color of the land of the dead, and pipes enabled communication with the deceased. Broken objects left at the grave site of a family member could be used by the deceased in the afterworld. Archaeological findings from the New York site also uncovered human remains with incisors filed into an hourglass shape, a common practice among the Akan of West Africa's Gold Coast. Additionally, some families decorated the coffins of loved ones with West African religious symbols. A coffin lid displaying the Sankofa bird, which symbolized the Akan maxim that "return to the past is the path to the future," was recovered from the excavation of the Negro Burial Ground in the late twentieth century. Free Blacks utilized West African burial rites to commemorate the deceased in funeral ceremonies during the early part of the eighteenth century, such as those led by Peter the Doctor, an African-born conjurer. Families like the Marrants commonly witnessed the performance of such rites, and many incorporated them in the ceremonies in which they laid their deceased loved ones to rest.[5]

While the Negro Burial Ground provided a "semi-autonomous" space for Black colonial New Yorkers to commemorate their dead according to their own beliefs and practices, it was not invulnerable to colonial realities stemming from racial proscription. Reports by local ministers that "heathenish rites" were "performed at the grave" by Blacks drew the ire of white colonial New Yorkers. Residents complained that late-night drumming and chanting from bereaved "Negroes" disturbed their sleep. In 1722, resolutions were passed that prohibited after-dark funerals and limited the number of people at these gatherings to twelve. Despite these restrictions, the Negro Burial Ground remained essential to the formation of Black racial identity and a vibrant site for Africana religious exchange.[6]

In the decades preceding the death of Marrant's father, colonial New York's Black population exploded. Increased cargoes of enslaved Africans began arriving in New York just as the numbers of American-born Blacks reached historic highs in the late 1740s. This population influx led to a revitalization of African-derived religious beliefs and established a competing source of religious authority for New York's Black residents. While an increase in American-born Blacks contributed to the growing Black community, the transatlantic slave trade was primarily responsible for the explosion in the local Black population. Between 1748 and 1774, there were at least 130 voyages between New York and Africa.

Of the nearly seven thousand slaves imported to New York from the beginning of the eighteenth century to the eve of the American Revolution, more than 40 percent came directly from Africa. Black slaves also arrived from Antigua, Barbados, and Jamaica. In 1755, census records listed enslaved people with comic, English, classical, and African names, suggesting that New York's Black population was a mixture of native-born, West Indian, and African peoples by the year of Marrant's birth.[7]

Religious Diversity in Colonial New York

From its outset, New York colony was culturally diverse. In the seventeenth century, the first Dutch settlers arrived as representatives of the recently formed Dutch West India Company. Following their independence from Spanish colonialism, the Dutch, eager to compete with other sovereign European nations, began trading in slaves off the west coast of Africa. Because the Portuguese and Spanish had long established strongholds in the region, the Dutch also went to Madagascar to acquire slaves to labor in their New World colonies. Although they were never able to compete with Portugal or Spain, Dutch traders were able to establish significant trade relationships with African nations on the west coast. The first enslaved Africans who arrived in the Dutch North American colonies came from modern-day Angola, Ghana, and Madagascar.

On their arrival at the Dutch colony of New Amsterdam, African slaves encountered Christian churches that were enjoying theological and institutional freedom since their recent independence from Catholicism under Spain's imperial regime. Because of their past history as Spanish subjects, Dutch settlers were suspicious of Spanish settlers and practitioners of Catholicism in general, factors that would play a significant role in the colony's race relations and religious history in later years. By the time slaves began to arrive from Madagascar, colonial authorities had ended the Catholic practice of liberating converted slaves. Initial waves of Catholic slaves from Angola who had arrived with the earliest Dutch settlers had eventually been freed and adopted into the fold of the Dutch Reformed Church. The second wave of Catholic slaves from Madagascar, however, were slaves for life without the intervention of religious assimilation. These African slaves likely saw their Catholic masters as violators of the rights established by the bonds of Christian brotherhood.[8]

Dutch settlers introduced African slaves to Protestantism in Calvinist and Reformed churches. Enslaved Africans were married and baptized in Dutch churches, and many attended worship services regularly with their masters. They were allowed to participate in these religious institutions, although their membership in Dutch Protestant congregations did not alter their status as slaves. Despite the efforts of the Reformed Church, preexisting African religious practices and beliefs remained operative among the colony's enslaved. Many continued to practice Catholicism, to which they had been previously exposed in Angola and Madagascar, much to the displeasure of Dutch and English settlers.[9]

Black New Yorkers also accommodated other aspects of Dutch culture. Many, like Isabella Baumfree, an enslaved woman born in Rifton, New York, in 1797, spoke fluent Dutch and attended Dutch Reformed churches with their masters. Despite the widespread use of the Dutch language, New York's Black community did not adopt Dutch cultural rituals uncritically; rather, they adapted aspects of Dutch Protestantism into their own unique religious culture. Most notably, the Pinkster festival exhibited a combination of African and Dutch culture. This festival originated as the Dutch version of Pentecost. The African practice of Pinkster, celebrated throughout the northern mid-Atlantic and New England colonies, combined features of African seasonal rituals and other cultural traditions. While Dutch settlers primarily celebrated with church attendance, baptisms, and confirmation, enslaved Africans—temporarily relieved from some of their labor—celebrated with dances, songs, storytelling, and, most important, the election of the Pinkster King. In many New England towns, centralized authority was vested in the Pinkster King, who was elected at the festival on the legal election day by those Blacks who gathered to select their own dignitaries, called kings or governors. For the Black communities that celebrated it, Negro Election Day became the highlight of the year. The Pinkster holiday in some New York and New Jersey towns served a similar function. The occasions provided slaves with an opportunity to feast, dance, and socialize, and to celebrate openly a distinct Black cultural tradition. Although that often meant satirizing whites' ways, the focus of these festivals was Black conviviality and leadership. Many popular kings enjoyed a long tenure. In Albany, New York, King Charles, an "old Guinea Negro" whose authority was regarded as absolute, ruled Pinkster from the American Revolution until about 1808. And some kings and governors had considerably more than ceremonial functions. In Newport, Hartford, and Portsmouth, informal systems of Black government existed alongside white county courts. On complaints by either whites or Blacks against Black offenders, the African American magistrate hearing the case would sentence the defendant, and a Black officer would punish him.[10]

Additionally, Pinkster celebrations continued within African American communities and were a staple feature of New York's African American culture into the 1820s. African elements of cultural expression were especially salient in music and dance. In the early nineteenth century, enslaved dancers from Long Island and New Jersey brought boards "five to six feet in length" and paid a shingle to participate in the "shingle dance" during the Pinkster holiday in New York City.[11] African dance and music were central to the ceremony, and the use of many instruments created an "orchestral style akin to the music of an African festival." Notably, differences in performance on the fiddle were highlighted by commenters. African musicians "plucked the bow energetically" in a "highly percussive style" that varied greatly from European methods of performance.[12] In later years when Marrant studied music in Charleston, he quickly gained wide popularity as a violinist. The possibility that his exceptional skill was inspired by the performances of musicians at Pinkster celebrations in New York underscores the generative influence of Africana culture on his development during adolescence.

Pinkster became the primary site of religious interaction between Dutch settlers and African slaves in colonial New York and much of the mid-Atlantic colonies.[13] An observance of the resurrection of Christ, Pinkster functioned both as an agriculturally based community gathering and as a deeply private religious occasion. The highlight of the celebration occurred when the "Holy Wind" swept through the gathering, "compelling powerful preaching and prophesying" and "speaking in tongues" by the participants irrespective of race, gender, or legal status. As with the deities of West Africa, when the Holy Ghost drove worshippers to ecstasy, they prophesied, spoke in tongues, and became a "mouthpiece of God." These moments of ecstasy replaced church baptisms as the primary mode of conversion within the Dutch Reformed Church.[14] (This ritual of prophetic ecstasy would inform Marrant's ministry among Cherokee and Creek Indian communities during subsequent sojourns in the Savannah low country.)

Because Pinkster services required neither perfect English, literacy, nor command of scripture, it was one of the most widely observed festivals in the mid-Atlantic colonies. Pinkster brought together worshippers from English, Dutch, German, and African cultures—a union possible in few places outside colonial New York.[15] The kind of cultural blending that Pinkster exhibits had likely been permitted by Catholic missionaries prior to the arrival of enslaved Africans to America. Many Catholic missionaries in Angola "regarded all aspects of the culture of the target country that were not directly contrary to fundamental doctrine of the church as immaterial and left them unchanged." Thus, some Blacks arriving in New York possessed Africanized rather than Protestant understandings of Christianity that informed their celebration of Pinkster.[16]

Though the influence of Dutch culture would diminish following British conquest in the early part of the eighteenth century, the impact of Dutch-inspired African culture would continue well into the nineteenth century in New York.

More recent research posits a more substantive role for traditional African religion in the formation of the American Pinkster tradition. The organization of the Pinkster festival can be traced to Afro-Iberian confraternities, or "brotherhood traditions," established in West Central Africa and introduced to the Dutch North American colonies by the charter generation of enslaved Africans in colonial New York. In the sixteenth century in urban centers such as Seville and Lisbon, Black brotherhoods had developed to foster group unity, shape collective identity, and provide systematized aid to community members in need. These organizations enabled Blacks in Spain and Portugal to "have their own chapels, to participate in processions with their own performances, to have Masses for the souls of the living and dead members, and to make sure that members received an honorable funeral and burial place."[17] (Public processions and funeral rites would play important roles in the ritual life of the African Lodge, the Black Freemason fraternal organization to which Marrant was chaplain during adulthood in Boston.) In West Central Africa, brotherhoods were critical to the development of "a Kongolese variant of Iberian Catholic procession culture."[18] The preexistence of Afro-Iberian brotherhood societies also explains the rise of mutual aid and benevolent societies in nineteenth-century New York. These societies perhaps constitute the institutional precursor to Black churches in New York and throughout urban centers in the mid-Atlantic and New England colonies. The organizing role of brotherhoods in the American Pinkster tradition underscores the likelihood that for Black families like Marrant's, participation in ritual and institutional forms of Christianity signified a multiplicity of meanings. In fact, the historian Sterling Stuckey notes that enslaved and freed Blacks frequently made special arrangements so that children and infants could attend ritual gatherings, thus ensuring the transmission of their culture to succeeding generations.[19]

Blacks encountered a variety of other European faiths in colonial New York and the surrounding areas. The Society of Friends (Quakers) was heavily represented on Long Island and in New Jersey, and exerted its influence on religious life in New York City. Although some radical Quakers advocated the end of slavery, most "continued to use slaves on farms and in households."[20] Rural Blacks were attracted to the Lutheran Church. Culturally and linguistically distinct from their Anglican counterparts, Lutherans were noted for exhibiting strong piety and racial "liberality." Because free Blacks were given "high-ranking positions in their churches," Lutherans attracted "other descendants of the original free blacks." Many of the children who appear on church registers can be traced to the charter generation of Angolan slaves in the seventeenth century. The Dutch Reformed Church, however, was "far less liberal." While Dutch evangelical fervor emphasized the need for spiritual rebirth, pietist attitudes regarding predestination continued to undermine "confidence in blacks' spiritual potential."[21]

Although their influence continued into the nineteenth century, the firm hold of the Dutch on the cultural and political makeup of New York began to wane following the British conquest in 1664. After briefly relinquishing control of the colony a little more than a decade later, the British exerted dominant influence over the religious and cultural life of colonial New York until the American Revolution. In an effort to secure the loyalties of disaffected Dutch settlers and to appease an ethnically diverse body of colonists, English rulers sought to foster a shared sense of belonging among the various European-descended settlers in New York. The stability of the colonial government depended on its ability to extend the benefits of British citizenship to all the white inhabitants of New York colony. Consequently, institutions and rituals that established British culture were of utmost importance to the success of British rule and the development of a cohesive white identity in colonial New York. The Anglican Church facilitated the development of a collective identity among white settlers as it provided a common liturgical language as well as systematized, uniform liturgical procedure and aesthetics for worship. While colonial governors formally extended the rights of English citizenship, the Anglican Church nurtured English sensibilities in the settlers and formed them into a community of loyal subjects. Colonial governors introduced the idea that adherence to Protestant religion and "obedience to the laws of England" constituted English citizenship. By providing the settlers with instruction in the English language and the doctrines of Anglicanism, the church enabled a cultural expansion that reshaped the boundaries of England beyond its continental borders, and redefined English identity from "primarily consisting of the external trait of having been born on the soil of England to positing certain internal traits of innate racial disposition as the essence of Englishness."[22] This process of Anglicizing the settler population not only established the line of demarcation that excluded Black New Yorkers but, equally important, "gave rise to the privileging of racial purity as the decisive principle of boundary maintenance" for inclusion by popularizing the myth of the Anglo-Saxon race. Through mythic reimagination of world history, diverse groups of people of European descent were incorporated into British identity.

The expansion of British culture in New York was largely aided by the missionary efforts of the Society for the Propagation of the Gospel in Foreign Parts

(SPG). At the onset of English rule in the late seventeenth century, the religious makeup of New York was perhaps best described as lacking any definite character. An array of Presbyterians, Quakers, Baptists, Anglicans, and a small number of Catholics constituted the Christian denominations in New York. In general, church membership revealed the "absence of religiosity" among the majority of New York's settler population. By the middle of the following century, however, the Church of England boasted a significant increase in Anglican converts as well as the "nearly universal use of the English language among American-born settlers." English-language instruction in addition to instruction in the fundamental doctrines of Anglicanism were the primary missionary aims of the SPG, and thus, the white settler population in colonial New York was thoroughly Anglicized by the time of Marrant's birth in 1755.[23]

The SPG's missionizing efforts were not limited to the white settler population. The SPG established Sabbath schools in an attempt to teach the catechism to enslaved Africans and Indian natives. These efforts aimed to spread not only Anglicanism throughout the colony but also fluency and literacy in English, thus establishing a fairly homogenized English culture. Elias Neau, a French-born Protestant minister, led the effort to promote both the doctrines of Anglicanism and English proficiency among New York's enslaved African population. Neau's career as the first SPG catechist in New York began in 1703. His instruction to Blacks included the basic tenets of Protestantism, lessons on the creation of the world, the singing of hymns and Psalms, and recitation of the Lord's Prayer as well as responses to the Anglican catechism. His conceptions of God, teachings about the creation of earth and humanity, and doctrinal positions regarding life after death and the work of salvation were "contained in proverbs and brief prayers" and resonated neatly with aspects of African theology. His conception of Jesus offered enslaved Africans "far greater hope and human dignity" than the Anglican Church. In Neau's teachings, Jesus was transformed into a "prophet of freedom" and the enslaved were encouraged to "find their own rebirth in personal suffering and human tragedy."[24] Although SPG authorities in London disagreed with Neau's pedagogical methods, the use of song and oral culture proved at least moderately successful among his Black pupils. Many of them had likely been raised in "the vibrant oral cultures of sub-Saharan Africa and the West Indies" and thus responded favorably to the familiarity of ritual rather than the doctrines of the catechism.[25]

Eventually, however, Neau acquiesced to the desires of the SPG authorities, adopting a more conventional method of religious instruction that emphasized Bible study and reading Anglican devotional materials. To accommodate this shift in teaching style, the SPG minister ordered transcriptions of the Lord's

Prayer in Akan and Mandingo languages as well as Spanish, Dutch, and French since many of his African pupils comprehended those European languages proficiently. Neau also adapted his teaching methods to better welcome "several Sailors, Negroes and Indians from Bermuda and other places" who attended his classes "when their vessels were in harbor." The sailors, he noted, often took reading materials such as "small tracts, books and catechisms so that they might learn at sea." Perhaps, as one scholar has suggested, Black New Yorkers used Neau's classes and reading materials for the benefit of literacy in English and to furnish their own understanding of Christianity.[26] Despite the zealous efforts of missionaries, "it is doubtful that the Anglican catechism classes obliterated all traces of past African faiths," since "scrubbing free the minds and souls of the continually arriving Africans would have required a much greater effort than that mounted by the timid Anglican divines."[27] The continued observance of African rituals and celebrations alongside the newfound interest in Christian literature suggests a strong possibility.

Although Elias Neau and other SPG affiliate ministers were diligent in pursuing African converts, they were met with little initial success. Many slave owners were reluctant to grant missionaries access to their workers, fearing that the time needed to instruct slaves would diminish the income generated by their labor. Additionally, there was some initial uncertainty regarding the effect of baptism on the legal status of their property. The chaplain of the fort, the Reverend John Sharpe, was suspicious that many Blacks were drawn to Christianity because they believed conversion "would make them free." The Reverend Robert Jenney of Rye, New York, concurred, adding that "most masters regarded baptism of slaves as useless and damaging to order and that slaves saw baptism as a ticket to manumission."[28] To assuage these fears and stem the tide of emancipation, the Dutch Reformed Church ceased slave baptisms—a "significant foundation for the codification of slavery in New Netherland."[29] Colonial officials subsequently introduced legislation that decreed that the legal status of Black slaves would not be altered by conversion. This statute eased owners' concerns, but it had the opposite effect on the enslaved themselves. Without the promise of manumission and limited opportunities for egalitarian worship, the Anglican Church was largely shunned by persons of African descent in colonial New York.

Africana Religions and Resistance in Colonial New York

While the Anglican establishment was mostly ignored, Blacks in colonial New York sought to establish vibrant, autonomous religious communities beginning with the arrival of the first eleven enslaved Africans to the colony in 1626.

Though their origins are uncertain, the charter generation of Black settlers were most likely born in Africa and had possibly experienced enslavement in Brazil or on a Spanish plantation in the Caribbean. The African pioneers would soon be joined by a growing slave population. The Dutch West India Company imported enslaved Africans to supply much-needed labor for the colony's food production. By 1644, enslaved Africans had established a sizable community. They had formed families and raised children and were reputed "loyal and hardworking" farmers, skilled laborers, and artisans. A petition for freedom to Governor Willem Kieft and the Dutch West India Company marked the earliest record of slave resistance in the New York colony. The petitioners received three hundred acres of farmland in southern Manhattan. "Negroes land," as the area would come to be known, constituted the geographic boundaries of the Black community and, perhaps more important to colony officials, established a buffer zone between Dutch settlers and Native Americans whose continuous attacks were a constant threat. The petition reveals how Black people manipulated diplomatic relationships between colonial governments and their enemies and allies to strategically position themselves for increased autonomy, an important strategy that would inform new directions in the Marrant family's collective future.

The petition and the creation of "Negroes land" provide an early example of African people attempting to re-create sovereign communities in New World locales. In Brazil, another Dutch colony that was contested by the presence of Catholic colonizers from Spain and Portugal, many African people formed *quilombo* communities to resist Dutch colonizers. As originally constituted in Angola, these communal institutions were politically and culturally unifying structures for people under constant military attack in the midst of political upheaval.[30] Within these military communities, African people re-created continental political structures. In the New World, these political states did not crystallize solely around "a royal lineage of divine kings"; rather, they also "gathered together diverse peoples in a lineageless community." The group identity of the charter generation of Africans in New Netherlands "best resembled the confraternities or brotherhoods found among Kongolese and Angolan Blacks living in Brazil."[31]

In North America, it was common for ethnically diverse African-descended people to form alliances in their struggle for freedom. Michael Gomez details the high occurrence of interethnic runaway attempts by enslaved persons to argue that colonial Black Americans often eschewed traditional ties of kinship and formed bonds around the mutual pursuit of freedom.[32] Additionally, scholars have noted the prevalence of runaway communities that populated the swamps and unsettled forest regions in places like Florida, Georgia, and South Carolina (Marrant's subsequent stops after New York). The existence of such communities in the mid-Atlantic and New England colonies has received much less scholarly attention; however, the petition signed by eleven formerly enslaved Africans in New York in 1644 exhibits how early Black Americans sought communal associations based on common interest when kinship relations could not be sustained in tumultuous New World political climates.

While there is no indication that this early New York community established armed or other violent resistance, subsequent Black communities certainly utilized violence to counter enslavement. Generally speaking, large-scale missions of overt violent attack were far less frequent in North America than in South America, the Caribbean, and Africa. Vastly outnumbered, Black communities were discouraged by their inability to mount reasonably successful militaristic campaigns. However, the relatively small size of the Black population in colonial New York did not altogether preclude the development of autonomous Black communities that sought to violently resist the New World order. While it is beyond the scope of this project, a study of the formation of ethnically diverse, autonomous colonial Black communities in North America is fertile ground for future scholarship. A comparative study of such North American communities with their counterparts in South America and the Caribbean would potentially uncover a more widespread presence of *quilombo* and maroon communities in North America and throughout the Black Atlantic world.

Free Blacks in Colonial New York

The free Black community in New York started small and grew slowly, but by the end of the seventeenth century, Black settlers had moved into King's County (Brooklyn), New Jersey, and Lower Manhattan. Because manumissions were increasingly rare, marriage and childbirth were vital to the growth of the free Black community. Consequently, family stability was highly prioritized. Also, the reinforcement of communal ties through extended kinship networks helped to solidify their tenuous existence.[33] Free Blacks like the Marrant family anchored a fledgling Africana culture in their "impromptu, unlicensed taverns" and public houses. These gathering spaces provided momentary relief from colonial political and religious surveillance. In the semiautonomous space of the tavern, early forms of African American dance and music were created by free and enslaved Blacks during Sunday "barroom frolics using banjos, drums, rattles, and horns and playing African songs mixed with European popular songs." The Sunday gatherings were "direct evidence of the survival of

African traditions" that arrived in New York from "disparate parts of Africa and the Caribbean." These tavern gatherings enabled free and enslaved Blacks to organize themselves into "nations or cultural units" that fused "religious beliefs and customary behaviors."[34] Elite whites were suspicious of the potential liaisons that could be formed with enslaved Blacks and sought to limit their unsupervised interactions. By the late seventeenth century, free Blacks in New York were prohibited from entertaining or harboring "any Servants or Helps, whether Christian or Negro" (a telling distinction) for more than twenty-four hours. Violators of the ordinance were subject to a fine of six shillings for serving liquor to slaves. Additionally, they could be enslaved or removed from the colony altogether.[35]

Where colonial taverns did continue to serve free and enslaved Blacks, narratives of violent resistance were likely rehearsed in the ears of patrons for generations. The story of the first African settler in New York, Jan Rodrigues, is exemplary. In 1613, Rodrigues, an explorer crew member on the Dutch vessel *Jonge Tobias* captained by Thijs Volcherz Mossel, traveled up the North American coast from the West Indies. Following a dispute between crew members, Mossel left Rodrigues behind after paying him his wages of "eighty hatchets, some knives, a musket, and a sword" to be used in securing the newly claimed territory on Manhattan Island.[36] The compensatory articles Rodrigues received as wages and his selection to protect the Dutch settlement suggest he had a military background. When a second vessel, the *Fortuyn*, arrived later that year, Rodrigues informed captain Hedrick Christiansen that he was a "free man" and labored as an interpreter with Rockaway Indians negotiating trade agreements between the two parties. When Mossel returned, he was angry with Rodrigues, presumably because he was working in the service of a competitor and had secured important trade agreements with locals for his rival explorer. In an ensuing fight, Mossel's crew injured Rodrigues before he was rescued by Christiansen's crew. The two vessels departed, leaving behind Rodrigues, the first nonindigenous resident of Manhattan Island, to father several children with Rockaway women.

By the time of Marrant's birth, stories of the 1712 rebellion had likely been added to the local lore. On April 1, 1712, two dozen or so Blacks armed themselves with stolen guns, knives, and hatchets and set fire to an outhouse in New York's East Ward. When the local settlers approached to extinguish the blaze, the rebels attacked them, killing eight and wounding another twelve. The settlers easily overpowered the rebels, however, once reinforcements arrived to provide aid. The rebels scattered—some hid in town while others sought refuge in the woods surrounding the city. By order of the colonial governor, the settler militia pursued the rebel fugitives and arrested those who remained in the city. Rebels secluded in the woods "committed suicide before the armed settlers could arrest them."[37] In the days following the rebellion, seventy alleged conspirators were arrested and twenty-one were convicted. Eighteen of the convicted rebels were sentenced to death; their executions were intended to strike terror in the heart of the Black community. As the historian Thelma Foote explains, "The executioners burned some condemned rebels at the stake, hanged others, beheaded all, and left their mutilated bodies outdoors to rot from exposure."[38]

Scholars have noted the role of traditional African ethnicities and cosmologies in solidifying bonds among conspirators. Days prior to the planned attack, rebels pledged their allegiance to one another by "sucking the blood of each others [sic] hands."[39] An Anglican minister, John Sharpe, suspected a nefarious liaison between free Blacks and African slaves in which African religion factored prominently. In his report to the SPG secretary, he alleged that "negroes [sic] slaves here of the Nations of the Caramantee and Pappa" were responsible for the recent rebellion. "A free negro," he related, "who pretends sorcery gave them a powder to rub on their clothes which made them so confident."[40] Many rebels, he alleged, believed the powder rendered them invulnerable to gunfire.

The colonial government's response to the 1712 insurrection included a series of legislative acts that restricted the autonomy of New York's Black residents. A number of the first several clauses of the newly instituted Black Codes targeted pubs and taverns explicitly by reiterating previously stated prohibitions on entertaining and selling liquor to slaves. For free Blacks, the key aspects of legislation were those that barred them from possessing "any Houses, Lands, Tenements, or Hereditaments in this colony." While these laws did not apply to Blacks who were already free, it all but assured poverty for newly freed slaves. As the historian Graham Russell Hodges surmised, "It seems rather that the assembly's intentions were to define blacks as slaves and to strangle any pursuit of freedom."[41]

The story of the 1741 insurrection was also well known throughout the colony by the time of Marrant's birth in 1755 and had likely been relayed throughout the familiar storytelling networks that were common in Black communities throughout the American colonies. While the international fallout between Catholic and Protestant imperial regimes created political loopholes that African-descended people used to their advantage, the suspicions aroused by colonial governments often brought a greater degree of scrutiny of Black communities. As a result, many of the freedoms that Blacks enjoyed in colonial New York were curtailed due to suspicions of white settlers that stemmed from the Dutch colonial history and recent liberation from Spain, as well as a broader rift between Protestants (Dutch and English) and Catholics (Spanish and French) in the competition to establish imperial regimes. Additionally, there was a general suspicion and fear of slave revolts in the North American colonies (the insurrection at Stono had occurred just two years prior, in 1739) and various international rebellions throughout the Caribbean territories. These violent uprisings coincided with the recent influx of slaves in North America, a grave concern given the rapid expansion of the African-descended population in New York at the time.

British New Yorkers were also wary of competition with French settlers to the north. The presence of French Catholics in the Canadian territory combined with English suspicions of a French and Native American alliance caused the threat of invasion to seem a certain, rather than merely plausible, reality. British settlers additionally feared possible collusion between French Catholics and African slaves due to perceived reciprocity between African religions and Catholicism. Catholic ceremonies and ritual, it was presumed, had an appeal with which the abstract doctrines of Protestantism could not compete. The combination of factors greatly impacted how events unfolded in late February 1741.

On February 28, 1741, a New York merchant, Mr. Hogg, was robbed of linens, medals, and coins (mostly Spanish) valued at roughly sixty pounds. Caesar (aka John Gwin), an enslaved man, was arrested for the robbery several days later. Notorious for theft and a supposed leader of "Negro bandits," Caesar was believed to be the father of the child of Peggy, an Irish house servant and an alleged prostitute. About a month later, a fire at Fort George, the official seat of the royal government, burned both the fort and a nearby chapel to the ground. Over the next several weeks, a series of fires throughout the city destroyed and damaged homes and stores of many of New York's leading merchants and government officials, several of whom owned slaves. Many residents suspected that these were purposeful acts of insurrection, and suspicions were aroused. The common denominator of destruction of goods and property was enough to connect the arson spree with previous robberies throughout the colony. As a result, Caesar and his alleged lover, Peggy, were interrogated in an attempt to uncover a conspiracy.

The suspicion of British colonists also implicated the international Black community. A fire at the home of a colonial officer, Sergeant Burns, just opposite Fort Garden the following day and another several hours later at a house near Fly-Market were attributed to the presence of "Spanish Negroes."[42] When Quaco, an enslaved man belonging to Mr. Walter, was overheard saying, "Fire,

fire, scorch, scorch, a little damn it, by and by," suspicions of revolution began to circulate.[43] The rumors of the Black uprising led to the apprehension of a recently purchased Spanish-speaking slave, who was taken to City Hall to be examined by magistrates. The interrogation was interrupted when Colonel Philipse's storehouse went up in flames later that same afternoon. While that fire was being attended, another blaze began that diverted attention from the effort. One witness claimed to have seen a Black man jump out the window of the burning building, adding credibility to the growing suspicion that "the negroes were rising."[44] The suspect was identified as Colonel Philipse's slave, Cuff, who had a bad reputation for mischief on account of his mostly absentee owner and the slave's corresponding abundant free time.

By April 1741, colonial officials had offered a reward of one hundred pounds to any white person for testimony leading to the discovery of persons responsible for the fires. Manumission and a twenty-pound reward were offered to enslaved Blacks for such testimony (their masters were to receive twenty-five pounds), while "free negroes, mullatoes, and Indians" would receive forty-five pounds and a pardon if they came forward with evidence leading to the arrest of conspirators.[45] Many residents, fearful that more fires were coming, moved their goods out of their homes and enlisted the assistance of Black laborers; they subsequently filed complaints of missing goods. Council members commissioned deputies to Black people's residences to look for stolen goods and also hoped that hideaways and other suspicious characters would be discovered by the searches; but their searches yielded neither suspicious persons nor missing goods.[46]

In the wake of the New York revolt, the Black community's autonomy was greatly curtailed. Blacks, whether enslaved or free, who had any associations with Catholic or Spanish-speaking whites were treated with wariness. Free Blacks in the mid-Atlantic colonies experienced a sharp decline in personal freedom. In 1751, the New Jersey General Assembly passed legislation that prohibited the unauthorized gathering of more than five Blacks. New York adopted similar measures in 1755, the year of Marrant's birth, and issued a public warning against "Negroes in this city of New York and in other parts of this province" who had "assembled . . . in Publick and Private" and had "uttered very insolent Expressions and in other ways misbehaved themselves." In response, older generations of free Black residents moved away to more rural surroundings as the number of emancipations fell dramatically throughout the eighteenth century.[47]

New York's free Black residents would come to be regarded as a pariah class by the early decades of the eighteenth century. Relegated to the status of aliens after the British reconquest of the colony in 1674, free Blacks were denied social privileges as British subjects, and ex-slaves were barred from inheriting land and devising land to their heirs.[48] Free Black widows like Mrs. Marrant were particularly vulnerable. When Lucas Petersen, a freeborn Black resident of colonial New York, could no longer support his ailing wife, Mary, he sent her to the city's church wardens and vestrymen for aid. Though temporarily relieved by their charitable donations, Mary was unable to escape poverty and received a pauper's burial in 1738.[49] Additionally, the intersection of white supremacy and patriarchy rendered Black women especially vulnerable to sexual exploitation at the hands of white men. Although social taboos regarding miscegenation encouraged white men to form conjugal relationships with white women, Black women were frequently victims of sexual assault, since neither statutory nor customary precedents mandated their protection. The large number of newspaper advertisements for the sale of mulatto children in colonial New York attests to the high occurrence of sexual exploitation of Black women.[50]

The decline in personal autonomy experienced by free Blacks in the wake of the New York Conspiracy of 1741 sheds light on what may have prompted the Marrant family's move after their father's passing in 1759. With the prohibitions against large gatherings of more than five people and greater degrees of scrutiny, the tavern may have ceased to provide the refuge from the dominant society that it once had. The Sunday gatherings and frolics were brought to a halt, and the informal networks of communication and commerce became more tenuous to maintain. News of opportunities in other American urban centers for greater degrees of autonomy may also have motivated the family's move. While New York would not be the "continuing city" they hoped for, perhaps the "one to come" could be found farther south.

Africana Religion in Colonial Florida and Georgia

The political sensibilities gleaned from their origins in New York colony were attested to by the Marrant family's constant movement throughout North America during John's formative years. Eager to exploit England's international conflict with Spain to their advantage following their father's death in 1759, the family moved to St. Augustine, the oldest European city in North America. The Florida colony was hotly contested by the Spanish and British Empires throughout most of the eighteenth century. Enslaved West Africans in Florida and in the British colonies of South Carolina and Georgia sought to exploit the imperial struggle to their benefit. News of fugitive slaves who escaped to Florida from British plantations seeking manumission in exchange for their conversion to Catholicism and four years of service in the Spanish army circulated in New

York newspapers and in bars and taverns by word of mouth. The former slaves established an all-Black and relatively autonomous settlement, Gracia Real de Santa Teresa de Mose (Fort Mose), just two miles north of St. Augustine. In addition to being the first all-Black settlement in North America, Fort Mose was also the northernmost defense against the British, who controlled the Georgia and Carolina colonies. Although temporary British rule between 1763 and 1784 eradicated the Spanish colonial border, "the St. Mary's River . . . demarcated a political, legal, religious, and cultural divide across which a new group of black and Indian refugees fled southward."[51]

Slavery in Florida permitted the formation of free Black societies. While Spanish Florida was not without anti-Black racism, enslaved persons enjoyed greater legal protections and more liberal manumission policies than their counterparts in the British colonies to the north. Features like the task system, paternalist relations between planters and slaves, an ability to use resources on the coast and the frontier, and a significantly smaller international slave trade account for a greater degree of autonomy experienced by enslaved Africans in Spanish Florida.[52]

Black communities in Spanish Florida existed within a complex web of cultural exchange that connected Africa, Europe, North America, and the Caribbean. Residents of Fort Mose drew on African, European, and Native American cultural sources to create new societies. Many of the earliest enslaved Africans formed maroon communities with Seminole and other Native American groups. These communities, like the Black community in New York and *quilombo* and maroon societies throughout the New World, strove for self-sufficiency, often raiding local plantations and trading with white planters. In urban centers like St. Augustine and Havana, Black communities developed rapidly in part because legal and religious protections made liberty and property ownership achievable. The enslaved earned wages and purchased their freedom, lived in their own homes, and formed their own societies.[53]

With such relative liberties available in Spanish Florida, the appeal of St. Augustine to Marrant's family was understandable. The lure of the Spanish territory was especially inviting given increasing restrictions to Black people's autonomy in the decades following the New York Conspiracy in 1741. The Spanish colony consistently attracted enslaved Blacks from Georgia and the Carolinas. The founding of Charleston in 1670 intensified hostilities between Spain and England in the North American colonies. As noted, many believed the New York rebellion of 1741 to have been, in part, instigated by recently arrived Spanish-speaking slaves. The enslaved rebels who partook in the Stono uprising in 1739 were, it is speculated, en route to Florida, where they hoped to find sanctuary in the Spanish territory. In fact, so many slaves attempted to cross into St. Augustine at the beginning of the eighteenth century that some scholars indicate the earliest roads to freedom ran south rather than north.[54]

The Marrant family moved in the opposite direction, however, heading north to Savannah after a brief eighteen-month residency in Florida. While their precise reasons for relocation are unknown, the decision to leave St. Augustine may have been motivated, in part, by political developments in the British colonies. The legalization of slavery in Georgia in 1750 increased the number of enslaved Africans transshipped from Charleston to Savannah. Many attempted to find sanctuary in Florida. To stem the tide of runaways leaving their colonies, British colonial officials increased their military presence to patrol routes of escape, thus making passage into Florida more difficult.[55] The increased Black population in Georgia, in conjunction with the relative disarray of Fort Mose following a defeat at the hands of the British nearly a decade before Marrant's arrival, most likely explains why the family would choose to eventually settle in Savannah.

Founded in 1733 by the Reverend James Oglethorpe, the Georgia colony was envisioned as an opportunity for rebirth for poor whites in London. Because Oglethorpe loathed the idleness of South Carolina planters, slavery was outlawed. To discourage plantation-style development, land allotments were limited to fifty acres for each settler in most cases. Silk and wine grapes were harvested since, unlike cash crops, they did not require slave labor. Oglethorpe's aversion to a slave society was partly rooted in a fear of a slave insurrection.

Opposition to the prohibition against slavery was challenged almost immediately in Georgia. Led by proslavery advocates Thomas Stephens and Patrick Talifer, opponents argued that slavery was necessary for the colony's economic and material survival. The Malcontents, as Oglethorpe's opposition group would come to be known, sought to remove him from leadership by raising complaints about the colony's fiscal management. When their complaints reached Parliament in London, slavery was legalized in the colony. The slave code that was passed in 1750 established that the slave-to-white population could not exceed a ratio of four to one. Additionally, the law forbade masters from administering harsh treatment or punishments for enslaved people's transgressions, and it mandated religious instruction and Sabbath observance.[56]

Several changes followed the seismic shift in the colony's history. Significantly, the colony introduced its first cash crop, rice, as wine and silk production continued to decline. Also important was the decision of colonial governors to institute a new land policy. The new policy, the headright system, distributed land allotments on the basis of households, which, for many Georgia settlers, now included slaves. The acquisition of larger land tracts enabled planters to develop larger plantations for rice cultivation. Also, for the first time landowners could bequeath their property to their heirs.[57] Inheritances of this type had previously been forbidden.

In the following decades, migrants from South Carolina and the West Indies flocked to Georgia in droves, eager to take advantage of the new opportunities in Savannah. From 1755 to 1765, most slaves arrived in Georgia from the West Indies in small groups of ten to twenty. By the mid-1760s, the size and frequency of slave cargoes arriving in Savannah had increased dramatically. Planter émigrés from South Carolina and the Caribbean had supplanted the founders in colonial government. The new leadership signaled a new direction in the colony's slave policy. In 1765, a new slave code was adopted. Using statutes established in Virginia and Jamaica as models, Georgia legislators passed much more restrictive laws that prohibited the sale of goods and alcohol to slaves without written permission from their owner. Written permission would also be required for slaves to leave the plantation. Also signaling the shift to Caribbean-style plantation society, the ratio of slaves to master was increased to twenty to one.[58]

By the time the Marrant family arrived in the early 1760s, the legalization of slavery in Georgia had resulted in unprecedented economic growth for Savannah. In 1765, when John Marrant was just four months shy of his tenth birthday, seventy slaves arrived at Tybee Island, the largest shipment the colony had seen to date. In 1755, the year he was born, Georgians shipped 2,300 barrels of rice, 50,000 pounds of deerskins, and 300,000 feet of lumber to London. By the time Marrant was seventeen, rice exports from Georgia exceeded 23,000 barrels annually. Deerskin exports had quadrupled to 200,000 pounds annually, and 2.2 million feet of lumber was shipped to London from Georgia. The increase in slave labor was directly responsible for the growth of Georgia's economy.[59]

The sudden growth of Georgia's economy had a profound impact on Black life in Savannah. The transatlantic trade on which the colony depended necessitated the development of port towns to support maritime laborers. As in other Caribbean port towns, Black seamen dominated the maritime industry in Savannah. Black sailors accounted for nearly a quarter of Savannah's population. The town also attracted fugitive slaves hoping to find passage on one of the vessels at the docks. The travels of seamen and bondsmen made for an "intricate pattern of connection" in which information, ideas, and outlooks were shared and exchanged.[60]

Many fugitive slaves and sailors in Savannah found refuge in Yamacraw, a neighborhood settlement on the west side of town. Known as a boisterous slum,

Yamacraw was a loose confederation of three smaller communities composed of residential, commercial, and merchant establishments. One of the communities was a biracial neighborhood in which sailors frequently lodged. It was not uncommon for white captains to share lodging with Black crew members. In other Caribbean port towns, neighborhoods like Yamacraw existed on the periphery of town, often occupying territory between indigenous people and settlers. Free people of color accounted for a large segment of the population, and it was not uncommon for free Black women, like Marrant's mother, to run drinking houses and keep small shops. Black women also exerted considerable influence in the market at Ellis Square. In market settings remarkably similar to their counterparts in West Africa and the sugar islands, Black women regulated prices and controlled the flow of produce. Such opportunities for limited autonomy may explain why the recently widowed Mrs. Marrant would have settled her family in Savannah.[61]

The religious and cultural diversity that Marrant encountered in New York, St. Augustine, and Savannah informed the development of his religious outlook in the subsequent years of his life. Black religious cultures from West Africa, West Central Africa, and the Caribbean profoundly impacted his understanding of religious storytelling and ritual performance during the subsequent years of his ministry. Marrant's understanding and eventual adoption of Euro-American Protestantism were filtered through Africana interpretive lenses. While no singular cultural or regional origin accounts for the African antecedents that developed in Marrant's Christian practice, comparative analysis of ritual practices in West Central Africa and their counterparts in the low-country region of the American South reveals how African religious epistemologies remained operative for Black people on both sides of the Atlantic during the colonial era. Many enslaved West Central Africans arrived in Spanish Florida, Georgia, and the Carolinas as practitioners of Africanized forms of Catholicism to which they had been exposed by Portuguese missionaries in their homeland.[62] The Marrant family likely gleaned vital intelligence from the networks of communication and cultural formation that enabled free and enslaved Blacks to form and maintain autonomous religious communities. Equipped with an understanding of colonial politics informed by the ritual and storytelling culture of the Africana community, Marrant would set forth on a journey in search of the city that was to come.

2. "Prepare to Meet Thy God"

Conjuring Initiation in Marrant's Narrative

In roughly 1766, the year he arrived in Charleston, John Marrant began his transition into adulthood. Despite the tragic loss of his father, and the series of moves that resulted from the subsequent lack of stability, he did well in school, having been "taught to read and spell" in Florida and "kept to school" until he had "attained [his] eleventh year" in Savannah. By the time he came to live with his unnamed sister and her husband in "Charles Town," he was a precocious adolescent who had determined that he would "rather learn to play music than to go to a trade." Noting "a strong inclination to learn" after he heard a band play while passing by a music school, he persuaded his mother and sister to hire a music teacher. Marrant proved a fast learner. In just six months, he could play the violin well enough to "play for the whole school." Soon he also took up the French horn, and after only a year had mastered both instruments. Marrant improved so quickly, in fact, that he was hired by the parents of his classmates to perform at local parties and balls in Charleston. Life as a working musician opened "a large door of vanity and vice" for the young Marrant, and he soon found himself "a stranger to want, being supplied with as much money as I had any occasion for." For two years he was "devoted to pleasure and drinking in iniquity like water," regularly passing his adolescent nights in local bars and taverns. Despite having unrestrained access to adult worlds of leisure and entertainment, Marrant felt himself "a slave to every vice suited to my nature and to my years."[1]

This chapter explores John Marrant's depiction of his call and initiation into prophetic ministry in *Narrative*. His portrayal of his call to ministry mimics phases of West African–based initiation rites. In West and West Central African societies, rituals of initiation marked the transition from adolescence to adulthood. The ritual communities employed symbols to communicate sacred meaning and instruction to initiates.[2] While variations of initiatory rituals are found throughout West and West Central Africa, five phases—call, wilderness seclusion, instruction from tutors or guides, physical impression, and communal reintegration, or covenant—represent a general model of initiation and provide the organizational structure for Marrant's autobiographical tale.[3] Biblical models of initiation follow a similar pattern, though such initiatory narratives typically dramatize the process by which an individual comes to understand and acknowledge his own prophetic identity. By narrating his call to ministry according to the pattern of Africana initiation, Marrant reveals that ritual and structural, rather than theological, modes of analysis informed his understanding of biblical Christianity. Biblical call narratives along with initiation rituals derived from traditional African societies formed the constitutive grounds from which Marrant drew inspiration for the depiction of his call to ministry in *Narrative*. His portrayal of his adolescent years set the stage for his prophetic call.

The Call

Marrant's life would turn in a new direction shortly after his thirteenth birthday. One evening, while accompanied by a friend on his way to a musical performance, he was drawn to a frantic scene in a local meetinghouse. When he looked inside, he saw "many lights in it, and crowds of people going in" and was told that "a crazy man was hallooing there." Curious, but unsure, he lingered at the entrance "that I might hear what he was hallooing about."[4] As one might expect for an adolescent, fate was determined by a dare. Accepting his friend's challenge to blow his French horn in the middle of the meeting, Marrant pressed his way into the crowded room and lifted the horn to his shoulder. But before he could blow a note, the Reverend George Whitefield began his address. "Looking round, as I thought, directly upon me, and pointing with his finger," said Marrant, "he uttered these words, 'PREPARE TO MEET THY GOD, O ISRAEL.'" The effect was staggering. "The Lord accompanied the word with such power, that I was struck to the ground, and lay both speechless and senseless near half an hour." When he regained consciousness, he was overcome with terror. The Lord's power accompanied the sermon as well, and Whitefield's words pierced him "like a parcel of swords." Marrant responded with a shout and let out a "halloo out in the midst of the congregation."[5] His shouting rose above the commotion of the gathering, and he was taken into the vestry so that the service could continue.

Marrant's account of his response to Whitefield's sermon is similar to patterns of spirit possession in initiation rituals throughout West and West Central Africa. In Black North American settings, spirit possession and shouting are generalized phenomena, while in West and West Central Africa, they are typically reserved for priests and acolytes. In both cases, the shout symbolizes that the recipient has received "special favor from the spirit that it chooses to drive out the individual consciousness temporarily and use the body for its expression."[6] The shout can be prompted by rhythmic speech, song, humming, hand clapping, or foot tapping—patterns of expression that replace ritual drumming in Black North American communities. In many but not all cases, spirit possession was attended by somatic responses that included the shout, dance, and meditative faint.[7]

Marrant's relation of his mystical experience emphasizes physical expressions consistent with Africana ritual forms—shouting, loss of consciousness, and visions of "the devil on every side of me"—rather than the theological merits of Whitefield's sermon. Zora Neale Hurston's ethnographic study of Black church life in the rural South reveals that experiences like Marrant's were fairly common. Often, the initiate would enter a semiconscious, trancelike state followed by a period of diminished physical ability in which "he does not know how to talk and can only express himself in inarticulate syllables." In many societies throughout West Africa, the Caribbean, and Latin America, spirit possession signified symbolic death and marked the beginning of ritual initiation. The initiate is usually kept physically immobile, lying on a mat for days. The imposed restrictions can induce a trance state.[8]

When the Reverend Oliver Hart visited him three days after Whitefield's meeting, Marrant was confined to bed, having not had "any food, only a little water now and then." His sister was obviously worried; his conditioned had not improved since he had come home ill three days earlier accompanied by two men. The doctors' treatments were ineffective, and unless her brother improved soon, she feared the worst. Hart had been sent by Whitefield to encourage Marrant, but Marrant was skeptical when the Baptist minister first walked into his bedroom and offered his hand in prayer. At first Marrant refused it, but Hart persisted and pulled him to the floor as he knelt in prayer. When he finished praying, Marrant felt worse than before. Hart was undeterred. So they knelt "a second time and after he had prayed earnestly we got up," wrote Marrant. He continued to worsen, and his sister feared death was imminent. Hart, however, remained steadfast and knelt to pray a third time. When he had prayed "a considerable time," Marrant found that he was "filled with joy" and that his soul was set at "perfect liberty."[9]

It is worth noting the duration of Marrant's fast. In Black North American seeking rituals, "three days is the traditional period for seeking the vision," explains Hurston. "Usually the seeker is successful, but now and then he fails." While most seekers "come through" in public worship meetings, some, like Marrant, "come after the meeting is closed."[10] It is also important to point out that Marrant and Hart pray three times before Marrant's soul is liberated. According to Hurston, "Three is the holy number and the call to preach always comes three times. It is never answered until the third time." Marrant's attending illness over the course of three days is also standard in Black call narratives, which Hurston describes as follows: "The man flees from the call, but is finally brought to accept it. God punishes him by every kind of misfortune until he finally acknowledges himself beaten and makes known the call. Some preachers say the spirit whipped them from their heads to their heels. They have been too sore to get out of bed because they refused the call. This never ceased until the surrender. Sometimes God sends others to tell them they are chosen. But in every case the ministers refuse to believe the words of even these."[11]

The initial rejection of the prophetic call is a common pattern in the Bible's call narratives as well. In some instances, the prophet refuses the call and must be coerced into service. Moses objects when he is called by God at the burning bush. He lists his deficiencies—noting, among other things, a stutter that he hoped would render him unfit for service.[12] In the biblical examples, the number forty signifies the ritual aspects of wilderness initiation. Jesus spends forty days and nights in the wilderness, and each of Moses's respective stays in the wilderness lasts forty years. Thus, the wilderness setting and the number forty are literary signifiers of ritual norms in biblical narratives.

Like Moses, Marrant initially was reluctant to accept the call, but once he was on board, his focus was singular. Besides adopting a strict regimen of fasting and prayer, he "read the Scriptures very much" and, despite his sister's pleading, stopped playing the violin and gave up manual labor. His sister was critical of his asceticism, and speculation that he had gone mad quietly circulated the neighborhood. Fed up with the perceived persecution, he "resolved to go to [his] mother" in Savannah. The journey from Charleston to Savannah took three days.

Marrant's narration of his prophetic call replicates many of the narrative features found in Bible stories. Moses turned aside to observe a continually burning bush; Marrant was drawn to the noise, lights, and frenzy of revivalism. In both cases, curiosity opened the door to prophetic awakening. God spoke to Moses in the burning bush; Marrant heard the call in the excitement of Whitefield's sermon. Marrant was struck to the ground under the power of God. The prophetic call of John Marrant at the meetinghouse in Charleston marked the first phase of his initiation.

Family Rejection

When he arrived in Savannah, the refuge he sought eluded him. At his mother's house, there were siblings who called him "every name but that which was good." At first, his mother was sympathetic to her son's plight, but after several weeks she "turned against me also, and the neighbours joined her, and there was not a friend to assist me, or that I could speak to." The family's ridicule was so intense that Marrant briefly "was tempted so far as to threaten my life."[13]

Social isolation caused by communal scorn was a commonly repeated theme in eighteenth-century Black American narratives. James Albert Ukawsaw Gronniosaw, the eighteenth-century Black Atlantic spiritual autobiographer, was born near present-day Nigeria. An heir to African royalty, he was lured into captivity by an English merchant who deceived him with the promise of a Western education. Gronniosaw was a precocious child and explains that his family held him in contempt because he possessed unique insight into spiritual matters at an early age: "I had, from my infancy, a curious turn of mind; was more grave and reserved in my disposition than either of my brothers and sisters. I often teased them with questions they could not answer: for which reason they disliked me, as they supposed that I was either foolish, or insane."[14]

Gronniosaw's inquisitiveness annoyed his siblings. His incessant queries about the great "Man of Power" who "resided above the sun, moon and stars" troubled his mother and angered his father. After lingering outside to observe a thunderstorm, Gronniosaw questioned his mother about the maker of creation and humanity, and when he would not be satisfied with her answer, he was threatened with punishment from his father if he was ever again so troublesome. Family contempt was not limited to parental disapproval; according to Gronniosaw, "[My] brothers and sisters despised me and looked on me with contempt," and "even my servants slighted me, and disregarded all I said to them." This dismal portrayal of family life intends to highlight communal recognition of Gronniosaw's spiritual identity rather than the backwardness of African society. The depiction of family persecution establishes Gronniosaw's marginal status and foreshadows his transformation into a prophetic hero by the narrative's end.

The link between family rejection and prophetic identity is established in biblical narratives as well. Jesus's family implored him to curb his public ministry because they doubted his sanity, while the scribes and religious leaders in Jerusalem believed that his spiritual authority was derived from a demonic, rather than divine, source.[15] Family rejection also played a major role in the Old Testament story of Joseph. When his brothers learned that Joseph was destined to rule over them, they were furious and began to plot his demise. His prophetic identity incited his brothers' wrath, and they sold him to Egyptian slave traders.[16]

The structural similarities between these examples and Marrant's narration are striking. In each case, family rejection stems from a recognition of the protagonist's unique spiritual abilities or religious practice. Joseph's brothers were angered because he possessed the gift of prophecy, and Jesus's siblings ostracized him with accusations of insanity. Gronniosaw was teased, disliked, and presumed to be insane, while Marrant was driven to ponder suicide. In each narrative context, family rejection signifies prophetic identity and foreshadows the protagonist's impending isolation.

Seclusion

While Marrant did not find the respite he sought at his mother's house, he was able to find solace in the uncultivated territory of the low country. In the sanctuary of the forest, he resumed the ascetic practices he had begun in Charleston—praying, fasting, and reading his Bible. At first, he stole away for brief moments, but soon he found himself staying in the woods "from morning to night to avoid the persecutors." His extended periods of isolation in the wilderness continued for weeks until, one day, the fourteen-year-old Marrant left home altogether. As he described in *Narrative*, "After spending some time in the fields, I was persuaded to go from home altogether. Accordingly I went over the fence, about half a mile from our house, which divided the inhabited and cultivated parts of the country from the wilderness. I continued travelling in the desert [*sic*] all day without the least inclination of returning back."[17]

Marrant's excursion was prompted by intense scrutiny from family and neighbors. His shift to the wilderness setting also conjures a narrative trope commonly used in Bible stories. Biblical prophets frequently endured isolation in uncultivated territory before embarking on a divine mission. After he was baptized by John and his prophetic identity was confirmed by a voice from heaven, Jesus was secluded in the wilderness for forty days of fasting and prayer. Similarly, before Moses led Israel from captivity in Egypt, he spent forty years in the wilderness, where he learned to herd sheep from his father-in-law, Jethro. He had fled to the wilderness after murdering a taskmaster for mistreating a Hebrew slave in Egypt. When he returned from the wilderness to Egypt, he was empowered to lead the people of Israel from bondage.

New members of early Black American Christian communities also turned to the wilderness to better understand transformative spiritual experiences. Hurston explains that it was common for Black supplicants to enter "into waste places and by fasting and prayer [induce] the vision."[18] In the Georgia and South Carolina low country—Marrant's stomping grounds—the association of uncultivated land with spiritual potency persisted among enslaved and free persons of African descent. The case of Gullah Joe, a Kongolese man enslaved in Africa and brought to the New World, is exemplary. Long after he arrived in South Carolina in the nineteenth century, he fondly remembered and longed for his wife, children, and other family members in Africa. He desired also to walk once more in the *feenda*, a Kikongo word meaning forest, where he likely "spent much of his youth in Africa collecting plants, trapping small animals, practicing the hunt, and otherwise learning to become a Kongo man."[19] The relationship between sacred land and social development in early African American spirituality is preceded by West and West Central African antecedents. According to Ras Michael Brown, "People of African descent . . . accepted that the physical landscape had sacred dimensions that had to be engaged for both the spiritual development of individuals and the well-being of communities. This notion, too, was embraced by many of the African societies from which the captives who landed in the Lowcountry originated."[20] The *feenda* was instrumental in the formation of Kongolese male identity, and this religious orientation was maintained among American-born persons of African descent in the low-country region of South Carolina. Eighteenth-century Black Christian communities adopted this ritual practice from West and West Central

African initiation societies. In many of these societies, initiation rites included "the stages of seeking in which the initiate endured seclusion in the wilderness and returned after a dramatic spiritual transformation." Several scholars have identified West African societies known as Poro and Sande as likely precursors for low-country seeking; however, "West-Central African antecedents have received much less attention."[21]

Wilderness initiation is a long-standing, widespread practice in many West Central African religious communities. In the Kimpasi association, one of the most important initiation societies in the Kongo region of West Central Africa, initiates were removed from the community and sent to the wilderness or another designated place outside the community where they were consecrated to *simbi*, or nature spirits. Kimpasi societies were commonly based in "uninhabited areas, especially densely wooded or secluded regions," and their ritual activity usually took place in outdoor, open enclosures "hidden by trees, logs, and thorny underbrush."[22] Living without the comforts of everyday life, initiates underwent extreme physical and psychological pressure. Seclusion provided them with extended time for reflection in an intensely focused spiritual environment designed to induce the contemplative journey. Initiates received wisdom of elders and the ancestors and were enabled to view both past and future from newly enlightened vantage points. Most important, they learned to understand and accept the cyclical nature of spiritual seasons and "take their place on the great wheel of life that turns elders into ancestors and children into adults."[23]

While the contemplative aspect of such practices often eludes observers not familiar with Africana religious traditions, the effect is evident in the life of the initiate. Wilderness seclusion enacts a narrative of death and resurrection and emphasizes the importance of communal support and cooperation. The initiate's vulnerability is underscored by exclusion from the community: apart from community, the individual, alone, cannot exist. Without communal support to transfer sacred knowledge regarding customs and rituals, the initiate has no lasting appreciation for group norms and long-standing traditions. Seclusion underscores the central importance of belonging to a social group and the value of one's responsibility to the larger society, without which the community disintegrates into chaos. Consequently, seclusion allegorizes the death from which the initiates will be delivered by integration into the community after the initiation process has been completed.[24]

The preceding evidence suggests that what Marrant's abrupt departure from home exhibits is not youthful impulsiveness but the beginning of the seclusion phase of ritual initiation.[25] When Marrant withdraws to the wilderness to contemplate his developing spirituality, fasting and prayer enable "clearer views into the spiritual things of God." But the insights he gains in solitude account for only a portion of his training. His formal instruction, which would emphasize the importance of communal membership, was not learned from family or communal elders but rather from an "Indian hunter" he happened upon during his journey through the forest.

Instruction

Marrant's encounter with the Cherokee deer trader was fortunate. In the days prior to meeting the trader, Marrant had found it difficult merely to survive. His lack of familiarity with the low-country wilderness was apparent—an encounter with wild bears nearly proved fatal. At night, he was forced to sleep in trees to find refuge from wild animals, and during the day, armed only with his Bible and a Dr. Watts hymnal, he struggled to obtain clean drinking water, procure food, and secure adequate lodging. On several occasions, he nearly succumbed to dehydration, starvation, and fatigue. When he was too weak to walk, it took him nearly an hour to crawl twenty yards to a meal of deer grass and muddied water that had recently been vacated by wild pigs. Unable to supplement his diet, he "prayed the Lord to bless it to me, and I thought it the best meal I ever had in my life." Throughout the entirety of the ordeal, however, his faith was strengthened. "The Lord Jesus Christ," he notes, "was very present, and that comforted me through the whole."[26]

Marrant's allusion to the presence of Christ likely intended to conjure images of Jesus's temptation in the wilderness. When Jesus went to the wilderness for forty days of fasting, he was tempted to forsake his prophetic calling for a life of wealth, ease, and pleasure. Like Marrant, he briefly considered suicide when prompted to jump from the pinnacle of the temple. When he sharply refused, his time of fasting was complete and angels attended to him shortly afterward. Similarly, Marrant overcame the suicidal thoughts that challenged him while fasting in the wilderness. "Not long after this," he writes, "I was sharply tried, and reasoned the matter within myself, whether I should turn to my old courses of sin and vice, or serve and cleave to the Lord; after prayer to God, I was fully persuaded in my mind, that if I turned to my old ways I should perish eternally."[27]

Determined to go on, Marrant began the next day's journey with newly found resilience. Bypassing wolves, bears, and other wild animals, he continued for several hours through the forest. Later that day, after he had concluded his afternoon prayers, he was discovered by an "Indian hunter" hiding in the wilderness. As recounted in *Narrative*, "As I was going on, and musing upon the goodness of the Lord, an Indian hunter, who stood at some distance, saw me; he hid himself behind a tree; but as I passed along he bolted out, and put his hands on my breast, which surprised me a few moments. He then asked me where I was going?"[28] Marrant explained that his destination was unknown; when the hunter asked him who he had been conversing with, Marrant responded:

> I told him I was talking to my Lord Jesus; he seemed surprised, and asked me where he was? for he did not see him there. I told him he could not be seen with bodily eyes. After a little more talk, he insisted upon taking me home; but I refused, and added that I would die rather than return home. He then asked me if I knew how far I was from home? I answered, I did not know; you are fifty-five miles and a half, says he, from home. He farther [*sic*] asked me if I knew how I did to live? I said I was supported by the Lord. He asked me how I slept? I answered, the Lord provided me with a bed every night; he further enquired what preserved me from being devoured by the wild beasts? I replied, the Lord Jesus Christ kept me from them. He stood astonished, and said, you say the Lord Jesus Christ do this, and do that, and do every thing for you, he must be a very fine man, where is he? I replied, he is here present.[29]

This question-and-answer exchange recounted Marrant's previous days in the wilderness prior to this encounter. Presumably, readers would already be aware of his difficulties in the forest, having read about them in the preceding pages, so the inclusion of this conversation in *Narrative* likely intends to communicate meanings that extend beyond the sequence of events related in the text. At the prompting of his instructor, John Marrant recites (perhaps as much for readers as for the hunter) that food, shelter, and protection come from the realm of the divine.

Marrant's encounter with the Cherokee hunter marks the beginning of his formal instruction. In this stage, the religious and ethical wisdom is communicated from elders to initiates in songs, riddles, proverbs, and sacred dances. The initiate learns the proper forms of worship and veneration to render to deities and ancestors.[30] Formal instruction stresses the interrelatedness of religion, life and death, sex and sexuality, social virtues, and self-identity. The relationship between seen and unseen realms that house the living and the dead is emphasized, as well as the interconnectivity of humanity with the created order.

While Marrant's initial conversation with the Cherokee hunter rehearses statements of belief pertaining to the spirit world, the forest had also long been the setting for teaching adolescents about the natural world in traditional West and West Central African communities. In addition to providing refuge from political rivals, forests in West and West Central African communities provided the training ground for male adolescent hunters—a rite of passage that continued to be practiced by many of their eighteenth-century descendants who inhabited the Georgia and South Carolina low country. Under the tutelage of master hunters and their fathers, boys "began their education in the ways of men," learning valuable lessons regarding hunting techniques, the value of medicinal herbs for both healing and harming purposes, and how to supplicate powerful nature spirits for successful hunts.[31] Hunting in the low country, as in Africa, also marked a transition into manhood and remained a male-dominated activity. As ancestors to generations of low country–born slaves, West Central African men "likely provided much of the instruction for activities such as hunting during slavery." Their twentieth-century descendants continued to use the Kikongo verb *tangisa*, meaning "to teach."[32]

In Marrant's case, his father could not provide knowledge of either spiritual or material worlds. As a result, the Cherokee hunter filled the role of male elder instructor in Marrant's depiction of this initiation phase. Because Marrant had endured ritual seclusion, he was ready to learn the more practical lessons of survival, but first, his instructor tested Marrant's fortitude to be assured that he was up to the challenge. When the Cherokee hunter threatened to take him home, Marrant responded that he "would die rather than return home." Only after Marrant professed his unwavering commitment did the hunter begin to teach him practical aspects of survival. Most important, he taught him how to hunt and trade deer, how to make a bed for sleeping, and how to protect himself from wild animals in the forest. These lessons reflect the questions the hunter posed during their initial conversation—"how I did to live," "how I slept," and "what preserved me from being devoured by the wild beasts."[33] After he could demonstrate an understanding that all food, lodging, and protection were provisions from God, he was ready to learn how to secure these for himself:

> Our employment for ten weeks and three days was killing deer, and taking off their skins by day, which we afterwards hung on the trees to dry till they were sent for; the means of defence and security against our nocturnal enemies, always took up the evenings: We collected a number of large bushes, and placed them nearly in a circular form, which uniting at the extremity, afforded us both a verdant covering, and a sufficient shelter from the night dews. What moss we could gather was strewed upon the ground, and this composed our bed. A fire was kindled in the front of our temporary lodging-room, and fed with fresh fuel all night long, as we slept and watched by turns; and this was our defence from the dreadful animals, whose shining eyes and tremendous roar we often saw and heard during the night.[34]

Numerous biblical stories demonstrate the centrality of guides in initiation tales. The most likely model for Marrant's encounter with the Cherokee guide is the story of Moses and Jethro in the wilderness. When Moses fled Egypt for the wilderness of Midian, Jethro, the priest of Midian, adopted him into his family. Moses married Zipporah, Jethro's daughter, and thus solidified kinship bonds with Jethro. Later in the Exodus saga, when Moses returned to the wilderness of Midian, he sought his father-in-law's counsel on how to organize the people of Israel, whom he had led to the wilderness after their escape from Egypt.

Marrant's Cherokee guide taught both practical and cultural lessons. Over the next several months, Marrant "acquired a fuller knowledge of the Indian tongue." His cultural expansion did not undermine his religious development. Under the tutelage of the Cherokee instructor, he continued to delight in "the sweet communion I enjoyed with God." In fact, as he reflected on his period of instruction under the hunter's guidance, he understood it as "preparation for the great trial I was soon after to pass through."[35] Marrant explains that the lessons taught by his Cherokee companion would prove invaluable in subsequent phases of the initiatory journey. His faith in God and his ability to wield the powers of the Cherokee language would certainly be put to the test in the next stage of initiation.

Marrant's relationship with the unnamed Cherokee deer hunter is instructive for understanding the formal and informal processes of cultural exchange that occurred between Black North American and Native American communities during the colonial and early republic eras. Since their arrival in North America in the sixteenth century, former slaves and free Blacks had fled to Creek communities in the Georgia and South Carolina low country. Known as *Estelvste*, a Creek word meaning "Black people," these Afro refugees were fully assimilated, learning the language and customs, sharing kinship ties, and rising to positions of influence within Creek society.[36] African Creeks created their own cultural institutions within the Creek Nation and asserted themselves in political and military affairs. They participated in the social life and took Creek women as spouses along with other privileges afforded by their adoption into Creek families.

The hunter's instructional relationship to Marrant may also be explained by corresponding relationships between elders and initiates in West African secret societies. In Poro and Sande societies, the *zo* were spiritual leaders who assisted initiates in the bush. Also called altar parents, these elders equipped initiates with rigorous training in "physical survival, social interaction, instruction in ethnic-group history, and art." In the Gullah communities of the Georgia and South Carolina low country, spiritual parents performed in roles similar to those of the *zo* during Christian seeking rituals. Spiritual parents, also called spiritual leaders, instructed seekers in the norms of good conduct and also the importance of generosity, communal allegiance, and group responsibility. In the wilderness, Black Christian seekers were taught "how to pray, an interpretation of the nature of God and Christ, concepts about death, and especially about the realities of life."[37]

For both Native and Black American inhabitants of the South Carolina low country in the eighteenth century, the association of uncultivated territory with spiritual potency persisted. In fact, one author suggests that Cherokee identity was so closely tied to land that the displacement of Cherokees west of the Mississippi River in the nineteenth century severed communal bonds between Cherokees and Blacks because they were removed from the grounds of their initial encounter where communal bonds first developed.[38] Marrant's choice of wilderness for the setting of his encounter with the Cherokee hunter symbolizes the seclusion and training that define the first two phases of initiation in many West and West Central African societies. Marrant's demonstration of endurance, knowledge, and fortitude propels him through ritual instruction. In the following phase of his initiation, his courage would be put to the test.

Physical Impression

To illustrate physical impression, the next phase in his initiation, Marrant relates a dramatic scene in which he narrowly escaped death by execution. After undergoing an initial period of instruction in which he learned to hunt and speak the Cherokee language, Marrant entered the Indian town with the hunter. Before he could enter, however, he was "surrounded by about fifty men, and carried to one of their principal chiefs and Judge to be examined by him." After he was examined, he was promptly taken into custody and held until he learned that he was scheduled to be executed the following morning. This news did not cause him to feel fear or trepidation but instead made him "very happy, as the near prospect of death made [him] hope for a speedy deliverance from the body." He spent the night praying and singing hymns to God, and in the morning, when he "was taken out, and led to the destined spot, amidst a vast number of people," he "praised the Lord all the way we went." Careful to highlight his stoic demeanor, he notes that "when we arrived at the place I understood the kind of death I was to suffer, yet blessed be God, *none of those things moved me*."[39]

Marrant's fearlessness in the face of death conjures patterns of Africana initiation. In many traditional West and West Central African societies, ritual death was a critical part of initiatory rites. While some traditional African groups expressed this concern symbolically, others enacted it literally through surgical procedures of circumcision or scarification. In Poro societies in Sierra Leone, initiates "underwent a symbolic death" that signified an end to their "prior lives and a rebirth to new ones within the society."[40] They were also scarified or circumcised in "dramatic ceremonies, dances, masquerades, performances, and visual displays" that depicted the perilous journey through the wilderness from death to life. In some ceremonies, the surgeon dressed in elaborate and colorful ritual garb and painted their faces so that they looked "as fierce and awe-inspiring as possible." As he approached the initiate, he may have jumped or danced wildly, displaying the knife to be used in the surgery. The drama was intended to inspire fear, yet "what is intended on the part of the [initiates] is courage." The initiates were watched closely and were not expected to exhibit any trepidation. Flinching or hesitation of any kind was considered disgraceful, and such a display would cause enduring shame.

The purpose of the physical impression was to celebrate courage. It was believed that the initiate's display of physical courage implied the moral courage necessary to carry on the life force of the society. For adolescent males, membership in the Poro was mandatory, and the rites of circumcision were commonly performed when they reached puberty. Successful completion of scarification signified the initiate's "ritual death and final graduation" to manhood. Additionally, he learned lessons in self-giving: the initiate, for the good and survival of the community, endured the pain of surgery without hesitation. The procedure also established the adolescent's identity within a particular ethnic group and joined him to the group's ancestors. Those who underwent the procedure together formed a bond that endured for their whole lives:

> It is to impress upon the initiate, in one intense, unforgettable moment, the reality of life and its requirements for the living. An initiation operation gives a clear message that to be self-giving and to sacrifice oneself for the sake of the community is an essential aspect of life, even if this means pain or may even demand extensive suffering. Furthermore, the operation is intended to tell the initiate that to know oneself and to appreciate the worth of others demands self-denial and a certain amount of suffering. Even to enjoy pleasure . . . some suffering is inevitable.[41]

Literary representations of death were common in the earliest Black narratives. As the eighteenth-century Black Atlantic author Olaudah Equiano explains in his spiritual autobiography, the fear of death loomed large in the minds of Black Atlantic writers, particularly when they entered new territories. Equiano, an Igbo descendant and native of Benin, was kidnapped in Africa and brought to the New World when he was a young child. He recalls the first time he boarded a slave ship:

> The first object which saluted my eyes when I arrived on the coast was the sea, and a slave-ship, which was then riding at anchor, and waiting for its cargo. These filled me with astonishment, which was soon converted into terror, which I am yet at a loss to describe, nor the then feelings of my mind. When I was carried on board I was immediately handled, and tossed up, to see if I were sound, by some of the crew; and I was now persuaded that I had gotten into a world of bad spirits, and that they were going to kill me.[42]

Ukawsaw Gronniosaw, the African captive who had been lured into slavery by the deceit of English traders, describes a scene eerily similar to Marrant's. He was taken from his parents' home in Bornu near Lake Chad by an English merchant who had promised "that if I would go with him I should see houses with wings to them walk upon the water, and should also see the white folks . . . and he added to all this that he would bring me safe back again soon." When they finally reached the Gold Coast after several hundred miles of marching over land, Gronniosaw was encouraged by the sound of drums and trumpets announcing his and other captives' arrival. His joy, however, was short-lived; he learned that he was to be put to death: "This account [reception] gave me a secret pleasure; but I was not suffered long to enjoy this satisfaction, for in the evening of the same day two of the merchant's sons (boys about my own age) came running to me, and told me, that the next day I was going to die, for the King intended to behead me."[43]

Unlike his literary contemporaries, Marrant was unmoved at the moment of death. His singular display of bravery signified his successful completion of this stage of initiation. As he found his fear waning and his faith growing, Marrant's prophetic identity was confirmed by a sign. Just before he reached the moment of death, his executioner granted him a moment to pray. He prayed at first in English and then fluently in the Cherokee tongue: "I fell down upon my knees and mentioned to the Lord his delivering of the three children in the fiery furnace, and of Daniel in the Lion's den, and had close communion with God. I prayed in English a considerable time, and about the middle of my prayer, the Lord Impressed a strong desire upon my mind to turn into their language, and pray in their tongue. I did so, and with remarkable liberty, which wonderfully affected the people."[44] The executioner was dumbfounded, unable to speak for five minutes. When he could finally talk again, he grabbed Marrant by the waist and vowed, "No man shall hurt thee till thou has been to the king." Marrant had transformed the executioner into an ally.

Having narrowly escaped execution, Marrant was led to the "king" and, for a second time, was asked to give an account of himself—how he came to their settlement, his age, and how he supported himself prior to meeting the hunter in the woods. When Marrant explained that he was guided and guarded by the invisible and omnipresent Christ, the Cherokee chief was confused, but the executioner, still deeply affected by Marrant's earlier display, "fell upon his knees, and intreated the king in [his] behalf." While the executioner pleaded for Marrant's life, the chief's eldest daughter entered and stood at Marrant's right side. Without speaking, she took the Bible from his hand, opened it and kissed it, and "seemed much delighted with it." The chief, perhaps alarmed by his daughter's infatuation with the Bible, ordered Marrant to read from the book. When Marrant read the story of the arrest and trial of Jesus, the chief was intrigued. When he asked why Marrant read Jesus's name with such reverence, Marrant replied, "Because the Being to whom those names belonged made heaven and earth, and I and he." The chief was unconvinced and insisted that "a man in their town" rather than the Almighty had created "the sun, and moon, and stars, and preserved them in their regular order." They debated until the chief's daughter intervened for a second time. Again, she took Marrant's Bible from his hand, opened and kissed it, then handed it back to him, telling her father that "the book would not speak to her."[45]

While the chief paused in disbelief, the executioner interceded again, begging that Marrant be allowed to pray. When Marrant began to pray, those gathered in the court, including the chief's daughter, cried out in agony just as Marrant had done during George Whitefield's sermon at the meetinghouse in Charleston. The chief was bewildered; he accused Marrant of witchcraft and sentenced him to be executed the following morning.

But the execution was delayed, and Marrant was kept alive in prison because the chief feared that "if he put [him] to death, his daughter would never be well." After several days, the Cherokee chief's daughter had not recovered from her trance despite the care she received from doctors and healers. When Marrant was fetched from prison two days later, he was ordered to heal the chief's daughter or face death by the sword. Marrant prayed for the princess to be healed, but "the heavens were locked to [his] petitions." He prayed a second time but "received no answer." After the third time he prayed, however, the chief himself was "awakened" and his daughter was "set at liberty." The dramatic transformation impacted the chief's entire household: "A great change took place among the people; the king's house became God's house; the soldiers were ordered away, and the poor condemned prisoner had perfect liberty, and was treated like a prince. Now the Lord made all my enemies to become my great friends."[46]

As Marrant settled into his elevated status, he assumed the customs and dress of the ruling elite. He learned to "speak their tongue in the highest stile [sic]," and over the next two months, he visited neighboring Creek, Catawaw, and Housaw communities, traveling in the company of fifty men provided by the "king." He was welcomed into each Native American community, passing freely throughout their territories unharmed. His exchanges with the indigenous nations perhaps shaped his understanding of colonial politics and also his practice of ministry. As Marrant described in *Narrative*, "When they recollect, that the white people drove them from the American shores, they are full of resentment. These nations have often united, and murdered all the white people in the back settlements which they could lay hold of, men, women, and children. I had not much reason to believe any of these three nations were savingly wrought upon, and there I returned to the Cherokee nation, which took me up eight weeks. I continued with my old friends seven weeks and two days."[47]

John Marrant's relation of his "Indian captivity" was certainly not original.[48] More than a century earlier, Captain John Smith had described a similar scene in which Pocahontas, the daughter of Chief Powhatan, rescued him from certain execution when she lay across his chest to forestall an executioner's fatal blow. Details, including Pocahontas's age and questions concerning her ability to exercise the authority needed to extend pardon, have led to doubts regarding the veracity of Smith's tale. Some dismiss it as outright fabrication, while others suppose that while Smith's relation dramatizes historical events, it also discloses Native American ritual practice. The historian Clara Sue Kidwell suggests that what takes place is an adoption ritual in which Pocahontas exercises social power typical of a woman in Powhatan culture. Her contention possibly sheds light on Marrant's encounter with Native Americans in the low country.[49]

Among the Cherokee, women exercised influence over military action and often decided whether prisoners were to be tortured, executed, or spared. By the time African captives arrived in the Americas, slavery had been well established in Cherokee society. The demand for slaves was filled by those who were taken as prisoners during war and military conflicts. Black slaves were acquired as captives from wars with British planters and also from raids of local plantations. Plantation raids, along with the enslavement and adoption of runaway slaves, explain the origins of Black slavery among the Cherokee. It was common for slaves to be spared during plantation raids, but whites were massacred. Typically, children, like Marrant, who were taken as captives were not put to death but were adopted into the families of elite members of society who could afford to provide for their care. Further evidence for the contention that Marrant's experience depicts ritual adoption or Cherokee rituals more generally can be found in accounts of male rituals pertaining to war and hunting. Cherokee men underwent periods of seclusion before and after military combat, and men and women captives who were freed "also underwent a period of confinement and ritual purification."[50]

Marrant also conjures Bible stories to illustrate the deeper spiritual meaning of his Indian captivity. His allusion to the story of Daniel illustrates how biblical storytelling impacted Black American religion in colonial America. Daniel, a Jewish captive exiled in Babylon, was sentenced to death when he defied an edict from the king of Babylon. He was thrown into a den of lions, but survived the encounter when the lions were forestalled by a sudden manifestation of divine presence. Daniel was delivered unharmed, and in the aftermath of his trial, he was exonerated, exalted, and made to prosper under the reign of the Persian king Darius.

Marrant's selection of Matthew 26, the chapter that depicts the arrest and trial of Jesus, as the text to be read as he faced his own trial before the Cherokee "king" is also telling. In this passage, Jesus, like Marrant, stood before his accusers against false charges that could result in a death sentence. As the soldiers approached to take Jesus into custody, his identity was revealed when Judas, his disciple, kissed him. In a similar way, Marrant's trial before the Cherokee chief and the court revealed his prophetic identity. The chief's daughter kissed Marrant's Bible to identify the source of his prophetic authority, but ultimately she recognized that power resided not only in the relic itself but also in the man who possessed the power to make the book talk.

Biblical models of ritual death include depictions of isolation and confinement. Often protagonists are restrained, struck, intimidated, or made to feel the pain of physical impression in some way. Joseph is bound and thrown into prison; the three Hebrew young men Shadrach, Meshach, and Abednego are bound and thrown into a flaming furnace; Daniel is thrown to the lions; Jonah suffers seclusion in a whale's belly; Peter is bound with multiple chains and imprisoned; and finally, Jesus is beaten before suffering a horrific crucifixion. In each case, the initiate's looming, presumed, or actual death is encountered in isolation from his community and involves the terrifying circumstances of a painfully horrific execution.

Inevitably, however, the heroes escape death by supernatural means. Joseph delivers a prophecy received by divine communication and is elevated from prisoner to government official. The three Hebrew companions of Daniel emerge from the flaming furnace with no evidence of being harmed by their fiery surroundings, while Daniel is unharmed after a night in a den of lions. After three days and nights in the belly of the whale, Jonah is delivered to Nineveh, where he proclaims his prophetic message. Peter's miraculous escape from prison is the result of an angelic visitation. And Jesus escapes the hold of death by God's miraculous power of resurrection. In each example, the protagonists escape death because of divine intervention.

Ritual death and resurrection was a recurring theme in American colonial literature as well. Marrant and other early American authors reenact ritual death and resurrection to conjure transformative spirituality in early American religion. The literary depictions of death and resurrection also conjure the physical impression phase of ritual initiation. While death and suffering find a host of literary representations, deliverance and resurrection are always attributed to divine intervention.

In Marrant's case, divine intervention came in the form of a sign. His prayers in the Cherokee language demonstrated the gift of tongues, a biblical sign that confirms that one possesses the gift of prophecy. Linguistic dexterity was common among the biblical prophets. Daniel, the Hebrew prophet who rises to leadership in the Babylonian Empire, learned to read and speak the Babylonian language. Conversely, although he is trained in the language and literature of Babylon, he prays to the God of Israel while facing Jerusalem, thus suggesting that ethnic identity primarily informs his spirituality. Fluency in multiple languages likely accounts for his ability to negotiate Babylonian religious and political terrains.

The prophetic gift was often represented by oral symbolism in other biblical lore. In Exodus, Moses at first is reluctant to accept the prophetic call. He hesitates because he presumes his slowness of speech (possibly a stutter) renders him unable to perform his prophetic duties. When prompted by God to take up the prophetic mantle, Isaiah initially objects that his "unclean lips" make him unfit for service. In the New Testament story of Pentecost, the religious authority of the apostles of Jesus is confirmed when "tongues of fire" descend on them, symbolizing prophetic utterance. As the tongues divided, and came to rest on each of them, they began to pray and exhort in other languages with fluency. In Marrant's case, the gift of tongues symbolizes not only oratorical eloquence but also his ability to interpret, or "hear," the message of the book and translate it into auditory forms of expression. His family's background in the Africana religious context of New York's Pinkster celebrations may have informed his understanding of the story of Pentecost. In the Pinkster tradition, the manifestation of the Spirit of God was signaled by the display of oratorical gifts—"compelling powerful preaching and prophesying" and "speaking in tongues."[51] For Marrant, the gift of tongues conjures both his oratorical skill and his prophetic authority to make the Bible speak. The sudden manifestation of his prophetic gift caused his life to be spared. Following the miraculous display, he was taken before the "king," where he underwent a final trial before his eventual release.

Reintegration

Marrant returned to his residence with the Cherokee later that year. It had been a long time—nearly two years—since he had last seen his mother or his siblings, and he found himself longing for the familiarity of home. He decided that he would return to his mother and acknowledged that "my affections to my family and country were not dead; they were sometimes very sensibly felt."[52] The journey home introduced reintegration, the final stage of his initiation. The resurrection theme in *Narrative* not only celebrates Marrant's successful endurance of trial and isolation but also anticipates a new identity that is allegorized by his family's inability to recognize him when he returns. The drama of recognition is acted out in reintegration, the final stage of ritual initiation.

In Africana religious societies, when initiates were reintegrated into the community after passing the tests of physical impression, they were expected to participate fully in the ritual life of the community as adults, taking their place among the living, the ancestors, and the yet to be born. The process of integration included charges to protect the community and revere both elders and ancestors given by spiritual parents. Integration into the community completed the symbolic death of seclusion, and thus the initiates were reborn. The children and adolescents who entered the wilderness returned as young men and women.

Marrant describes his reintegration into his community near the conclusion of *Narrative*. The shift back to familial environs was signaled by his admission that "affections to my family and country were not dead; they were sometimes very sensibly felt, and at last strengthened into an invincible desire of returning home." Though dissuaded by the Indian chief, Marrant, after the trifold utterance of prayers, began the journey home.

His first encounter back in Savannah revealed the extent to which he had fully embraced (and been embraced by) Native American culture. When he arrived at a neighboring family's home, his appearance, "purely in the Indian stile [sic]," frightened his unsuspecting hosts. Since it was near dinnertime, he approached their door to ask if he could join them for the meal, but first he lingered outside unnoticed. When they saw Marrant wearing "the skins of wild beasts . . . a long pendant down my back, a sash round my middle, without breeches, and a tomohawk [*sic*] by my side," they were frightened and ran away. They may have thought he was a member of a raiding party and possibly feared for their lives. Marrant helped himself to the dinner the family had abandoned and ate "very heartily" while they hid in a nearby barn. He settled into their home and waited for them to return to greet him. At one point, he noticed a young girl who "stood peeping at me from behind a barn," but when he tried to approach her, "she fainted away, and it was upwards of an hour before she recovered." It would be another two hours, until almost nine o'clock, before they all reentered the home to greet him.

After about two days, the family had settled into a more familiar routine. Marrant conducted Sabbath prayers with several families and about seventeen other individuals. He remained with them six weeks before continuing to his mother's house. He was delighted to see his uncle's familiar face and asked about the well-being of his mother and sisters. But his uncle did not recognize him and consequently would not receive him as a guest. Turned away from his uncle's house, he continued to Savannah. Once he arrived, he found an old classmate who also did not recognize him but allowed him to spend the night. Marrant asked his classmate about the well-being of his family:

> I asked him if he knew Mrs. Marrant, and how the family were? He said, he had just left them, they were all well; but a young lad, with whom he went to school, who, after he had quitted school, went to Charles-Town to learn some trade; but came home crazy, rambled in the woods, and was torn in pieces by the wild beasts. How do you know, said I, that he was killed by wild beasts? I, and his brother, and uncle, and other, said he, went three days into the woods in search of him, and found his carcase [*sic*] torn, and brought it home and buried it.[53]

Marrant was moved to tears by his classmate's story. After sharing a meal and prayer with his host, he went to sleep, awoke the next morning for prayer, and traveled to his mother's house one block away. When he arrived at his mother's house, his family did not recognize him either. Because of his customary Cherokee attire, he drew everyone's attention, but no one recognized him.

It was common for the prophet's identity to be concealed in reintegration scenes from biblical narratives as well. Notably, in Genesis, the patriarch Joseph was reunited with his family after having been estranged from them for a prolonged period in which he survived a tumultuous ordeal of seclusion, instruction, imprisonment, and near execution. His brothers did not recognize him, and

Joseph concealed his identity. He required his youngest brother, Benjamin, to be brought before him. It was Benjamin, his youngest sibling, through whom Joseph's reintegration into his family was facilitated.

In other biblical narratives, the process of reintegration was facilitated through women. For example, Peter's reintegration into the Judean community of believers following his miraculous escape from prison was facilitated not by the youngest sibling, but by a maid, Rhoda.[54] Before the devotees gathered for prayer, Rhoda, having recognized Peter's voice, announced his presence to those gathered at the house of Mary. The others did not believe her, and Peter's reintegration was delayed. Rhoda, however, was resolute and insisted that it was Peter that she had heard. Eventually the others came to accept her testimony, and Peter was recognized and restored to fellowship among them. Thus, Peter rejoined the group by the testimony of a woman.

Similarly, women were first to proclaim Jesus's resurrection in the Gospel narratives. The men, however, needed more convincing following the women's testimonies. In fact, in several Gospel accounts, Jesus was not recognized by people who knew him when he first appeared after his crucifixion. In each instance, his identity was concealed and only women recognized him.

In Marrant's case, the biblical tropes of ritual reintegration are combined. His younger sister—both a female and his youngest sibling—facilitated his integration into the family by announcing his identity. Like the community of disciples in the biblical model, Marrant's family did not believe her testimony. As he recalled:

> My youngest sister, eleven years of age, came in from school, with a book under her arm. I was then sitting in the parlour, and as she passed by the parlour door, she peep'd in and seeing a strange person there, she recollected me; she goes into the kitchen, and tells the servants, her brother was come; but her report finding no credit, she came and peep'd again, that she might be certain it was me; and then passing into the next room, through the parlour where I was sitting, she made a running curtsy, and says to my eldest sister, who was there, it is my brother John! She called her a foolish girl and threatened to beat her.[55]

Marrant's youngest sister was the only one who recognized him. In *Narrative*, the biblical trope of recognition in which either the youngest sibling or women facilitate ritual reintegration is collapsed in the character of Marrant's youngest sister. It is also worth noting that Marrant points out that his sister had just come home from school and carried "a book under her arm." Is it possible that she recognized her brother because she was also literate and possessed the power to make the book talk? Did book literacy also suggest the power to conjure scriptures? Marrant's reintegration takes place when his youngest sister is eleven years old—the same age as he was when his formal education ended and he had learned to read. Perhaps she was the only one who could recognize, or "see," John Marrant when he reentered the community because Marrant had identified her gift and she recognized the same in him.

Marrant is not the only Black Atlantic author for whom a sister represents familial attachment. Fellow Black Atlantic authors Olaudah Equiano and Ukawsaw Gronniosaw both identify sisters who facilitate their separation from their families when their respective journeys begin. Equiano and Gronniosaw also express a singular fondness for their youngest female sibling. In Gronniosaw's account, Logwy, his "beloved sister" whom he describes as "quite white, and fair, with fine light hair," exhibited "every sign of grief that can be imagined," crying "most sadly" and "wringing her hands" when he left with the English merchant. Though Gronniosaw was "the more willing" to part company with siblings who "despised me, and looked on me with contempt," he was "truly concerned to leave" his "one sister who was always exceeding fond of me."[56] Equiano "cried and grieved continually" when his sister was violently "torn from me, and immediately carried away" in the middle of the night "while we lay clasped in each other's arms." His profound grief left him "in a state of distraction not to be described." For several days he was despondent and "did not eat any thing but what they forced into my mouth."[57]

Except for these affectionate relationships, both Gronniosaw and Marrant portray familial relations that could be described as tenuous at best. Gronniosaw looks forward to separating from his family because of strained relations stemming from their annoyance at his queries into profound spiritual matters. Marrant, who endured the scourge of his family because of his religious devotion, annoys his siblings and neighbors. Both authors, however, reserve special affection for a sister, singling her out as the relative to whom familial attachment is most strongly felt. But in Marrant's *Narrative*, the trope is revised. His younger sister announces his reintegration into the community. In Gronniosaw's and Equiano's respective autobiographies, separation from their sisters is permanent. Marrant's youngest sister, however, like the women at the tomb of Jesus, is the first to proclaim his return. He employs language consistent with resurrection to dramatize the scene: "She ran and clasped me round the neck, and looking me in the face, said, 'Are not you my brother John?' I answered yes, and wept. I was then made known to all the family, to my friends, and acquaintances, who received me, and were glad and rejoiced: Thus the dead was brought to life again; thus the lost was found."[58]

The resurrection of John Marrant reintegrated him into his community, and the dead was made alive again. In the same allegorical sense that his seclusion represented initiatory death, his reintegration with family, friends, and acquaintances represented the continuity of life and the African cosmological understanding of the interconnectedness of the living and the dead.

Covenant

As adults in the community, initiates are expected to marry and ensure the continuance of the life of the community. Marriage, along with vows of commitment and reverence for the community, constitutes a communal covenant that is considered eternally binding and sacred. Having completed the initiation, the initiates successfully transition from adolescence to adulthood and assume the responsibilities necessary to ensure future generations of the community.

Marrant expressed his understanding of covenant when he assumed the role of preacher among a community of enslaved Africans in Charleston, South Carolina. On his return to Charleston, he lamented the lack of religious instruction among the enslaved. He organized a small community of about thirty persons and began instructing them in prayer and scripture. He describes his sense of covenantal commitment to the larger African American community in the following: "During this time, I saw my call to the ministry fuller and clearer; had a feeling concern [sic] for the salvation of my countrymen: I carried them constantly in the arms of prayer and faith to the throne of grace, and had continual sorrow in my heart for my brethren, for my kinsmen, according to the flesh."[59]

The transition from childhood into adulthood reflects the transformative goal of contemplation as discussed by Barbara Holmes, who understands initiation as a contemplative practice, or at least as a practice that affords multiple possibilities for transformative contemplation. Initiation understood as transformative contemplation provides an illuminating lens through which religious phenomena can be evaluated. This lens is particularly informative for phenomena occurring in moments of intercultural contact. The making of the New World involved the subordination of African societies to European colonial powers. Many scholars presume that the cultural contact of this historical moment resulted in subordinated Africans adopting European religions and religious orientations and consequently the eradication of African traditional religious communities. However, scholars who rigidly hold to such a model of acculturation fail to understand the complexities of exchange that are involved in moments of cultural encounter. As Holmes explains, moments of encounter necessarily involve varying degrees of acculturation, particularly in those instances where power relationships are unequal; however, cultural exchange is never unilateral even when inequitable: "Africans were not likely to supplant one belief system with another. Religions were layered upon another, and then they were tested for their efficaciousness. Throughout African history, indigenous beliefs coexisted with Islam and Christianity. If a certain emphasis developed, it was because a particular faith system seemed to improve the lives of the people. Conquerors could only affect surface practices; the prioritizing of religious allegiances remained with the people."[60]

While the formation of Black Christian communities has been commonly interpreted under the analytical rubric of conversion, West and West Central African initiation rituals may better explain the religious transformation John Marrant describes in his autobiographical *Narrative*. Although the Bible provided the narrative models through which his formation was depicted, Africana ritual forms determined the meanings assigned to the texts he produced.

3. Exodus

Conjuring Retaliation in Marrant's Narrative

Of the numerous biblical stories that populated the religious imagination of Black America during colonial times, perhaps none resonated as widely as the Exodus story. Its popularity among Blacks battling legal enslavement and social proscription is understandable given that it narrates the supernatural deliverance of enslaved people. The centrality of Exodus in African American religious history is well documented, but many studies of the Exodus story in Black religious experience suggest that Black readers' hermeneutical lens derives solely from their political status as slaves.[1] In most cases, however, the religious orientation of the Black reading community has not been widely considered.

One exception, Zora Neale Hurston's fictitious *Moses, Man of the Mountain*, renders the Exodus narrative from the cultural worldview of Black Americans. While her characters' perspectives more closely reflect those of her twentieth-century ethnographic studies, *Moses* demonstrates how a Black religious worldview was utilized to interpret Exodus. Moses, the central character, is portrayed as a conjure man who speaks in Black dialect. Hurston's tale is informed by a keen insight into the religious lives of Black Americans and grounded in the religious imagination of twentieth-century Black Floridians, not those of eighteenth- and nineteenth-century African Americans who witnessed or experienced slavery directly. As North America's first Black ordained minister, John Marrant, in contrast, provides a firsthand interpretation of Exodus by an eighteenth-century Black religious authority figure. In fact, his interpretation of Exodus in *Narrative* establishes a seminal moment in African American religious history.

Near the conclusion of *Narrative*, John Marrant presents a retaliation tale in which a South Carolina planter's wife, Mrs. Jenkins, mysteriously dies after she orders her husband to terminate the religious meetings of the enslaved people on their property. In his depiction, Marrant conjures thematic and structural elements of the Exodus story to illustrate how divine aid assists the enslaved to overcome their enslavers. "It pleased God," narrates Marrant, describing Mrs. Jenkins's death after a sudden illness, "to lay his hand upon their Mistress."[2] This same tale motif in which the enslaved violently throw off the shackles of enslavement by divine intervention was more overtly espoused in the preaching rhetoric of his contemporary David Margrett, a fellow Huntingdon minister whom Marrant may have encountered in Savannah. Marrant's redeployment of the Exodus story utilizes two symbols, blood and wilderness, to illustrate a pattern of retaliation. This symbolic pattern is also identified in the respective narratives of Nat Turner and Frederick Douglass. Though both Turner and Douglass explicitly disavow the practice of conjure, their narratives include motifs that signify conjure as an agent of divine retribution. Turner insisted that his possession of spiritual and intellectual gifts, rather than "conjuring and such like tricks," was responsible for the influence he exerted over the minds of fellow slaves, adding that he "always spoke of such things with contempt."[3] Similarly, Douglass reluctantly accepted a protective herb from an elder adviser who insisted the root contained properties that could protect its carrier from racial violence. Despite both narrators' stated distrust of conjure, their autobiographical narratives utilize biblical symbols to allegorize supernatural retribution for slavery. Marrant also deployed biblical symbols to depict divine confrontation with and to pronounce spiritual condemnation on the institution of American slavery. The previous chapter discussed his depiction of wilderness initiation relying on structural parallels to biblical stories. In each case, the authors use wilderness and blood to signify ritualized prophetic initiation and direct confrontation with oppressive rulers. Taken together, these symbols, read within narrative structures derived from traditional Africana storytelling cultures, reveal retribution tales for injuries suffered at the hands of enslavers.

The Power of the Blood

After narrating the conclusion of wilderness initiation, Marrant demonstrates the first sign of his ministry; he conjures the Exodus. Marrant's choice of the Exodus as the sign of his ministry is based on the biblical example of Jesus. In the Gospel of John, Jesus's ministry begins with the transformation of water into wine. This miraculous sign is the first that confirms Jesus's prophetic identity. Within the symbolic and structural world of biblical narratives, this moment mimics the transformation of water to blood by Moses in Exodus.

The story of Israel's escape from Egypt was a dominant theme in biblical literature as well. Moses, the story's central prophetic figure, meets all the narrative criteria for biblical prophetic identity. His birth is marked by divine intervention via a miraculous escape from death; as a child, he is noticed for exceptional beauty and unique qualities; he receives special training and education as a member of Pharaoh's court; and he undergoes ritual initiation in the wilderness—in fact, the five stages of initiation discussed in the previous chapter are present in his story (divine call at the burning bush; seclusion in the wilderness; instruction at the feet of Jethro; physical impression enacted by Zipporah, Jethro's daughter; and reintegration into his community in Egypt after he receives a message for their deliverance from bondage). When he prophesies the deliverance of his people to Pharaoh, one of the signs of their emancipation is the transformation of water into blood, an ominous foreshadowing of the final plague— death to the firstborn in every household of Egypt. The death plague takes the life of Pharaoh's son and the firstborn son in every household in Egypt. Pharaoh finally agrees to release Israel, and Moses leads them from Egypt across the Red Sea and into the wilderness. In the Exodus story, the plague of death is not enacted until lesser plagues prove ineffectual.

Other versions of the Exodus narrative avoid the death plague altogether. Abram's escape from Egypt does not require the plague of death. When Abram goes to Egypt because of a famine, he conceals his relationship with Sarai, his wife, saying instead that she is his sister.[4] Abram fabricates this relationship because he fears the Egyptians whom he supposes will kill him to take Sarai, his spouse. Abram's fear is nearly realized. Though his life is spared, the Egyptians capture Sarai and take her into Pharaoh's house to be his wife. However, Pharaoh's house is besieged with plagues, and Sarai's virtue is preserved. Pharaoh sends Abram out of Egypt with his wife and all his possessions, and Abram escapes Egypt with all of his people and increased possessions.

The same narrative pattern of escape can be observed in Abraham's account in Genesis, chapter 20. Although the setting has shifted to the land of Gerar, and Abram and Sarai are now named Abraham and Sarah, respectively, the structural elements of the story are unchanged. Abraham returns to the Negev region where he had been just before entering Egypt. He enters Gerar and says that Sarah is his sister instead of his wife. Sarah is taken to King Abimelech, and plagues are brought on Abimelech and his household because of her. Abraham and Sarah are sent out of the land, and Abraham increases his material possessions in cattle, servants, and silver.

The next repetition of the story in Genesis 26 involves Isaac, one of Abraham's sons. Like Abraham, Isaac is driven into a foreign land due to famine. He is warned in a dream, however, not to go to Egypt but to go to Gerar instead with his wife, Rebekah. Fearful of the jealousy of his neighbors, Isaac pretends Rebekah is his sister. This time, however, the king discovers that Rebekah is Isaac's wife before she is taken. The king proclaims that no one is to touch Rebekah lest punishment be brought on the land. Isaac and Rebekah leave Gerar with family and increased possessions. Thus, plagues of any kind are avoided altogether.

When John Marrant conjures the Exodus near the close of the fourth edition of *Narrative*, he explains that the commencement of the American Revolution prompted his swift departure from North America. Up until that point, he had lived in Charleston with his brother and found employment as "a house Carpenter" on a South Carolina plantation. It was there that Marrant began instructing enslaved children and their parents:

> I used to spend my time in reading God's Word, singing Watt's Hymns and in Prayer, the little negro children would often come round the door with their pretty wishful looks, and finding my heart much drawn out in Love to their souls, I one evening called several of them, and asked them if they could say the Lord's Prayer, &c.... I used to go to prayer with them before we parted; this continued without interruption for three or four months, in which time, by the children acquainting their parents with it, I soon had my society increased to about thirty persons.[5]

Marrant's "society" mediated, if only temporarily, the harsh realities of enslavement by offering the enslaved communal bonds of support on the Jenkins plantation. However, the familial environment of fellowship and learning would be short-lived. Mrs. Jenkins, the plantation mistress, "became acquainted with our proceedings," writes Marrant, "and was full of rage at it, and determined to put a stop to it."

The mistress's efforts to break up the society began with the interrogation of two of Marrant's young pupils. After the children were brought before her, they were asked to recite the Lord's Prayer, and Mrs. Jenkins demanded to know who taught them. When the children answered, Marrant was brought into direct confrontation with the slave-owning Jenkins family. Mrs. Jenkins resolved to put an end to Marrant's meetings and sent her husband to intimidate Marrant and his society of pupils. As Marrant recalled:

> She then stirred up her husband against us . . . and made him promise to examine further into the matter, and break up our meeting; which he then very soon did, for a short space; for he, together with his overseer and negro-driver, and some of his neighbours, beset the place wherein we met, while we were at prayers; and as the poor creatures came out they caught them, and tied them together with cords, till the next morning, when all they caught, men, women, and children were strip'd naked and tied, their feet to a stake, their hands to the arm of a tree, and so severely flogg'd that the blood ran from their backs and sides to the floor, to make them promise they would leave off praying, &c. though several of them fainted away with the pain and loss of blood, and lay upon the ground as dead for a considerable time after they were untied, I did not hear that she obtained her end of any of them.[6]

Mrs. Jenkins insisted her husband flog Marrant, but Marrant threatened to "take the law of him, and make him pay for it." The threat of legal action stalled Mr. Jenkins, and a conversation ensued. In Marrant's narration, he and Jenkins debate the ethical responsibilities of slave owners to slaves in light of Christian doctrine. According to Marrant, he wields better command of legal policy and Christian doctrine than does Jenkins.

Of particular interest in Marrant's description of Jenkins's assault is the ground saturated by the blood of the enslaved. In the Exodus story, Moses's initial sign to Pharaoh, the conversion of water to blood, foreshadows Israel's retaliation and the death of Egypt's sons.[7] Marrant also deploys blood imagery to foreshadow divine retribution. Although Mrs. Jenkins succeeds in driving him from the plantation, Marrant has the final word in the saga when Mrs. Jenkins is seized with a mysterious illness: "In about two months after I left them, it pleased God to lay his hand upon their Mistress, and she was seized with a very violent fever, which no medicine that they could procure would remove, and in a very few days after she was taken ill, she died in a very dreadful manner, in great anger with her husband, for not preventing their meetings, which she had heard they continued, notwithstanding all her endeavours to stop it."[8] The death plague is enacted on Mrs. Jenkins because, like Pharaoh in Exodus, she refused to allow the people of God to worship freely in the wilderness. Her harsh treatment of enslaved laborers causes their blood to flow. The blood imagery foreshadows divine retribution, which is realized by her untimely demise.

Nat Turner

The Exodus narrative was also conjured by the repetition of wilderness initiation and blood symbolism in Nat Turner's narration of his spiritual autobiography in *The Confessions of Nat Turner*. Turner, the leader of the 1831 rebellion in Southampton, Virginia, spent extended time isolated in the woods before he planned his revolt. He escaped from his owner's Virginia plantation in 1829 and was secluded in the woods for thirty days but returned after he received a divine commission. In *Confessions*, related to Virginia attorney Thomas Gray, he explains that he was directed by the Spirit to "return to the service of my earthly master," where he should "seek first the kingdom of God."[9] The plantation slaves were dismayed by his return, claiming that "if they had my sense they would not serve any master in the world." When Turner was back on the plantation, his wilderness consecration took on new effect. Like Marrant, he adopted ascetic practices that distinguished him from peers and augmented his prophetic authority. At every opportunity, he withdrew into the seclusion of the woods to better understand the revelations of the Spirit. Like the Kimpasi initiates in Kongo whose rituals equip them with a better understanding of spiritual seasons, Turner learned "the knowledge of the elements, the revolution of the planets, the operation of tides, and changes of seasons."[10]

In *Confessions*, blood imagery also triggers retributive justice. Turner, like Marrant, was consecrated in the woods before commencing his antislavery heroics. Shortly after returning to the plantation, Turner received a vision that inspired him to rise up in rebellion against slave owners in Virginia. He describes a cosmic battle in which streams of blood resulted from fighting between Black and white spirits, and a voice from heaven was heard saying, "Such is your luck, such you are called to see, and let it come rough or smooth, you must surely bare [*sic*] it."[11] The blood imagery in Turner's narration signals rebellion. The image of blood flowing in streams and the voice of the Spirit sound a call to rebellion. While Turner does not initially understand the vision of battle between white and Black spirits, the repetition of blood patterns in subsequent visions drives home the point.

Following this revelation, Turner received a second vision while laboring in the field. He saw what he describes as *"drops of blood* on the corn as though it were dew from heaven." He also describes "hieroglyphic characters, and numbers, with the forms of men in different attitudes, *portrayed in blood*." He shared news of this revelation widely, communicating it to both white and Black residents in the neighborhood. In particular, he notes the effect of his news on Etheldred T. Brantley, a local white man reputed for his wicked treatment of the enslaved:

> About this time I told these things to a white man, (Etheldred T. Brantley) on whom it had a wonderful effect—and he ceased from his wickedness, and was attacked immediately with a cutaneous eruption, *and blood oozed from the pores of his skin*, and after praying and fasting nine days, he was healed, and the Spirit appeared to me again, and said, as the Saviour had been baptised so should we be also—and when the white people would not let us be baptised by the church, we went down into the water together, in the sight of many who reviled us, and were baptised by the Spirit—After this I rejoiced greatly, and gave thanks to God.[12]

For Turner, the appearance of blood—on the corn in the field, oozing from Brantley's pores, and flowing in cosmic visions—symbolized an apocalyptic battle in which the powers that upheld American slavery would be defeated. As he and his band of rebels marched from plantation to plantation in revolt, they likely imagined themselves accompanied by the death angel who wreaked havoc in Egypt just as they sought to do in Southampton, Virginia.

Turner's reference to the "blood of Christ" in his description of the miraculous signs that inspire his rebellion is also noteworthy. "The blood of Christ," he declares, "had been shed on this earth, and had ascended to heaven for the salvation of sinners." The appearance of Christ's blood in Turner's visions, however, does not signal the reconciliation of humanity and God but rather announces that "the great day of judgement was at hand."[13] The concern was for earthly, rather than cosmic, justice. The association of the blood of Christ with the redemption of captives in America may have precedence in traditional West and West Central African religion. Samson Fatokun, an African church historian, notes that expiatory sacrifices were common in these religions. As in the Christian maxim, "bloodshed is necessary for remission of sin," blood occupies a significant place in the Yoruba concept of expiatory sacrifice and can avert evils in the land. In fact, such sacrifice is incomplete without the shedding of blood—the blood of animals, or even (in extreme cases) human beings, is believed to have both "propitiatory and purifying power." The victim's blood stands as a substitute for the offender and gives satisfaction or cools the hot anger of the offended deity.[14]

Among the Abaluyia in Western Kenya, blood sacrifices were performed to bring about peace rather than hostility. During the *omusango* ceremony, the ritual slaughter of a sacrificial dog enacted an end to intercommunal hostilities. The blood of the sacrificed animal stood in place of the blood of the men from the communities that had been spared by the slaughtering of the dog. The ceremony is comparable to animal sacrifices practiced for generations throughout the region. According to the religious studies scholar Lucas Nandih Shamala, "The Israelites of the Old Testament times and other Near Eastern groups (extra-biblical groups) were quite familiar with these types of sacrifices, which sealed peace covenants and ensured peace for the parties involved. A striking example of this notion is the Christian Church, which was founded on the belief in a crucified Christ who shed his blood for the salvation of humankind."[15]

The notion of expiatory sacrifice may also help illuminate ritual sacrifices performed by Turner and his coconspirators on the night of the rebellion. Turner and six fellow conspirators slaughtered a pig in the woods before they commenced their attack on the planters of Southampton. Nearly forty years earlier in Haiti, Boukman Dutty, who is described as "a Papaloi or High Priest," performed a similar ritual slaughter of a pig in the wilderness at the commencement of the Haitian Revolution. After the animal was sacrificed, Boukman gave instructions to rebels, and "after Voodoo incantations and the sucking of the blood of a stuck pig, he stimulated his followers by a prayer spoken in creole." The expiatory sacrifice was widespread throughout New World diasporas and was also a constitutive element of traditional African indigenous religion.[16]

Turner's reference to the blood of Christ invokes the redemption of slaves in Southampton, Virginia, rather than the whole of humanity. In fact, notions of universal salvation through expiatory sacrifice are without precedent in traditional African religion. According to Samson Fatokun, "While indigenous religion has references to cases of sacrifices undertaken by some individuals (savior-gods) for the liberation of their different communities from one calamity or the other, the notion of a single individual taking away the sins of the 'whole world' through a single act of expiatory sacrifice finds no parallel to Africa."[17] In Turner's narrative, the blood of Christ signals resistance to the forces of American slavery and redemption from bondage. The reconciliation of human beings, either individually or collectively, to God does not appear central to Turner's conception. Turner's deployment of blood symbolism in *Confessions* seems more in line with epistemologies informed by African conceptualizations of expiatory sacrifice.

Frederick Douglass

Wilderness seclusion also preceded blood symbolism and retaliation against slavery in Frederick Douglass's autobiographical *Narrative of the Life of Frederick Douglass* (1845). Douglass fled to the wilderness after his petition for protection from his overseer, Edward Covey, was dismissed by his owner. In the wilderness, Sandy Jenkins, an older slave, passed along herbs to Douglass that "would render it impossible for Mr. Covey, or any other white man, to whip me" if worn on his right side. He reluctantly accepted Sandy's herbal protection, noting his skepticism regarding conjure, and returned from the wilderness. Back on the plantation, the stage was set for a showdown with Covey.

In his depiction of his conflicts with Covey, Douglass employed blood symbolism to signal meanings beyond the surface of the text. Douglass explains that he had been brutally beaten in an earlier fight with the overseer. Covey kicked Douglass repeatedly when he complained that he was too sick to work; when Douglass was unable to stand, Covey struck him with a hickory slat, and "the blood ran freely" from a large wound on the side of his head. Douglass's description of his appearance after this first fight emphasizes bloodshed to amplify his suffering: "I then presented an appearance enough to affect any but a heart of iron. From the crown of my head to my feet, I was *covered with blood*. My hair was all *clotted with dust and blood*; my shirt was *stiff with blood*. My legs and feet were torn in sundry places with briers and thorns, and were also *covered with blood*. I suppose I looked like a man who had escaped a den of wild beasts, and barely escaped them."[18]

When Douglass and Covey next face off, Douglass had returned from the wilderness and he was carrying Sandy's protective root. This time when Covey tried to strike him, he "resolved to fight" rather than succumb to another beating. He explains, "Suiting my action to the resolution, I seized Covey hard by the throat; and as I did so, I rose." Covey, taken aback by Douglass's newfound resolve, called for Mr. Hughes to help subdue him. Hughes was greeted by a kick to the ribs when he arrived to help, and with Hughes out of commission, Douglass and Covey fought for nearly two hours. When the dust settled, Douglass notes, he had not been whipped by Covey at all. He credits the dramatic confrontation with Covey as the turning point in his career as a slave. Not only did he experience a rejuvenated determination for freedom and greater self-confidence, but Douglass explains that he was never again whipped. In fact, by the end of the scene, the structural elements of the story have been reversed. Covey, not Douglass, is covered in his own blood. Douglass pinpoints the role reversal, reminding the reader, "He had drawn no blood from me, but I had from him."[19]

The retaliation tales related in autobiographical narratives of Marrant, Turner, and Douglass raise important questions regarding the role of orthodox theology in Black people's adoption of Christianity during the colonial era. Their depictions suggest that for some early Black Christians, the enslavement of African people was irreconcilable with Christian faith; consequently, resistance to enslavement was sanctioned in the religious reflections of leading Black religious figures. According to the interpretations of these biblical exegetes, violent retaliation against slavery was sanctioned by God and constituted a moral imperative within the ethical reflections of Marrant and other early Black Christians.

The autobiographical narratives of John Marrant, Nat Turner, and Frederick Douglass suggest that the association of retaliatory conjure and the Exodus may have been ubiquitous in the religious thought of early Black Christians. Yvonne Chireau's study of conjure in African American religious history uncovers a standard narrative structure employed to relate accounts of supernatural retaliation. Chireau provides the following description: "These [conjure] narratives nearly always focus on some sort of human suffering, and they inevitably articulate a link between conflict and supernaturally induced misfortune.... [T]hey describe sudden illness, with symptoms of headache, deafness, and unusual physical debilitation—all precipitated by conflict or emotional injury."[20]

The autobiographical accounts discussed in this chapter follow this narrative pattern. In Marrant's text, the account begins with the suffering of slaves caused by the brutal beating they receive at the urging of the mistress. Mrs. Jenkins's sudden, incurable fever is attributed to a supernatural source. As Marrant states, "It pleased God to lay his hand upon their Mistress." By the end of the saga, the fortunes have been reversed. Mrs. Jenkins is bedridden and at the point of death while the enslaved continue to gather in the woods for worship and mutual edification.

David Margrett: Exodus and Religious Resistance to Slavery

The recognition of the Exodus as a pattern for retaliation narratives may have been shared widely by eighteenth-century Black Christians. The case of David Margrett, a Black Methodist missionary from London, is illustrative. In 1774, Margrett was sent to North America to minister to enslaved laborers at the Bethesda Orphanage in Savannah. Selina Hastings, Countess of Huntingdon and founder of the Huntingdon Methodist Connexion, inherited the orphanage when her most notable minister, George Whitefield, passed away in 1770. Whitefield desired that the orphanage be used as a college to train ministers to evangelize Native Americans. When the property came into Hastings's possession, there were roughly fifty enslaved people there whose primary responsibilities included growing rice and other crops for food. The Reverend William Piercy, who was temporarily placed in charge of Bethesda, along with Robert Keen, a London merchant who handled the countess's American affairs, agreed that Margrett was the most suitable choice to evangelize the slaves at Bethesda, since many of the white ministers "deemed themselves too great to speak to any but white people."[21] Margrett, an alleged former slave who had resided in London at least seven years, had enrolled at Trevecca College in Wales, where ministers in the Huntingdon Connexion received training for ministry and some received Christian ordination. Having completed his studies a year earlier, he was chosen to accompany a white minister to the American colonies, where he would evangelize the slaves at Whitefield's orphanage.

When Margrett arrived in 1774, his first stop was in Charleston, where Marrant was living at the time. It did not take long for Margrett to make an impact. Within three days of his arrival, complaints about his preaching and his behavior began to be addressed to Selina Hastings. At the invitation of his host, Patrick Hinds, Margrett preached a sermon in a Baptist meetinghouse, and his discourse included an unsettling interpretation of the Exodus narrative. He delivered a damning message of judgment to American slave owners. "Remember," he warned, "that the children of Israel were delivered out of the hands of Pharo [sic] and he and all his host were drowned in the Red Sea and God will deliver his own people from slavery."[22] His preaching aroused the anger of local whites, and even his friends feared violent repercussions in response to his incendiary preaching. Forced to flee from Charleston to avoid execution, Margrett arrived in Savannah after just two short weeks. In Savannah, Margrett was cautioned to avoid the kind of preaching that had gotten him run out of Charleston, but despite these warnings, he reiterated his message of temporal deliverance to the enslaved. In Savannah, it was reported that he told the enslaved laborers at Bethesda that he had been sent to America as "a second Moses and should be called to deliver his people from slavery."[23] Fears of insurrection circulated throughout Savannah, and Margrett was soon a wanted man once again—a bench warrant was signed for his arrest. Shortly thereafter, Margrett confided to Piercy that the Lord had commanded him to take an enslaved woman as his wife even though she was already married to another enslaved man. When Piercy refused to arrange the relationship, Margrett insisted that a different, unmarried enslaved woman was to be his wife. This request was also denied, and for the remainder of his time in North America, Piercy noted that Margrett was found "amongst the poor ignorant negro slaves, I mean wenches, continually."[24]

Although Margrett's actions angered Piercy, he was not so upset that he wanted to see Margrett hanged. When Piercy learned that the men who sought Margrett's life in South Carolina had come to Savannah to hang him, he made quick arrangements to have Margrett board a vessel for London.

Of particular interest in David Margrett's saga is his allusion to the story of Exodus as a central component of his message to the enslaved. Whereas Marrant's redeployment of Exodus is rendered discreetly, Margrett's rendition is more overt. In both narrations, God's divine intervention promises deliverance to slaves. Margrett, however, explicitly pronounced himself a "second Moses," suggesting that the desired freedom would result from human agency. Understandably, Margrett's sermons caused tremendous alarm throughout the white community, and there was "continual apprehension of an insurrection among the slaves."[25] Marrant, in contrast, attributed the work of retribution wholly to divine agency. Consequently, his teaching did not inspire the fear of rebellion, but nevertheless Mrs. Jenkins objected to her husband that religious instruction "was the ready way to have all his negroes ruin'd."[26]

Also noteworthy concerning Margrett's proclamation is his claim that certain enslaved women were to be betrothed to him in marriage. While Piercy saw these proclamations as evidence that Margrett was led by "the Devil and the lust of his own heart," Margrett's actions may have been inspired by his interpretation of biblical retaliation stories.[27] In the Genesis retaliation narratives, the threat to Israel's future was signified by the capture of the patriarchs' wives. It is possible that Margrett's actions and proclamations concerning enslaved women at Bethesda were intended to mimic the abduction of the patriarchs' wives in the stories from Genesis, thus dramatizing the injustice of slavery suffered by the Black community. In the Genesis accounts, when the patriarchs' wives are abducted, plagues of retribution afflict the ruling elites, and the women are subsequently released from bondage. Margrett's alleged advances toward enslaved women, both married and single, allegorized the vulnerability of the enslaved community and posed a threat to their survival.

Margrett may also have chosen to allegorize the material history of enslaved women in Georgia. As the religious studies scholar Alexis Wells-Oghoghomeh explains, episodes of sexual vulnerability profoundly shaped African women's experience of enslavement prior to their arrival in America. In many West African societies, European colonialism rendered African women vulnerable to sexual exploitation. Many women were offered to Europeans as sexual and domestic partners for those who lived onshore along the coast. Foreign travelers and traders in West Africa helped themselves to the "plethora of available" African women. In addition to the sexual and domestic services, some women functioned as cultural and linguistic liaisons who "forged commercial partnerships between local elites and foreigners." If these relationships extended beyond a specified amount of time, the women could be treated as wives. These coerced domestic arrangements could be beneficial for the women as well, and many utilized sexual partnerships to curry favor with Europeans and also to enhance opportunities for "the social, political, and economic advancement of the women's children."[28]

The Atlantic historian Pernille Ipsen describes interracial marriages between free and enslaved women and European traders in Gold Coast trading posts as "key economic and social institutions" that enabled culturally and socially inept European men to integrate into West African society. Known as *cassare*, it was a practice through which African families negotiated political and economic alliances through the marriage of their daughters to European traders. For more than three centuries, *cassare* marriages were widespread across many West African regions. Ipsen notes that though such marriages offered a degree of social advancement within the shifting landscape of West African society during the upheaval of the transatlantic slave trade, European traders, as a general rule, regarded African women as guilty, corrupt, and promiscuous.[29]

In light of African women's history of vulnerability via the transatlantic slave trade, Margrett's attempted exploitation of enslaved women may be explained by depictions of captive women's sexual vulnerability in the biblical saga of Exodus. In the accounts of the patriarchs found in Genesis, the wives of the protagonists were rescued from the households of captors who threatened exploitation. If it is the case that Margrett's interpretation was informed by enslaved women's history of exploitation in Africa, then it should be noted that the enslaved women's material history, rather than the doctrines of Euro-American Protestantism, informs Margrett's reading of Exodus. As Wells-Oghoghomeh notes, "This experience of capture, removal from kin ties, economic dependency, and sexual vulnerability burrowed into the collectives of enslaved women whether they were marched to another West African household, the barracoon of a European slave factory, or the dark hold of a Savannah-bound slave ship."[30] These memories also became fixtures in the psyches of the men and children who suffered alongside them, and they persisted even as enslaved women and men began new lives in the New World.

The pattern of retaliation identified in these Bible stories—suffering, confrontation, and supernaturally induced misfortune—can be traced in the material history of African American rebellions and insurrections more broadly. During the New York Slave Revolt of 1712, a rebellion allegedly organized to retaliate against harsh treatment by slave masters, conspirators swore an oath in blood and consumed "an enchanted powder" that they believed rendered them invulnerable.

Denmark Vesey, who, like John Marrant, worked as a carpenter in Charleston, employed conjure rituals during his 1822 conspiracy. Vesey, an alleged leader in the African Methodist Church, recruited artisans, laborers, and field hands to participate in an insurrection conspiracy headquartered at the church. Religious faith became a tool for both unifying and motivating participants. However, according to religious studies scholar Chireau, "While Christianity gave justification to the noble but dangerous cause of freedom fighting, ritual action was the catalyst." Additionally, Vesey also deployed an exegesis of the Exodus narrative to incite his followers to action. As Rolla Bennett, an enslaved woman owned by the former governor of South Carolina, confessed, Vesey exhorted the enslaved to "rise up and fight against the whites for our liberties." Bennett further explained that Vesey read from the Bible "how the Children of Israel were delivered out of Egypt from bondage. . . . He then read in the Bible where God commanded, that all should be cut off, both men, women and children, and said, he believed, it was no sin for us to do so, for the Lord had commanded us to do it."[31]

The association of conjure rituals and rebellion may have cultural antecedents among religious groups deriving from West Africa and West Central Africa. Among the Akan of West Africa, oath-swearing rituals were a central feature of the political culture. Taking an oath was a sacred act that involved ingesting ceremonial food or drink made from a variety of substances—gunpowder, water, blood, rum or other strong drink—potent enough to cause serious harm or even death if the terms of the oath were violated or if the oath was taken disingenuously. Described by many Europeans as "drinking fetish" or "eating fetish," oathing ceremonies were enacted to "seal commercial contracts, to consecrate peace treaties between nations, or to ensure the loyalty of soldiers and their commanding officers to the war aims of a polity." As one Ga-speaking informant relates, each element in the "drinking fetish" signified a different means of death if the terms of the oath were violated: "Water means an unhappy death in the sea . . . *the blood means a violent death by gunshot or sword* . . . the [millet] that all the blessings of the earth's fertility will be denied him, if he breaks the oath."[32]

The pervasiveness of oath swearing among West and West Central African religious communities obscures the specific cultural origin of oath-swearing rituals among enslaved Blacks in North America. However, in both North American and African contexts, oathing rituals were enacted to secure the loyalty of soldiers during war.[33] One of Vesey's most influential "lieutenants" was Jack Pritchard, or Gullah Jack, an acknowledged priest of African tradition. Gullah Jack was a leader in the Gullah Society, a church-based association composed of Blacks from Carolina plantations and the Sea Islands. Commonly known as a "sorcerer," Gullah Jack engaged in spiritual practices, including readings, prayers, and oaths. Additionally, he distributed poison to be used in preemptive attacks on planters and whites.

Poison was a purported weapon in the collective arsenal of Vesey's alleged revolt, but it was far more commonly deployed in "acts of personal defiance." In many instances, eighteenth-century African Americans turned to poisoning as a means of resolving offenses. Because slavery and poison were viewed as forms of spiritual evil, some enslaved Blacks settled grievances by poisoning their masters. Legislative responses in Georgia and South Carolina attest to planter concerns regarding the high incidence of poisoning in the region. South Carolina's Negro Act of 1751 stated, "That in case any slave shall teach or instruct another slave in the knowledge of any poisonous root, plant, herb, or other poison, whatever, he or she, so offending, shall upon conviction thereof, suffer death as a felon." According to eighteenth-century Georgia legislation, anyone convicted of poisoning was sentenced to death.[34]

Slave owners, as well as their mistresses, had reason to fear poisoning by slaves as retribution for ill treatment. Chireau notes the case of Sambo, a North Carolina slave convicted of conspiring to poison his slave mistress "to make her better to him." Sambo was found guilty of planning to give "touck," a harmful potion made of wild herbs widely known among Native and African American conjurers. The association of conjure with African and Native American culture was so common that one eighteenth-century doctor referred to conjure traditions as "Indian or Negro poison."[35] The association of retaliatory conjure with African and Native American cultural influence is instructive for understanding John Marrant's account of his conflict with a plantation mistress in Combahee, South Carolina. The well-documented tradition of poison raises suspicions concerning the possible role of conjure in the mysterious death of Mrs. Jenkins. It is plausible, and perhaps likely, that Marrant's wilderness initiation under the tutelage of his Native American instructor included training in the curative and toxic properties of local botany. If Mrs. Jenkins's sudden, mysterious illness was the result of conjure, then one can reasonably infer that the combination of the wilderness motif and blood imagery in Black freedom narratives signifies divinely inspired retaliation against oppression.

After the death of his employer Mrs. Jenkins, Marrant returned to Charleston and lived with his sister and her husband until the outbreak of the American War of Independence. In the late fall of 1775, he was impressed into the service of the British navy aboard the fourteen-gun war sloop *Scorpion*. Throughout the volatile eighteenth century, Royal Naval press gangs marauded the Atlantic rim, forcibly conscripting sailors into service. Long considered "a prerogative of the crown," press gangs supplemented formal systems of recruitment during heightened periods of maritime aggression. Both Black and white sailors tried desperately to avoid the press, but impressment was especially dangerous for free Blacks like Marrant. Since the fear of enslavement was an abiding threat, most Black seamen were reluctant to sail to the Caribbean, where there was a greater possibility of being sold into slavery. Unless Black seamen could prove that they were free men, they were assumed to be slaves.[36]

The fear of enslavement was not the only racially determined difference between Black and white seamen. The divisions of labor and hierarchies of status assigned aboard ship reflected racial stereotypes and presumptions of Black inferiority. Most often, Black sailors "filled special billets as cooks, officers' servants, or musicians, reinforcing their distinction from the seamen proper."[37] Marrant explains that he was pressed into service "as their musician, as they were told I could play on music."[38] Maritime musicians were frequently men of color and were often cast in the limelight as their skills were called on to gather crowds for recruitment in ports of call. Black Sam, an enslaved seaman who was described as "a good drummer and fifer," absconded from the *Comet* at Charleston in 1777. Two years later, Abraham, a seafaring runaway, was found drumming up a berth of recruits on the wharfs in Charleston. Though music making was not exclusively the domain of Black sailors, these instances of Black seafaring musicians underscore how racial identities were signified by forms of labor throughout the Atlantic world. Consequently, Marrant's inclusion of his employment as a musician aboard the *Scorpion* evinces a common pattern of employment marked by his racial identity.[39]

The American literary scholar Vincent Carretta posits that "Marrant may have fabricated his career" in the British navy, since Carretta was not able to find "his name on any of the muster lists recorded before, during, and after the *Scorpion* was stationed off the Carolina coast."[40] However, Marrant's allegorical rendering of his time at sea suggests that a symbolic, rather than literal, reading might better explain the meaning he sought to convey. Marrant concludes *Narrative* with a relation that allegorizes his time at sea. He notes with remorse that while he was aboard the *Scorpion*, "a lamentable stupor crept over all my spiritual vivacity, life and vigour; I got cold and dead."[41] He was revitalized, however, by a miraculous display of God's power. While he was traveling the Atlantic seas in service of His Majesty's Navy, a violent storm washed him overboard. Engulfed by waves and drowning in the sea, Marrant had all but given up hope of survival when he was suddenly washed back onto the ship's deck by the tumultuous waters. Before he could catch his breath or come to his senses, high waves and gusting winds tossed him back into the ocean a second time. In the open sea, he was submerged beneath the water but, as before, was miraculously washed back on deck a second time. This time, he fastened a rope to his waist to secure himself to the ship, but the storm's force washed him overboard a third time. Fully immersed in the sea, Marrant remained in the water "about eight minutes." Not only did he contend with the relentless waves, but "several sharks came round me; one of an enormous size, that could easily have taken me into his mouth at once, passed and rubbed against my side." Facing imminent peril, Marrant "cried more earnestly to the Lord than I had done for some time," and miraculously, he was rescued when he was washed back on deck by the force of the storm. Safe aboard the ship, he attributed his renewed sense of direction to his oceanic baptism, noting, "These were the means the Lord used to revive me, and I began to set out afresh." Lest the biblical parallels go unnoticed, Marrant was careful to point out that "he who heard Jonah's prayer, did not shut out mine."[42]

Marrant's telling of his near-death experience at sea conjures images of the Bible's story of Jonah and the whale. His adaptation of the epic tale to his own context reveals how water recalled African rituals and spiritual forms in early Black Christian communities. The tale follows the narrative pattern of the biblical story of Jonah and allegorizes water baptism. The dramatic account of his immersion (three times) in the "American seas" establishes a pattern of signification that utilizes water as a symbol for ritual initiation. Within the narrative framework of Exodus, Marrant's dramatic tale of renewal by water immersion conjures the biblical story of the Israelites' crossing the Red Sea. When the Egyptians discovered their male heirs had been slaughtered, their army pursued Israel in hopes of exacting revenge. Israel escaped to the Promised Land and avoided the wrath of the Egyptians. In Marrant's case, His Majesty's Army ensured his protection from would-be American captors.

Over the remainder of his naval career, Marrant saw combat several times and sustained life-threatening injuries that would plague him for the rest of his life. No longer fit for combat, he was deployed in the West Indies, and after a three-month stay in the hospital, he was discharged. The injuries he suffered from the battles of his military engagement brought his naval career to an abrupt end. Following his discharge, Marrant arrived in London, where he lived with "a respectable and pious merchant" and developed a reputation for his Christian piety and respectability.[43] It was during this time in London that Marrant attended Trevecca College and received his ministerial ordination in the Huntingdon Connexion, an offshoot branch of the Methodist Church founded by the Countess of Huntingdon, Selina Hastings.

Hastings was a towering presence in the early history of the Methodist Church in England. The Huntingdon Connexion emerged in the latter half of the eighteenth century against the backdrop of substantial diversity among the Christian sects of England. Protestant dissenters could be categorized as belonging to one of two groups: assimilationists and separatists, the former recognized as part of the Church of England while the latter was characterized by a constant agitation for religious freedom. Amid the upheaval of religious institutions and ideologies during the tumultuous eighteenth century, doctrines regarding creation and the nature of God were hotly debated throughout England. While the Church of England emphasized the need for personal piety and discipline, since it did not convene to resolve doctrinal matters, theological innovation was widely encouraged among the competing Protestant sects. It was against this backdrop of ambiguity (and church corruption) that the revivalism movement emerged. Although revivalists embraced the solemnity of the high church tradition of the established church, they rejected the joyless discipline of earned salvation.[44]

Selina Hastings converted to the revivalist movement in 1739 when she was thirty-two years old. She would not meet George Whitefield, the Huntingdon Connexion's most notable preacher, until three years later when Whitefield returned from a preaching expedition in North America. It was during this initial encounter that Hastings was first persuaded to consider Whitefield's Calvinistic approach to Christianity; prior to their meeting, she had leaned toward John and Charles Wesley's Arminianism. Although Hastings was devout during the years immediately following her conversion, it would not be until decades later, in the 1760s, that she would begin to build her society through networks of individual ministers and the chapels that were dependent on her patronage.[45]

The establishment of Trevecca College in 1768 was critical to the growth and development of the Huntingdon Connexion. It was there that young ministers like Marrant learned the art of open-air preaching, a staple of Methodist revivalism in both Wesleyan and Huntingdon sects. Since most congregants in the Huntingdon chapels were working-class and could not independently support their own preachers, itinerant preaching was necessary for most Huntingdon ministers. Chapels in the Huntingdon Connexion shared leadership responsibilities via committee. Unlike her counterpart John Wesley, Hastings was less reticent about the administration of the sacraments and worship taking place outside the church. Consequently, open-air tent meetings and extemporaneous, rather than rehearsed, preaching added to the dynamism of worship and attracted a substantial working-class following in England. The relative freedom of expression also attracted independent clergy, as well as clergy from other denominations (including the Church of England) into the Huntingdon Connexion. Under the tutelage of Huntingdon ministers like William Romaine and Thomas Wills, aspiring ministers like Marrant could hone their preaching skills as they satisfied the requirements for ordination.[46]

In the summer of 1875, just three months after receiving Christian ordination in the Huntingdon Connexion of the Methodist Church, John Marrant departed London for America. Throughout his time in London, Marrant was able to remain in touch with his brother in America through an exchange of letters. Though none of the correspondence survived, their transcontinental communication ultimately determined Marrant's return to North America. Marrant relayed that he was eager to attend to the ministerial needs of his countrymen. His designation of the group of Black Loyalists in Nova Scotia as "countrymen" demonstrates the degree to which the political realities for the eighteenth-century transatlantic world had been transcribed by race. It also underscores that for early Black Atlantic communities, the bonds of communal belonging endured despite the physical and temporal separation that resulted from the disruptions caused by the American Revolution. Because he had endured the trials of isolation during his wilderness initiation in Georgia and also during his naval service, Marrant understood the importance of maintaining the social bonds of community. As a minister ordained in the Huntingdon Connexion, he was equipped to utilize the symbols and rituals of evangelical Christianity among the Black Loyalists to solidify the bonds that time and distance had nearly severed.

Marrant's "countrymen" had arrived in Nova Scotia following the war. Some came as the property of Loyalist masters who fled Charleston and other Loyalist strongholds as they were captured by the Patriot army, but most had self-emancipated, escaping to British army lines after the proclamation of John Murray, Lord Dunmore, the last colonial governor of Virginia, in 1775. Dunmore had promised liberty to slaves in exchange for some capacity of service to the army. At first, scores, then hundreds, of enslaved people found their way to British ships in search of the "godly deliverance" that was "brought by the soldiers of the king."[47] Some estimates suggest that between six thousand and ten thousand undocumented enslaved people left Charleston aboard British vessels in 1782; others posit that as many as twenty-five thousand enslaved people had fled South Carolina plantations by war's end. In addition to liberty, Lord Dunmore's Proclamation also ensured the former slaves would be given land in Nova Scotia.[48] Though they could not be sure what Nova Scotia held in store, an uncertain future in freedom, they reasoned, was better than the present certainty of bondage. As free people they could assemble themselves, build communities, and establish churches. As one scholar reasoned, "Whatever it might be . . . it could not possibly be worse than where they had come from. Could it?"[49]

Marrant's account of his ministry in Nova Scotia is related in *A Journal of the Rev. John Marrant*, his second autobiographical publication.[50] A complete analysis of this text is the subject of chapter 4, but in the introductory story in *Journal*, he resumes where *Narrative* ends—crossing the treacherous waters of the Atlantic Ocean. After he had received approval from Lady Huntingdon to lead the Black Loyalist community in Halifax, Nova Scotia, Marrant headed back to North America aboard the *Peggy*, and for a second time the sea would be the setting for a trial by water.

During the first three weeks of travel, the ship lacked all the conventions of etiquette, resulting in swearing, card playing, and a generally raucous environment. Marrant's first attempt to convince passengers to modify their behavior fell flat, but in the fourth week, the tide began to turn. When "it pleased God to send a violent storm," the passengers cried "for God to have mercy upon them, and called for the minister to pray for them" because "a heavy sea, which almost filled the cabin," threatened to overtake the vessel. At first, Marrant dismissed their cries for help, saying "they must pray for themselves," but when water had to be removed from the cabin, he led them in prayer. From the deck he observed, "The sea seemed to be all on fire; running mountains high." After a night of prayer, however, all was calm "as though there never had been any storm." That night, everyone aboard the ship joined him in prayer, and the whole affair was described as "sweet work." Several passengers marveled at the display of God's power in the ferocity of the storm, and Marrant's prophetic status was established.

Seizing the opportunity afforded by his recognized status as a man of god, he persuaded the captain to prohibit swearing and card playing for the remainder of the voyage. A fine of one penny was collected for every violation, and Marrant aided the crew in making repairs to the ship. For the remainder of the trip, instead of swearing and card playing, the ship was filled with "reading, praying, singing of hymns, and preaching." He even led the sailors in Bible study, a sign of his acknowledged spiritual power after he had calmed the storm.[51]

Marrant's depiction of his journey back to America conjures images of the biblical story in which Jesus calmed a storm at sea. Like Marrant, Jesus was asked by shipmates to rescue them from impending doom when a violent storm suddenly arose. He rebuked the storm and the winds, and the sea was instantly calm. The disciples were so amazed they asked each other, "What manner of man is this?" and marveled at his command over the storm.

The power to control weather was a designation of spiritual authority reserved for prophets in many of the Bible's stories. When Moses commanded the Red Sea to separate, a strong eastern wind caused the sea to recede into walled columns so that the Israelites crossed from bondage to freedom on dry land. When the Egyptian army tried to pursue them, the walls collapsed and the army was drowned. The Old Testament prophet Elijah also demonstrated power over the natural elements when he prophesied that a drought would afflict Israel for three years. It was also by his word that the rains returned and the severe famine ended. Irregular climate patterns and weather events also contextualized the story of Elijah's ascension. When he was taken to heaven, a chariot driven by horses of fire appeared, and Elijah was ushered away in a whirlwind, leaving his pupil Elisha behind. As Elijah ascended, his mantle fell to Elisha, who used it to strike the Jordan River. The waters parted, and Elisha crossed the Jordan in the presence of the prophetic company gathered from Jericho. When they witnessed Elisha's power over the natural world, they realized that Elisha had assumed the prophetic authority of Elijah, his predecessor.

The association of spiritual power with bodies of water was well established within the religious cosmologies of eighteenth-century Black seamen. The maritime culture created by Black sailors in the New World reflected the spiritual sensibilities of traditional African religions. Throughout West and West Central Africa, water was regarded as a mythical element, and the symbolic perception extended to its use in rituals. In the Kongo-based cosmology of low-country slaves from West Central Africa, the *kalunga*, a watery line that divides the material and spiritual worlds, is associated with ancestors and other divine beings. For many Kongolese people enslaved in the New World, the Atlantic Ocean, along with other smaller bodies of water, was a passageway to the spirit world and part of the spiritual landscape that made supernatural power accessible.[52] In West Africa, traders, fishermen, and warriors believed their lives were dependent on vital connections to nature and ancestral spirits who resided below rivers and seas. The boats they used to navigate sacred waters were a means to access the ancestral realm. Consequently, West African boatmen regarded vessels as both "workplaces and connections to the spirit world."[53]

Black seamen in the New World continued to believe in the presence and power of *simbi* spirits, Kongo nature spirits that function as intermediaries between the living and the dead. In colonial low-country Black communities, the *simbi* played a vital function in forming and maintaining a cultural cohesive bond. As Ras Michael Brown explains, "Although it may seem that the simbi as nature spirits belonged to a realm removed from the activities and concerns of human society, they were always profoundly interested in those who inhabited their domains. They often initiated relationships with the living by communicating through dreams or by 'seizing' those who ventured near their abodes. They commanded storms, floods, and droughts to remind people of their obligations to the simbi and bestowed blessing for proper veneration."[54] The presence of *simbi* in South Carolina discloses a system of religious thought that informs how the Bible's stories of storms, floods, and calamity on the seas were interpreted by African-descended people in America.[55] Marrant's divine encounters crossing the Atlantic Ocean as described in *Narrative* and *Journal* underscore the profound spiritual importance of bodies of water within the Africana religious landscape.

Olaudah Equiano notes that during his time at sea it was commonly assumed that storms and weather-related events were the result of supernatural forces. He recalls a night at sea when a violent storm washed one of the crew overboard; Equiano feared the man was lost because "the white people did not make any offerings at any time." Importantly, Equiano discloses the belief within traditional Africana cosmologies that water domains are governed by spiritual beings. "As the waves were very high," he reasoned, "I thought the Ruler of the seas was angry, and I expected to be offered to appease him." When a group of Grampus dolphins surfaced near the ship, he reckoned the storm and lost passenger signified divine retribution for neglecting "the rulers of the sea." He was so certain that the water spirits had to be appeased he hid "in the fore part of the ship" when the wind stopped and the storm grew calm, for fear that he would be offered in sacrifice to appease them.[56] While he makes no mention of *simbi* or other African-derived water spirits, his belief that spiritual beings govern bodies of water reveals an orientation to the material world that reflects traditional African cosmologies.

Marrant's second escape from pending death at sea placed him in elite prophetic company. The same can be said for his models, the ancient prophets of the Bible. When he was still a small child, Moses was rescued from the Nile by Pharaoh's daughter after his mother placed him in a basket of reeds to escape Egyptian soldiers. As an adult, facing almost certain death at the banks of the Red Sea, he commanded a strong wind and the waters to form columns so that Israel escaped slavery in Egypt. In the New Testament, Jesus underwent the initiatory rite of baptism when John the Baptist immersed him in the Sea of Galilee. When he emerged from the water, Jesus possessed power to perform miracles, many of which exhibited an ability to manipulate water. In one tale he calmed the storm by the power of his voice; in another, he walked on water in the middle of a storm at sea. Jesus's power over water can be traced to his initiatory baptism by John in the Sea of Galilee.

Because Marrant's self-construction is modeled on the main characters of the Old and New Testaments—Moses and Jesus—he echoes the structural patterns of their narratives in his respective accounts of his trials by water. In *Narrative*, Marrant admits reluctantly that in his six years and eleven months aboard the *Scorpion* "a lamentable stupor crept over all my spiritual vivacity, life and vigour" and that he felt "cold and dead."[57] His spiritual death was dramatized when he was overtaken and nearly drowned. Aboard the *Peggy* in *Journal*, however, Marrant is steadfast in the midst of "the passengers, in general, swearing and playing at cards all day, and impatient with a gracious God."[58] In fact, his display of fortitude alters the ship's environment, causing others to conform to his example.

The contrasts in Marrant's respective accounts mirror differences in the initial and subsequent water narratives found in the stories of Moses and Jesus. Moses was, at first, drawn from the Nile, while Jesus was baptized by John in the Jordan. In both instances, the prophetic protagonists were the passive recipients of the water's blessing. Moses was rescued, while Jesus was cleansed. In subsequent encounters, each demonstrated his power over the water. Moses parted the Red Sea and drew water from a rock; Jesus walked on water, silenced a storm, and directed Peter to a miraculous catch of fish. In Marrant's second trial by water, he also demonstrated power over the raging sea. His prayer calmed the ocean "as though there had never been any storm."

In *Journal*, Marrant's exhibition of power caused crashing waves to subside. When he moved into action, he assumed authority not only over the sea but also over the ship. The atmosphere changed, and the passengers, once dismissive of his religious authority, now conformed their behavior to his standard. The transformation of the sea (from rough to calm) mirrored the transformation of the ship. The raucous environment disappeared, and after the storm, according to Marrant, "we had no swearing on board; but, instead . . . reading, praying, singing of hymns, and preaching."[59]

While Marrant's narration of his trials at sea conjures the aforementioned biblical stories, the Bible was likely not his only source of inspiration. His miraculous display of power also mirrors accounts of High John the Conqueror, a popular hero in African American folklore who commanded authority over both natural elements and social atmospheres. According to some accounts, High John "came *dancing over the waves* from Africa," while others maintained that he traveled with the enslaved "in the hold of the slave ship." Renowned for his "great physical strength," High John was "a flamboyant character" who overpowered foes "more by an audacious display of his power than through any subtlety or cunning."[60] Though not explicitly religious, he was a symbol of salvation and shares many heroic attributes with Christ. In the beginning High John "was not a natural man"; rather, he began as "a whisper, a will to hope." Over time, as the storytelling community heard and internalized the ethical norms and moral lessons espoused by the High John tradition, "the whisper put on flesh." When the High John narratives had been conjured into reality, "High John de Conquer was a man in full, and had come to live and work on the plantations, and all the slave folks knew him in the flesh."[61]

When the lessons and principles of High John narratives were enacted, the spirit of High John the Conqueror was conjured into material reality. He took the form of a man and revived the spirit of the enslaved by affecting change from within. The internal dynamics of transformation were realized in external communal expressions. Somber slave quarters were filled with laughter and song upon the arrival of High John, whose power was conjured into nonhuman, material forms as well. According to the legend, High John left America, disappearing into the waters on his way "back to Africa, but he left his power here, and placed his American dwelling in the root of a certain plant." Anyone in possession of the root could summon High John or use it to "call on nature to protect people from harm." This "radical form of protection" demonstrates how African American mythic characters were conjured to establish communal ritual norms.[62]

In Marrant's case, he did not specify the source of his power to control the wind and sea, saying only that when he reached dry land, he and his shipmates "went into the woods, and on ours knees, returned God thanks for landing us once more on shore."[63] On Tuesday, November 24, he and three others paid twenty dollars to hire a boat and sailed to Halifax.

4. "My Travels in Nova Scotia"

Ritual Healing and Communal Restoration in Marrant's Journal

⫙

In the aftermath of the American Revolution, the quest for political and civic freedom took on added dimensions. Loyalists, the dispossessed colonists who remained faithful to His Majesty's Crown, fled the former American colonies and dispersed to the British imperial territories in North America and the Caribbean. The wealthiest among white Loyalists returned to London "to forget that they had ever been American" or to the British Caribbean colonies, where they hoped to amass new fortunes in the profitable slave-based sugar economy. The "middling sorts" found refuge in Nova Scotia. Though less fortunate than their counterparts in Britain and the Caribbean, many had been slave owners and were accustomed to having the benefit of slave labor for routine domestic and rural chores.[1] Most white Loyalists had previously worked in urban trades and found the transition to agrarian life difficult. Nova Scotia's thick forests, rocky soil, and harsh winters did not lend themselves to agricultural success. Land grants of one hundred acres were allotted to private soldiers and heads of household, with another fifty-acre allotment for each additional family member, and field officers were promised thousand-acre allotments. But after two years, many settlers had yet to receive grants for their promised land allotments.[2]

The situation was even worse for the more than ten thousand free Blacks who had been resettled in the surrounding districts of Nova Scotia's urban centers following the American War of Independence. Like their white counterparts, Black Loyalists had done "perilous, dirty, exhausting work," risking their lives as "spies amidst the Americans" and as "guides through the Georgia swamps" in service of His Majesty's Royal Army. They had also been promised land on which they could build homes and establish small farms. In reality, however, fewer and smaller plots were assigned to Black settlers, and land allotments outside the towns often were not arable. A few received land grants comparable to those received by their white counterparts, but most Black Loyalists received no land at all. At Preston, the Black community near Halifax, Black settlers had to perform public labor to earn provisional rations that whites received freely.[3]

When the first wave of Black refugees arrived in Halifax in 1783, British colonial officials dispersed them throughout the province. Black Loyalists principally settled in Birchtown, Brindley Town, and Little Tracadie, "all-black settlements in Loyalist Nova Scotia and the only grants of land made directly to free black people" following the war.[4] A substantial Black enclave also formed at Preston near Halifax, but the largest group of free Blacks settled just outside Shelburne. Roughly five hundred refugees had settled in Shelburne during the first summer after the war, many of whom had been enlisted to help with the construction of the town. Under the leadership of Colonel Stephen Blucke, described as "a Mulatto man" born in Barbados, Black settlers began to organize a town for themselves. Blucke had been an officer of the Black Pioneers, a separate company of guides and spies, during the war. Under his leadership, they built schools, paved roads, and established meetinghouses for worship and public gatherings.[5] They named the settlement Birchtown, after Samuel Birch, the British general who had sheltered slaves from vengeful masters in New York at the close of the American Revolution. As the first free Black settlement in British North America, Birchtown's Black Loyalist community aimed to demonstrate, especially to their former masters in the so-called southern republic, that they were capable of building and maintaining a free society. Most important, Birchtown was to be a testament to the "international revolution devoted to incipient stirrings of democracy around the world as well as to freedom from slavery."[6]

Religious life would be central to visions of freedom cast by Black Loyalist settlers. Free Blacks arriving in the 1780s were "thrust into a crackling atmosphere" of revival.[7] Characterized by their enthusiastic worship, participants in the revivalist movement were disparaged by some members of more established traditions. Sermons that stressed the importance of direct communication with the Spirit and services that encouraged enthusiastic worship (shouting, speaking in tongues, extemporaneous prayer) ran afoul of the more conservative Anglican Church— itself an extension of royal authority. In Loyalist settlements such as Halifax and Shelburne, large Anglican majorities pervaded the religious landscape. Opportunities for muted protest against the British Crown along with the relative openness to modes of expression more closely associated with Africana spirituality may have encouraged some Black settlers to embrace evangelical Christianity. Pervasive racism, however, caused Black Christian congregations to grow separately from white churches. In Birchtown, the Methodists were led by Moses Wilkinson, a blind former slave who had absconded from his master in Virginia and fled to the safety of the British Continental army. Without regular oversight from denominational authorities, Black Methodists were free to interpret scripture and develop doctrines best suited to their own spiritual needs.[8] David George, the Baptist minister who had run away from his master in Virginia, counted fifty Black families as part of his congregation in Shelburne. George publicly lauded the virtues of freedom and exhorted his followers to live "free from the contaminations of a lost outside world."[9] The Huntingdonians were led by Marrant, who, like George and Wilkinson, inspired a "tradition of religious anarchy" among his followers, insisting that former slaves understand that they were not only free from slavery, but also free to govern themselves.[10] Under the guidance of Black clergy, free Black Christian communities in Nova Scotia "were in effect independent black branches only loosely tied or . . . completely untied, to any white hierarchy."[11] The relative autonomy of these early Black Christian communities inspired an attitude of "obstreperousness towards human authority" that was reinforced by racial separation and geographic isolation.[12] From their pulpits, Black preachers reformulated their parishioners as "a select group uncontaminated by the sins of the white world."[13] The chapels that housed their worship were the centers of their respective communities. Since, "generally, people of one denomination settled in one location," communities were largely defined by the chapels to which they belonged.[14]

This chapter explores John Marrant's ministry in Nova Scotia. As Black Loyalist communities organized themselves into congregations, Black ministers adapted Africana ritual expressions—shouting and baptism—to Christian contexts to inspire the growth of autonomous religious institutions and also the formation of new collective identities as free people. Ritual shouting and baptism attracted and accommodated diverse bodies of Black Atlantic worshippers and enabled disparate religious identities to cohabitate in a single communal space. Despite the efficacy of ritual performances of baptism and shouting, Black churches were not impervious to interdenominational rivalries. This chapter also explores intraracial and interdenominational rivalries within Black Loyalist communities. Black ministers routinely challenged one another's authority and competed for members and communal influence. However, Nova Scotia's unforgivingly harsh winters and recurring outbreaks of smallpox decimated Black Loyalist communities and compelled interdenominational cooperation. In the chapter's final section, I examine John Marrant's response to widespread communal suffering and argue that his adoption of the structural forms of Bible stories discloses Africana religious orientations as it relates to healing and salvation within Black Loyalist communities.

Shout for the Lord Has Given You the City

When the *Peggy* pulled into Beaver Harbor about twenty leagues east of Halifax, the Reverend John Marrant remained aboard. After several days he disembarked, in the latter part of November, and headed toward Halifax, where he was greeted by William Furmage, a fellow Huntingdonian minister and his former classmate at Trevecca College.[15] Later, Marrant was reunited with several former neighbors, family members, and friends from South Carolina. Marrant was invited by Furmage to preach at the chapel in Halifax. Initially, attendance was sparse, but when he preached to "a large concourse of people" on December 8, the response was overwhelming. Marrant notes, "Many [in the congregation] were crying, 'What shall I do to be saved.'" According to the account in *Journal*, the demonstration confirmed that "divine power" attended Marrant's ministry. The shout "proved the conversion of several present," and, he notes, there was "no small stir" caused by his eventual arrival in Birchtown.[16]

Over the course of the next month, Marrant's popularity soared among the Loyalists in Preston and Birchtown. In one of his first sermons, he established his ministry in the prophetic tradition of Moses. "For Moses truly said unto the fathers, a prophet shall the Lord your God raise up unto you of your brethren," he proclaimed. "Him shall ye hear in all things whatsoever he shall say unto you." Again, the Spirit manifested power. "Ten of them were pricked to the heart," writes Marrant, "and cried out, 'Men and brethren what shall we do to be saved,'" while "groans and sighings were heard throughout the congregation."[17] In his evening sermon, Marrant read from the Gospel of John: "The hour is coming, in which all that are in the graves shall hear his voice, and shall come forth." He notes, "The Lord was truly present with us, so that there was groaning, and sighing, heard throughout the congregation." The presence of the Spirit was manifest; Marrant was unable to speak for five minutes.[18]

The persistence of the shout ritual as a unifying structure for African American identity formation may be attributed to its appearance in the oral culture of Black folklore. The cultural historian Sterling Stuckey's analysis of symbolic depictions of the shout in the folktale "Brer Rabbit in Red Hill Churchyard" uncovers underlying African-centered religious orientations primarily directed toward the veneration of ancestors.[19] In the tale, various animals gather in a cemetery as Brer Rabbit emerges atop a grave playing a fiddle. The animals dance wildly, but when Rabbit stops playing, they arrange themselves in a circle. When Rabbit resumes the music, the animals dance intensely and shout. At the sound of their shouting, the earth opens and the spirit of Simon rises from the grave. The music stops so that Simon can address the animals gathered in the cemetery. At the conclusion of his address, Simon disappears, Brer Rabbit resumes the music, and the animals rejoin the dance. As Stuckey explains, the "Red Hill Churchyard" tale conjured mythic dancers like those in Suriname who "face the drum and dance toward them, in recognition of the voice of the god within the instruments," just as the animal characters danced for Brer Rabbit when he played the fiddle.[20] He also notes that the violin was utilized to summon the spirits of the ancestors in the Mali Empire and among the Songhai of Upper Volta.

Descriptions of the shout portrayed in the "Red Hill Churchyard" folktale bear important similarities to the worship service that Marrant describes in *Journal*. In both accounts, shouting enables communication with the world of the Spirit. In the oral account analyzed by Stuckey, Simon's spirit is summoned when the animals shout and dance in the form of a circle. Marrant conjures divine presence when he declares that all who are in their graves would arise. His preaching and Rabbit's violin stir their respective audiences into a frenzy, and in both stories, the shout subsides when the divine presence manifests.[21] In the "Red Hill Churchyard" tale, the excitement abates when Simon begins his address, and Marrant is silently reflective while the Spirit communes with the worshippers in Birchtown. In both stories, ritual shouting enables divine communication.[22]

Shouting also factored prominently in the ministry of Boston King, the Methodist preacher who had escaped from slavery to the Royal Army in Charleston. As he explains, his wife "was struck to the ground, and cried out for mercy" when she heard the Methodist minister Moses Wilkinson preach the first year they arrived at Birchtown. She shouted for nearly two hours until someone summoned her husband to her aid. When he arrived, King was "struck with astonishment at the sight of her agony." After six days, she was delivered and "the Lord spoke peace to her soul." Three years later, King began "to exhort both in families and prayer meetings" in the Methodist society led by Wilkinson. As he concluded his sermon in Preston, "the divine presence seemed to descend upon the congregation" of Black Loyalists gathered to hear him. As King relays, "Some fell flat upon the ground, as if they were dead; and others cried out aloud for mercy."[23] Like Marrant, King may have recalled shouting rituals like the one he describes from his days among slaves in Charleston. His father had been kidnapped in Africa and brought to South Carolina as a slave when he was young. King recalled that his father "lost no opportunity of hearing the Gospel, and never omitted praying with his family every night," and that he often "went into the woods and read till sunset" in solitude—a pattern of Christian formation strikingly similar to Marrant's.[24] If the shout opened the path to Christianity for King's father in the same way it did for Marrant, then King's knowledge of the shout may have been inherited from his African-born father.

Ritual shouting may have factored prominently for many of the former slaves brought to Nova Scotia from South Carolina. Prior to the American Revolution, Charleston was "the principal port of entry for slaves." Large numbers of enslaved Africans from Sierra Leone and Senegambia arrived in the Carolina colonies to supply labor demands for rice and tobacco crops. Because of the specificity of labor demands in the region, Carolina planters were more keenly aware of the ethnic identities of imported Africans. This development led to a high number of African Muslims in the Carolina low country.[25] The dense concentration of ethnic Africans in South Carolina aided in the development of distinct rituals, codes of ethics, and spiritual orientations within Black religious communities. Some African Muslims who were enslaved in the Carolinas may have continued to observe the fifth pillar of Islam. As some scholars contend, the shout symbolically reenacted the hajj, or pilgrimage to Mecca. Highlighting a linguistic connection between the Arabic word *sha'wt* and the English word *shout*, at least one scholar posits African Islamic origins for the shout ritual. *Sha'wt* refers to the completion of one tour around the Kaaba, the building at the center of what some Muslims believe to be Islam's most sacred mosque. Similarities in performance reinforce the linguistic hypothesis between the two rituals. As Islamic studies scholar Sylviane Diouf explains, Sea Islands shouters in Georgia and South Carolina turned counterclockwise "around a sacred object, such as the church itself," in the same way as "the pilgrims do in Mecca." For enslaved Muslims and their descendants, the shout enabled entry into contemplative reflection and enabled worshippers to re-create "the major event of the most important pilgrimage a Muslim can make."[26]

In the analyses offered by Stuckey and Diouf, circular dance or movement is critical to the performance of the shout. The animals in the "Red Hill Churchyard" folktale form a circle before they commence their dance. The Sea Islands shouters referenced by Diouf move around the Kaaba, encircling it as they pray. In many descriptions of the shout (also commonly known as the ring shout), participants dance or shuffle rhythmically in a circular, counterclockwise direction while others sing, chant, and keep rhythm via bodily percussion. Neither King's nor Marrant's respective narrations of the shout included descriptions of dance or rhythmic movement (though one can hardly imagine those attending a church, having been moved to tears by powerful demonstrations of preaching and song, easily resisting the urge to dance). Black preachers may have barred dancing, or excluded descriptions of dance from their accounts, because they wanted to distinguish their gatherings from "Negro frolicks," which were "frowned on and eventually forbidden in Shelburne" by white Loyalists who were disturbed by the "drumming, jumping, dancing and singing" of Black revelry.[27] Demonstrations of Black enthusiasm, both sacred and profane, were targets of legal proscription by white church and government officials. David George, a Baptist minister, was prevented from holding camp meetings in the woods when he learned "the White people were against me" the first year he arrived in Shelburne. He had begun to hold nightly services while Birchtown was still under construction. The gatherings were well attended and filled with the same spirit of enthusiasm found among the worshippers in Marrant's and King's congregations. "Black people came [from] far and near" to hear George preach and to join in the communal singing of sacred hymns. When their worship reached its climax, George "was so overjoyed with having an opportunity once more of preaching the word of God, that after I had given out the hymn, I could not speak for tears." Many in the audience listened intently; however, "the White people, justice, and all, were in an uproar, and said that I might go out into the woods, for I should not stay there."[28]

White surveillance of Black worship aimed to intimidate and dissuade Black Loyalists from full expression of their newly found freedom. Boston King admitted that "when any of the White inhabitants were present, I was greatly embarrassed, because I had no learning, and I knew that they had." When King ventured outside the relative safety of Black Loyalist enclaves to Chebutco in central Nova Scotia, he was "met with some persecution from the baser sort" despite the fact that several residents "began to seek the Lord in sincerity in truth" after they had heard him preach.[29] The presence of white worshippers in their religious services was a legitimate cause for concern for Black Loyalists. Mixed-race audiences especially drew the ire of the surrounding white community. During Marrant's first week in Nova Scotia, he was received well by Irish Catholics who attended his service. But when he returned to preach for them again the following week, he "was prevented, by the violence of the Irish Romans."[30]

Biblical models of storytelling explain how Black preachers may have conceptualized the political implications of ritual shouting. In the story of Moses's successor Joshua, when the community of Israel prepares to enter the Promised Land, they are instructed to march around Jericho for seven days—once a day for six days, and seven times on the final day. At the conclusion of the seventh march on the seventh day, the priests are told to "make a long blast" using the ram's horn and the trumpet, at which time "all the people shall shout with a great shout." The sound of Israel's shouting army caused the walls that protected Jericho from invasion to fall flat, leaving the city vulnerable to plunder.[31] Marrant's sermon in which he pronounced himself the successor to Moses conjures Joshua's story, since Joshua assumed Moses's leadership role following his death. It was Joshua who led Israel into possession of the Promised Land. Marrant and the other Black preachers in Nova Scotia hoped that by raising the shout, they might inspire their flocks to take possession of the lands they had been promised.

The contemplative elements of the shout reveal its generative role in African American identity formation. Within the broad nexus of Black Atlantic religious cultures, the shout enabled disparate religious identities to cohabitate in a single ritual space. Since the shout allowed for multiple expressions of spirituality, Marrant's ability to "stir up a shout" explains why he could attract and accommodate a diverse body of Black Atlantic worshippers.

Baptized into the Death of Christ

Despite the growing number of souls under Marrant's leadership, the bond that established the spiritual relationship between pastor and flock had not yet been solidified by the start of his first winter in Nova Scotia. On Christmas Day, he declined to administer the sacrament because he still doubted the sincerity of some parishioners. Over the next week, he preached several times a day, noting, "The Lord was pleased to rise and shine in the hearts of those that were wounded." During each sermon, the Spirit accompanied his preaching with power, and the response from the people was overwhelming—four couples were joined in marriage, there were seven that "God was pleased to awaken," and "many precious souls" were added to his congregation. He also notes that he baptized ten people. After performing the baptisms, the spiritual bond that held them together as a community was more firmly established. The next week, on New Year's Day, he offered the sacrament to those gathered for service.[32]

For the remainder of January, Marrant visited Black Loyalist communities, adding members to the Huntingdon Connexion. When he arrived in Green Harbor, he learned that none there had been baptized. His sermon that afternoon explained that those who believed and were baptized would be saved from damnation. Stirred by his message, "the greater part of the people would not go home" after service, so Marrant "got no sleep this night; but conversed with them till five o'clock" in the morning. As he met and talked with congregants, he learned "that the master of the house, with his wife and seven children had not been baptised."[33] Noticeably unsettled by this revelation, Marrant preached a sermon the following morning that examined the identity of John the Baptist, the prophet who baptized Jesus in the Sea of Galilee.[34]

Over the next several weeks, Marrant circulated through various Black Loyalist communities urging residents to be baptized. In a number of his next sermons during the nearly month-long tour, powerful messages espousing the necessity of baptism were accompanied by demonstrations of God's Spirit.[35] The multitudes groaned, wailed, and exclaimed, "What shall we do to be saved." His final sermon of the preaching mission set the stage for the ritual that was to ensue. The prophet who had twice survived the perilous waters of the Atlantic went from town to town throughout the neighborhood announcing to the formerly enslaved residents that "the Spirit of God did move upon the waters."[36]

Marrant concluded his brief mission and returned to Green Harbor in late January. In Green Harbor, his attention was focused on his hosts and their seven children—none of whom had been baptized. He ordered the parents to prepare their children for baptism at once. When they gathered the next day, he reminded them that eternal life was promised to those who do good.[37] "The power of God," he reflected, "was present to wound, and to heal." The baptism ceremony continued into the following morning. Marrant's next sermon explained that water immersion joined the initiates in the death of Christ.[38]

Following the sermon, many of those gathered returned home weeping. The master of the house, his wife, and three of their children were left to consider "much upon the nature of the ordinance they were about to submit to." At ten thirty that morning, the people made their way through the snow to the chapel for the baptism. Before proceeding, Marrant repeated the story of the resurrected Christ who commissioned his followers to baptize and teach in the authority of the Spirit.[39] The people's ecstatic response to both his sermon and the baptism ceremony confirmed the presence of God:

> My soul was filled with the glorious power and love of God; I could perceive solemnity in the faces of all the people within the audience of my voice; so that the convincing power of God was manifested; instead of nine, the number of the family, there were added to it twelve, which made twenty-one; and in the time of baptising, I desired all the grown people to kneel down upon their knees; fourteen kneeled, then did I lift up my voice aloud to the Lord for the baptising Spirit to fall upon us; and here I would have my readers take notice, that, for about five minutes, I was not able to speak, being overpowered with the love of God; when, rising from my knees, I looked upon the people, and saw tears in their eyes, and the congregation at large, filled with solemnity. I took the bason [sic] in my hand, and attempted to baptise them; when I had baptised five, the rest were fallen to the ground; however I baptised them on the floor, while they were crying out, and saying, "Lord Jesus have mercy upon us."[40]

At the height of the drama, Marrant called for the children to be brought forward.[41] He took two of them in his arms and made the other five kneel. They were baptized "with tears running down their cheeks." His prayer for God's blessings on them was barely audible above the sound of the weeping throughout the congregation.

The emphasis on baptism in Marrant's Nova Scotia ministry may have stemmed from recollections of Africana models of Christian formation in Georgia and South Carolina. As one scholar has noted, preparation for the baptism ritual in the low country "was unlike preparation for baptism in any Christian context other than African American."[42] In the Sea Islands, baptism rituals included stages of wilderness seeking and also instruction with community elders. Often they were concluded with ecstatic processions of singing and weeping, similar to the congregational responses to Marrant's preaching described in *Journal*. Protestant baptism rituals had attracted West and West Central Africans and their descendants to Christianity in the American South. Water baptism helped to mediate cultural and religious exchange among enslaved Africans of various ethnicities beginning during the Middle Passage and continuing upon their arrival at Carolina plantations. The persistence of the gravitational pull of the baptism ritual on the Black Loyalists in Nova Scotia "likely reflects the results of the cultural and religious interactions that occurred between Africans of varied backgrounds."[43]

Accounts of baptism among Black Loyalist religious groups were prevalent. As revival spread throughout Loyalist communities, baptismal rites were central to the formation of early Black Christian communities.[44] At Halifax, "many hundreds" of Black settlers were baptized by Dr. John Breynton, the Anglican rector of Saint Paul's Church, during the first year of Loyalist migration. "They daily crowd to me for Baptism," Breynton reported, "and seem happy with their prospects of Religion and Freedom." Roger Viets, the Anglican rector from Cornwallis, baptized sixteen Black settlers at Digby years before it was established as a parish. When he arrived to lead the congregation in 1786, he found that "large numbers of Brindley town blacks were baptised as Anglicans." Though they had been baptized as full members, Black Anglicans seldom attended church, choosing instead to supply their spiritual needs with Black ministers whose authority was vested in ritual knowledge rather than clerical status. Joseph Leonard, a Black Loyalist settler, not only led worship services in his home but also baptized children and new members and "was administering the communion sacrament to some 60 black families." When Charles Inglis, Nova Scotia's first Anglican bishop, visited Halifax in 1791, he "reproved Leonard for these irregularities." Leonard, in turn, asked to be ordained, explaining that the congregation desired complete autonomy and separation from the white church. Inglis neither ordained Leonard nor recognized the institutional autonomy of Black Anglicans, though they visited Saint Paul's, and other white Anglican churches, only sparingly.[45]

For some Black Loyalist congregations, opposition to the freedom signaled by autonomous baptisms occasioned displays of white rage and racial violence.[46] David George grew his Baptist congregation to include more than fifty families within two months after he began to baptize congregants at his Shelburne residence. The admission of white candidates for baptism caused outrage among some whites. William and Deborah Holmes, a white couple who lived near Shelburne, were candidates for baptism in George's congregation, much to the displeasure of their relatives and neighbors. To prevent the spread of biracial fellowship and potential affirmations of mixed-raced spiritual kinship, Holmes's family put a stop to the baptism. As George recounts, "Mrs. Holmes's sister especially laid hold of her hair to keep her from going down into the water." When Mrs. Holmes insisted on her right to be joined in fellowship with Black worshippers, "forty or fifty disbanded soldiers were employed," George recalled, "who came with the tackle of ships, and turned my dwelling house, and every one of their houses, quite over." The mob of white rioters intended to destroy the meetinghouse where the Black worshippers gathered, but "the ring-leader of the mob himself prevented it."[47] Marrant may have been careful in administering the sacrament because clerical autonomy attracted the attention of white people who intended to suppress expressions of Black religious and political freedom. David George's treatment attests to the potential violence Black ministers faced if they allowed their autonomy to be displayed too openly.[48]

Marrant's emphasis on the association of water and spiritual potency in the sermons preceding the baptism is also noteworthy. He identifies water as the locus for divine activity—"the Spirit of God did move upon the waters." In many Africana religious cosmologies, bodies of water separated the land of the living from the realm of the dead. The spirits of some ancestors, deities, and nature spirits inhabited a world that was a "complementary inversion" of the material world of humanity. Passage between the two worlds could be achieved by the enactment of water rites in which initiates were immersed in bodies of water to enable communication with ancestral and nature spirits. As the religious historian Ras Michael Brown explains, "The journey from one to the other requires passage through the water (*n'langu*, *m'bu*, or *kalunga*), which serves as both a window or door and a great barrier between the two lands. Movement through the water establishes connections between the realms of the living and the dead and represents processes of transformation."[49] Consequently, Marrant's sermonic proclamation that "many of us who were baptized into Jesus Christ were baptized into his death" likely signaled traditional African as well as Christian meanings for those gathered.[50]

One of Marrant's final sermons preceding the baptism at Green Harbor explored the identity of John the Baptist. Some early Black Atlantic Christian communities held John the Baptist in the highest prophetic regard since his baptism catalyzed the public ministry of Jesus. Baptist congregations led by George Leile, a former slave and Baptist minister who settled in Jamaica following his master's death during the American War of Independence, "attached more ritual significance to and displayed more reverence for the biblical figure John the Baptist, who baptized Jesus, before he began his ministry." Leile's Baptist congregations were distinguishable from other Jamaican Christian groups in their emphasis on two central elements: "the inspiration of the Holy Spirit; and Baptism, in the manner of John the Baptist."[51] Marrant's identification of John the Baptist as a prophetic model on which his baptism campaign was founded may uncover shared understandings of water initiation with Leile's Baptist group, despite divergent denominational affiliations. In early Black Christian communities, biblical exposition helped to make African water immersion rituals intelligible to the broader community. Marrant's sermonic expositions that precede the baptism ceremony at Green Harbor help to explain how Black Christian communities developed unique understandings of Bible stories and fused biblical symbols with preexisting ritual structures from Africana religious traditions.

Also noteworthy among Black Loyalist ministers is the emphasis on baptizing in natural bodies of water. David George located a spot outside in the woods, "in a valley between two hills, close by the river," to baptize new members. A "great number of White and Black people came" to be baptized, but colony officials ended his meetings.[52] Baptism factored prominently for Black Loyalist communities settled in other parts of the British Empire. George Leile, the Baptist minister credited with spreading the faith to the Caribbean, had been born into slavery in South Carolina and spent time in Savannah exercising his gift of exhortation on plantations in the years prior to the war. In Jamaica, his congregations grew rapidly as he implemented baptism rituals to establish congregational membership. "At Kingston," he reported, "I baptize in the sea, at Spanish Town in the river, and at convenient places in the country."[53]

The insistence on baptizing in natural bodies of water underscores the enduring association of spirituality with the natural landscape in early Black Christian worldviews. David George explains he baptized congregants "in the creek which ran through my lot" at his Shelburne residence even though some "had been converted in Virginnia [sic]."[54] The desire for baptism despite prior conversion in Virginia may also underscore an abiding need to establish a spiritual connection to the physical landscape. For some former low-country slaves, baptism completed the wilderness-seeking ritual required for an individual to be considered a "full-fledged, trustworthy church member and a Christian." Immersion in natural bodies of water "imbued the rite with much spiritual meaning in addition to the inherent meaning of the baptism itself. Immersion into these waters provided a merging of the physical and spiritual in an ideal location for just such a connection to occur." As settlers in new lands, Black Loyalists had no ancestral or spiritual ties to the spatial geographies of Nova Scotia. Faced with the same crisis as their ancestors who were the first to arrive in the American South, the Black Loyalists performed rituals to establish ties to the land. "Baptism in the creek or river," notes Ras Michael Brown, "ensured complete engagement with the spiritual landscape and . . . the natural environment where the land of the living intersected with the land of the dead."[55] Brown's analysis raises the possibility that water immersion rituals may have also been attempts to connect with nature spirits believed to inhabit the natural landscape. These ancient spirits, known as *simbi*, predated the appearance of human ancestors, having always existed in the elements of nature.

Brown posits that wilderness-seeking rituals practiced by low-country slaves included attempts to locate and commune with *simbi* spirits to establish bonds with the land on which they depended for food and protection.[56] Such ritual orientations seemingly persisted among their counterparts who migrated to Nova Scotia.

While *Journal* does not include accounts of baptisms by Marrant in natural bodies of water, the story of Marrant's own baptism in the Atlantic Ocean was likely included in the sermonic proclamations and more informal exchanges with congregants that preceded the baptism accounts he describes. As discussed in chapter 3, Marrant recounted the story of his near death aboard the *Scorpion* near the conclusion of *Narrative*. He was washed overboard and immersed in the waters of the Atlantic Ocean three times. While in the water for many minutes the third time, he was encircled by several sharks, including "one of an enormous size, that could easily have taken me into his mouth at once," but instead "passed and rubbed against my side." When he "cried more earnestly to the Lord than [he] had done for some time," he was miraculously "thrown aboard again." The immersion in the Atlantic proved to be "the means by which the Lord used to revive me," Marrant noted, adding that he "began now to set out afresh."[57]

Water initiation signaled rebirth and reemergence in Africana religious contexts as well. For Nkimba initiates in Kongo, water immersion was the final stage of spiritual transformation and "entailed leaving the spiritual domain (land of the dead) to reenter normal society." As their spiritual journey came to an end, initiates washed white clay (the color of death in many West Central African cosmologies) from their bodies to mark the transition back to the community in the land of the living. Low-country Christian initiates, according to one scholar, experienced baptism "as the means of washing off the spiritual and physical residue of their passage."[58] As one scholar explains, membership in Christian communities distinguished Black residents as "a select group uncontaminated by the sins of the white world."[59]

Marrant's extemporaneous sermons and casual encounters with residents also likely included retellings of his journey back to America aboard the *Peggy*. In the opening narrative of *Journal*, he recounts how he calmed the storm at sea and changed the atmosphere aboard the ship. The demonstration of power over the natural elements established his prophetic authority both among his shipmates on the *Peggy* and among the members of the Huntingdon Connexion who heard and circulated these stories throughout their community. The retelling of these accounts legitimized Marrant's authority to baptize and to perform the sacred rites that signified rebirth in both Christian and Africana religious contexts.

Beware the Yeast of Pharisees

While ritual performances of baptism and shouting helped to gather disparate ethnic Africans into cohesive religious communities, Black churches were not impervious to conflicts stemming from intraracial and interdenominational rivalries. When David George was attacked by a mob of white rioters after attempting to baptize a white couple in Shelburne, he sought sanctuary in Birchtown. Birchtown's Black community provided refuge from further attacks from white mob violence, but, George noted, "my own color persecuted me there" when he began to preach.[60] Moses Wilkinson had already established a sizable Methodist following by the time George arrived in Birchtown that winter, and perhaps perceived the Baptist minister's arrival as jeopardizing the potential growth of his own congregation. Following the persecution in Birchtown, George returned to Shelburne with his family and resumed his ministry there.

Violet King, wife of the Methodist minister Boston King, was "the first person at Burch Town that experienced deliverance from evil tempers" in the Methodist church led by Moses Wilkinson. Despite this distinction, "she was not a little opposed by some of our black brethren" when she "exhorted and urged others to seek and enjoy the same blessing." When the white Methodist minister Freeborn Garretson visited Birchtown to regulate the society and form the members into classes, he commended Violet's faith and "encouraged her to hold fast her confidence, and cleave to the Lord with her whole heart."[61] King's favorable depiction notwithstanding, Garrettson and Wilkinson, "the Arminians"—Marrant's pejorative moniker for the Methodists—were frequently depicted as ministry rivals in *Journal* and were the targets of considerable acrimony.[62]

Marrant's initial troubles with "the Arminians" began in the middle of the spring in 1786. He had spent his first winter in Nova Scotia working tirelessly to advance the Huntingdon Connexion. Throughout the winter, he preached to large bodies and small companies of people and visited members from house to house in the communities surrounding Birchtown, Shelburne, and Halifax. When he returned to Birchtown in April, he found "they were all gathered in the chapel" to hear his evening sermon "for the Arminian had been amongst them, endeavouring to draw them away, and had drawn some of the weak ones away." Rumors that he had drowned had been circulated in his absence, so,

Marrant recalled, "the people all rejoiced to see me once more." In his sermon from the Gospel of John, he narrated a story of conflict in which the Pharisees challenged the prophetic authority of Jesus. "In the last day," he read, "that great day of feast, Jesus stood and cried saying, 'If any man thirst, let him come unto me, and drink. He that believeth on me, as the scripture hath said, out of his belly shall flow rivers of living water.'"[63] Jesus had emphasized the witness of scripture and his power to evoke new spiritual life in followers to validate his ministry in answer to the Pharisees' challenge. Marrant seemingly used the same strategy to respond to Garretson. Prophetic authority was evinced by the prophet's relationship to his followers, and not vested in church affiliations or clerical hierarchies. There was a "great outpouring of God's spirit" in response to his preaching so that when he "came out of the pulpit, they would not let my feet touch the ground." The congregation worshipped all night, and "the chapel was filled, all praising of God in prayer, and singing" when he arrived the next morning. By the conclusion of the morning service, those who had "been drawn aside through error, came, trembling, and expressed great sorrow because they had been deceived, and had joined the Arminians."[64]

With the Arminian threat looming, Marrant remained in Birchtown for nearly a month teaching classes and reestablishing order within the congregation. Membership within the Huntingdon Connexion grew weekly, and he gradually ventured into the surrounding towns and neighborhoods to attract new members. At Barrington, however, evidence of Arminian meddling resurfaced. His host "seemed somewhat shy" to receive him, though he was strongly recommended, presumably because "the Arminians had been there, and had told them falsehoods, desiring them not to let me go into the chapel to preach." Days later he learned that "there was a great division among them." Some residents sided with Garretson's Arminian faction, while others declared "they would have their names taken out of the book."[65]

The rivalry with the Arminians continued to intensify when Marrant returned to Birchtown in late April. After a prayer meeting one morning, several people came to him requesting that he present their petition for tools and supplies to the governor in Halifax. Initially, he refused, advising them to seek the aid of Colonel Stephen Blucke, but Blucke, they informed him, had been unresponsive. A week later, he "collected the people together" to inquire "into those things they had, and found they really stood in want of more." Marrant compiled a list of supplies—"tools, spades, hoes, pickaxes, hammers, saws and files, such as they should want, and blankets"—and sailed for Halifax to present their petition to Governor John Parr on May 14, 1786. Ten days later, he arranged to have the supplies sent to Birchtown with explicit instructions that nothing was to be distributed before his arrival. When he arrived at Birchtown days later, however, he "found the town in an uproar." The supplies had been given to the Arminians; even worse, Moses Wilkinson, "the old blind man, who preaches for the Arminians," had sold the meetinghouse and threatened to limit its use exclusively for Arminian preachers. Marrant was outraged and "answered him, that the place was built for the people at large, not more for one connection than another." Determined to assert their right to what they effectively deemed public space, Marrant's church elders "demanded the key, and were denied, but they took it away."[66]

That evening, a multitude of people assembled in anticipation of Marrant's address, but Moses Wilkinson stepped into the pulpit to prevent him from speaking. As Marrant recounts in *Journal*, "The doors were opened, and the people went in and prepared for preaching. The old man, in order that I should not preach, came and sat in the desk, and began to give out an [*sic*] hymn, but nobody would sing with him until I came in, and he not knowing that I was in, I gave out the same hymn over his head when the house rang with the praises of God."[67] Wilkinson tried to regain control of the meeting and "went immediately to prayers," but when "some of the people touched him and asked him whether he knew what he was about," Marrant stood to take the lead. He began to pray, and when Wilkinson heard him, he stepped down from the pulpit, left the chapel, and was seen no more that night. When he discovered the missing supplies the next day, Marrant threatened legal action if "the king's property" was not returned immediately. The supplies were returned the following day.[68]

Over the next several weeks, Marrant resumed his ministry without further interference from rival ministers. He remained in Birchtown, "setting all right again" for the remainder of June. At month's end, he traveled to Jordan Falls, a Loyalist stronghold on the Jordan River near Nova Scotia's southern coast, but soon learned that Freeborn Garretson had returned to stir up dissension among his followers. "The Arminian preacher," he explains, "had been among them and insinuated into their mind that I was not right." He returned to Birchtown on July 4 and discovered that Garretson planned to meet with members of his congregation in the chapel later that night. That evening, Marrant entered the chapel "but was not discovered by the preacher, nor them that accompanied him." He sat "pretty close to the pulpit, that nothing should slip" his notice. Garretson began the service with a hymn, followed by a prayer, and then "told the people he should not preach, but read Mr. Wesley's society book, and expound from that, and shew them how the order of their society was, and it was the best order that could be adopted." Regarding Marrant, Garretson also added that "he was very sorry that they had a man come from England, and was not of Mr. Wesley's society, and had sown the seeds of discord." "He even went so far," Marrant marveled, "as to call me a devil."[69]

Garretson continued, but he was interrupted by one of the elders from the Huntingdon Connexion who stood in defense of their leader. Boldly addressing the white Methodist minister, he warned, "If he came to preach the Gospel of Christ, for to preach it; if not, to come down out of the pulpit." The elder's stern reprimand continued, "You had no business to rail against a person that you never discoursed with, nor have seen," he stated, "but this one thing we know, we never heard the Gospel of Christ till he did come, and we know that God hears not the prayer of a sinner." Garretson, in response, demanded that they choose between the two sects once and for all. Those who wished to join the Methodist congregation could remain in the chapel; those siding with the Huntingdon Connexion were asked to leave. All remained seated and looked to Marrant for direction. As Marrant relates, "The people all fixing their eyes upon me, I stared about five minutes to see if any person or persons left the place, and finding that they would not go without me, I thought I would give them leave to go on with their plan, and see how far the devil could go. So I moved towards the door, and the whole house moved and went out, all but fourteen."[70]

The congregational movement in response to the direction of their leader validated the minister's authority. Like Jesus in the story of the conflict with the Pharisees, Marrant's authority was established by scriptural knowledge (the source of ritual instruction) and his relationship to his followers. Garretson, by contrast, read from the Methodist Book of Discipline instead of the Bible. He also neglected to perform vital rituals that enabled the collective worship needed to establish lasting ties between church members. Consequently, members of the Huntingdon Connexion were unresponsive to his song and his prayer.

Accounts of competition from rival ministers during his North American ministry were included in Garretson's own journal. While he makes no direct reference to the dispute with Marrant, his disdain for branches of Protestantism outside the Methodist tradition is evident:

> With regard to the Doctrine taught by the Methodists, I have had no reason to doubt of its veracity, and conformity to the Holy Scriptures, from the first day I embraced it. As for the principles taught among other denominations of Christians, I am willing to think and let think: only, it appears to me unreasonable, that persons should continue in this, or the other persuasion, merely because their parents brought them up in that

belief. While I have the use of my understanding, I can never embrace the Doctrine of unconditional Election and Reprobation; it is unsupported by Scripture, as well as repugnant to sound Reason, to suppose that the gracious and merciful Creator, should from all Eternity, consign the far greater part of the human race to eternal fire! I have never yet conversed with the Defenders of this horrible Decree, but who frequently contradict themselves.[71]

It is important to highlight that Garretson's primary objections pertain to doctrines of election and reprobation—concerns rooted in theological rather than ritual models of Christian formation. In the Gospel tradition conjured by Marrant, Pharisees routinely challenged Jesus on issues of doctrinal orthodoxy. They sought to impose strict adherence to religious codes, often neglecting more nuanced applications of scripture that enabled deeper communion with the Spirit. In many of the stories of confrontation, Jesus rebuked the Pharisees and reprimanded them for their inflexibility. In the account related in *Journal*, Marrant ordered Garretson to come down from the pulpit when he and his followers reentered the chapel. At first, Garretson, perhaps taken aback by the Black congregation's bold demonstration of authority, hesitated to leave the pulpit. Marrant restated his demand, bidding him to "come down again, and told him, that if he did not come down by fair means, that I would force him out of it." Garretson, somewhat amazed, came down from the pulpit and walked out of the chapel, and "the door was made fast" behind him. The Huntingdon Connexion had stood their ground against the white minister's attempt to usurp their congregational autonomy.[72]

Poverty, Famine, and Plague

While intraracial and interdenominational rivalries were a thorn in the side for many of Nova Scotia's Black Loyalist ministers, the threat paled in comparison to challenges arising from poverty, famine, and plague. Crippling tariffs imposed by the British government on the province's fledgling cod fishing and whaling industries all but collapsed Shelburne's postwar economy. Many white merchants fled to Halifax, while some sought refuge back in the United States. Black Loyalists near Shelburne, wedged between economic hardships and the racist attitudes of their fellow white settlers, faced an even more precarious situation.[73] Some fell victim to ruthless traders who kidnapped and sold free Blacks in the West Indies. Others who remained in Shelburne were "forced into indentures so punitive that they might as well be in chains."[74]

Boston King lamented "the wretched circumstances of many of my black brethren at that time, who were obliged to sell themselves to the merchants, some for two or three years; and others for five or six years."[75] Though Black Loyalists fought vigorously to keep their families together, the choice between indentureship and starvation compelled many to hire their children to "white slaveholding loyalists and those who wanted to convert the impoverished free black labour force into slaves."[76] Horrific stories of "children fraudulently held in indentures far beyond what had been understood to be their contract" were common in Preston and other Black Loyalist strongholds.[77] White Loyalists, many of whom had owned slaves in the American South, sought to uphold de facto slavery, regularly circulating notices of sale and auctions throughout the province. Black residents, "strikingly conscious of their rights . . . through knowledge of the Dunmore and Clinton proclamations," mounted fierce resistance to attempts at reenslavement.[78] Some, like Phebe Martin, an indentured servant who was kidnapped in Halifax and advertised for sale in the Bahamas, sought legal protections against reenslavement. In court, Martin acknowledged that she and three other Black servants were indentured to Captain Thomas Hamilton, but she insisted that never "did she or any of the others think of themselves as Hamilton's slaves."[79] Court records chronicle Black settlers' fierce attempts to resist reenslavement in Loyalist Nova Scotia, but religious communities remained central to collective efforts for social advancement.[80] John Marrant's *Journal* demonstrates how healing rituals were deployed to prevent Black settlers from resorting to old identities rooted in slavery and subjugation.

During his visit to Ragged Island in February 1786, Marrant was warned not to enter the house of an older couple because the man's wife was "an abandoned woman, one that had been on board a man of war all the last war." His designation of the woman as "abandoned" is intriguing since the historian W. Jeffrey Bolster notes that some "less fortunate wives abandoned by their husbands turned to prostitution to support themselves and their children" while their husbands were away at sea.[81] During the era of the transatlantic slave trade, maritime culture initiated Black women into racialized, enslaved modes of existence in which deplorable acts of sexual violence became routine.[82] Despite the relative archival silence pertaining to Black women's experiences in the Royal Navy, accounts like that of Alexander Falconbridge, a British surgeon, help elucidate some of the hardships Black women suffered while aboard ship and subject to sailors who were "allowed to have intercourse with such of the black women whose consent they can procure" and men who were "permitted to indulge their passions among them at pleasure."[83] Marrant, perhaps jolted by memories of his own spiritual stupor while in the service of the Royal Navy, ignored their warnings and knocked on the door when "it was impressed upon my mind to go in and see them."[84]

When Marrant entered the house, the woman accused him of being a "pick-pocket" and attacked him with tongs and a poker from the fireplace. Marrant grabbed her to restrain her and she began to calm, but when he let her go, she attacked him again. Marrant ran from the house and took refuge in an empty barn nearby. Alone in the barn, he prayed for strength:

> I kneeled down, and laid my complaint before my God, and lifting my hand up which was then bleeding, and the blood trickling all over my face, begging the Lord to search my heart, whether I had lost these drops of blood for the gospel of Christ, and the good of souls; that he would be pleased to show me a token for good, so that I might not deceive myself. The Lord was pleased to pour down his blessing upon my soul, in answer to my poor petition; then was I strengthened and encouraged to go back, and said, If it is his will that I should spill more blood, in his cause, I was willing, for I know that he will not let the words return void.[85]

When he returned to the house, she attacked him again, but he avoided her most dangerous blows. After he was able to subdue her, he spoke to her about the suffering and death of Jesus. "The Lord furnished me with words," he noted, "particularly out of St. Matthew's gospel, chapter xxvii." After several moments of silence, he began to pray and "felt much of God's spirit." He continued, and "about the middle of the prayer, she fell from off the bed, as though she was shot, and screamed out with a loud voice, and stretched herself off, as though she was going out of the world." Marrant rose from his knees, placed a "smelling bottle to her nose, and washed her face with cold water." He prayed again but found that he "was shut up," so he left her lying on the floor and went to her son's house to alert her family of her condition.[86]

When Marrant arrived at the son's house, his clothes were torn and he was covered in blood. Marrant explained that the woman had attacked him and that she was at home, unconscious on the floor. Her son and daughter-in-law went to check on her, and when they found her, she was unharmed, but unable to respond to their questions. They placed her onto a sled and dragged her through the snow to their house. Panic swept through the neighborhood as the woman "continued as though she was dead." Her family contemplated calling a doctor, but Marrant assured them that "she was only sin sick, and no doctor in this life could cure her; but there was a good physician in Gilead, and in his good time he would apply his balm of Gilead to her soul." Marrant prayed with the woman once more before leaving, but "the poor creature was slain worse, and cried out—she was sinking into hell." Weary from the evening's events, Marrant advised everyone to get some sleep. The woman cried out all night, imploring God for mercy.[87]

Over the next several days, Marrant checked on her frequently, but her condition did not improve and she continued in anguish. Three days later, however, during his evening sermon, she "got up, and praised God in a remarkable manner" much to the amazement of all who were present. When Marrant spoke to the woman after the service, "her joy was so great, that she could not express herself." After she apologized and "begged me to pardon her for the blood she had spilled," she hugged him tightly "round my neck, then sat down again, and was not able sometimes to speak for five or six minutes, being so filled with the peace of God."[88]

The abandoned woman's story is instructive for understanding the communal nature of healing and spiritual regeneration in early Black Christian communities. While she was in torment and unresponsive to those around her, communal support was essential to ushering her through the experience. Her son and daughter-in-law rushed to her side to ensure her safety, and they transported her to their home, where she could be better looked after. For three days, Marrant prayed at her side, while family and friends attended to her needs. A communal response was also needed in the winter of 1787 when David George took ill returning to Shelburne from a preaching engagement in Preston. Unable to stave off the effects of the brutalizing winter without provisions, George "got frost-bitten in both my legs up to my knees, and was so ill when I came towards land, that I could not walk." Members of his Baptist congregation, however, met him at the riverside, carried him home, and attended to him until he was somewhat recovered. "Afterwards, when I could walk a little," George recalled, "I wanted to speak of the Lord's goodness, and the brethren made a wooden sledge, and drew me to Meeting."[89]

The stories of infirm Black Loyalists transported by their communities conjure the biblical story of Jesus healing a man who suffered from paralysis.[90] The paralyzed man was brought to Jesus on a bed by his neighbors and was lowered into the house through the roof. When Jesus saw the man's faith, he forgave his sins and the paralysis was cured, thus linking the man's illness to his need for repentance. In Marrant's parable, the woman's paralysis was an outward sign of the trauma that plagued her during her days aboard the ship. Additionally, for the woman in Marrant's account, healing was a communal matter. She, like the paralyzed man in the biblical account, relied on communal support to facilitate her spiritual and physical restoration.

The abandoned woman's reintegration into the community was facilitated by the ecstatic worship that took place over the course of the three days that she remained in trance. Spiritual transformation, like physical healing, was often a communal affair for Black Atlantic religious communities. As Jason Young explains,

> Most observers discuss spiritual ecstasy as an individual experience, something that, in a given ritual context, occurs to a certain person: a particular flailing and flinging of the body to and fro. But this is clearly not the case. For indeed, the faithful regarded religious excitement and ecstasy as community events. The community produces the ecstasy, and the trance only emerges once the community of believers conspires to create the necessary conditions—a particular percussive rhythm, a certain hymn, a special ritual practice (i.e., baptism). In this way, ecstasy does not belong to the individual as much as it belongs to the entire community. God does not speak to the person in trance as much as through the person in trance, the body in ecstasy being little more than a vessel, a line of communication through which the community comes into closer contact with God.[91]

Marrant's rendering of the story of Jesus and the paralyzed man not only reveals the communal nature of biblical transformation but also underscores the relationship between one's physical and spiritual health. In early Black Christian communities, healing required both communal and spiritual care. As Young explains, "In the moment of ecstasy, the body in trance is not controlled (or even controllable for that matter). Rather, the spirit that moves through the body and, by extension, the body itself is communally shared and protected."[92]

Marrant's own bout with illness also began in the winter of 1787. After the dispute with Freeborn Garretson had been resolved, he "determined to stay home for the summer" attending to instruction and administrative duties at the Anglican school in Birchtown.[93] That summer, he preached in the surrounding villages only once a month, but by fall he had resumed a more robust preaching itinerary. His sermons were met with "the shouts of the people, and the groans of poor sinners," but violent storms and freezing temperatures regularly hampered his travel as winter rapidly arrived. In January 1787, a vicious snowstorm prevented his safe passage from Birchtown to Jordan Falls. Unable to travel beyond Shelburne by water, Marrant and company sought passage through the woods, but they were overtaken by the storm and lost their way. When they finally arrived in Green Harbor a day later, Marrant was too exhausted to preach. After morning service the next day, he did not preach again for nearly two weeks, and when he resumed preaching, he preached only during the morning services due to constant fatigue. Weeks later he felt well enough to travel but had to be assisted and was forced to walk slowly while leaving Ragged Island. By the end of February, he was able to walk unassisted from one side of the room to the other but was still unable to preach because his "sickness continued increasing till the 6th of March." Despite a communal outpouring of care—"the people did all that they could, and gave the best attendance that laid in their power"—his illness was prolonged due to inadequate provisions. A bed "stuffed with straw, with two blankets, without sheets," and a diet of "fish and potatoes, and sometimes a little tea sweetened with treacle," he lamented, were "very poor nourishment for a sick person in the state I was then in." His health continued to fluctuate throughout the remainder of the winter.[94]

The combination of famine, disease, and cold ravaged Nova Scotia's Black community throughout the winter of 1787. That year, the Royal government canceled rations to immigrants, and a wave of smallpox swept through Black Loyalist settlements.[95] Additionally, untenable farmland combined with an extended rainy season resulted in widespread crop failure and famine throughout Loyalist Nova Scotia. The combination of famine and unemployment rendered David George, like many of Birchtown's residents that winter, "so poor that [he] had no money to buy any potatoes for feed." Without the aid of benefactors from London, the Baptist minister might have succumbed to cold and starvation during the treacherous winter months. Divine assistance, however, arrived in the form of Mr. and Mrs. William Taylor, British Baptists who had recently settled in Shelburne. Mrs. Taylor donated to George's fledgling mission and gave him "money enough to buy a bushel of potatoes; which one produced thirty-five bushels."[96]

Other Black Loyalists were not so fortunate. Some in Birchtown, according to Boston King, were "compelled to sell their best gowns for five pounds of flour, in order to support life." Unable to subsist on the meager produce of their mostly unfarmable land, some "killed and eat [sic] their dogs and cats," while others simply "fell down dead in the streets, thro' hunger." Because employment opportunities were increasingly scarce, Black laborers like King sought work away from Birchtown. He "worked all night" building a chest to supply the order of a man in Shelburne, but when "to my great disappointment he rejected it," King worried that his family would not survive since he "had but one pint of Indian meal left for the support of myself and wife." Walking home to Birchtown, he "fell down several times, thro' weakness, and expected to die upon the spot," on account of being "pinched with hunger and cold."[97]

Marrant tried valiantly to grow a thriving ministry despite the onset of cold and starvation, but as Nova Scotia's long winter lingered into the months of early spring, the smallpox epidemic continued to devastate the Black Loyalists. In late March, the Jordan River was still frozen, so Marrant and his companions traveled from Shelburne to Birchtown through the woods. About halfway, they discovered "two women in the road" who were at the brink of death. One of them "was lying down and just expiring," and "the other stood over her weeping." One of the boys in the company ran to Birchtown for help, while Marrant stayed behind with the ailing women, who told him that they "had both been over to Shelbourn [sic] to beg something to eat," but had only been able to find "a little Indian meal, but had not strength to reach home with it." Marrant grabbed some rum from his knapsack. He tried to warm the women with "a little of it to drink and rubbed her face with some." The help from Birchtown arrived just as one of the women passed away. The team of rescuers "took the charge of the living woman, and got her to town as fast as they could," and later returned to "bring the dead body of the other woman" back to Birchtown for funeral preparations. Days later, Marrant eulogized the deceased woman, and over the next few days, his own health declined rapidly.[98]

Early symptoms of smallpox mirrored those of common cold and flu viruses, so it is understandable that Marrant mistakenly thought that he had only "got a fresh cold" at the onset of his illness. Body aches, fever, and vomiting are common signs for a variety of mundane illnesses.[99] But when he "spit blood for eight days continually," it was clear that something more serious was happening. For ten days, he was unable to walk. A doctor, called in from Shelburne, gave him two pounds of honey on credit and advised him to "drink honey in everything I used." He was confined to bed and did not preach for nearly a month. When he returned to the pulpit in late April, he was still not fully recovered. As he started his sermon, he "began to bleed in the pulpit and was taken out of the pulpit, and staid in doors till the 6th of May." Though preaching duties were temporarily suspended, he continued to receive visitors "who were continually coming begging, and . . . were perishing for want of their natural food for the body."[100]

He resumed his mission in midspring, drawing large crowds throughout the Black Loyalist towns near Shelburne and Halifax. "The Lord was present to wound and heal," recalled Marrant, but an exceptionally rainy spring extended into summer, making travel difficult. When he returned to Birchtown in early July, he was "not very well" and was "taken with a violent fever." He vomited blood for seven days, but on the eighth day he "attempted to perform divine service, it being the Lord's day, and seeing a crouded [*sic*] multitude coming from the neighboring villages round about." The church elders warned against it, but he undoubtedly assured them that he would be cautious. However, midway through the service, Marrant got caught up in the excitement of worship. As he later recalled, "About the middle of the discourse, I found myself pretty warm, had much liberty, so exerted myself, forgetting my former illness. But before I concluded, I was nearly strangled with blood. The blood came running out at my nose and mouth, so that the people were all frightened. They took me out of the pulpit and carried me into my house, which was next door to the chapel, where I laid for two hours in that condition."[101]

Marrant's depictions of his bout with smallpox emphasized violent eruptions of blood. On two occasions, he was unable to complete sermons because of spontaneous bleeding. Both times, the eruption of blood replaced the proclamation of the preached word, since on both occasions he was unable to finish preaching. In *Narrative*, Marrant utilized blood imagery to conjure rebellion; however, in *Journal*, blood imagery conjures plague. Biblical accounts in the Old and New Testaments utilize blood imagery to symbolize individual and communal illness. In the story of Exodus, Moses's transformation of water to blood symbolized a series of plagues that would befall Egypt if it continued to hold Israel in bondage. The plagues preceding the final plague of death included pestilence and boils, signaling threats to Egypt's communal health. In the Gospel tradition of the New Testament, a woman's prolonged illness is characterized as an "issue of blood." While the nature of her ailment is not specified, her suffering is symbolized by a prolonged bodily discharge of blood.[102] Marrant's depictions of eruptions of blood in *Journal* conjure biblical stories in which blood signifies communal or individual bodily affliction.

Prolonged bouts of illness continued to hamper Marrant and other Black Loyalist settlers in Nova Scotia due, in part, to inadequate material resources. During the early years after they arrived in Nova Scotia, Black Loyalists resided in makeshift homes consisting of tents, huts, and pit houses—crude structures composed of a six-foot hole dug in the ground and a pitched roof made of logs and covered with sod or bark. The floors, lined with "planks or sometimes just with leaves," was all that protected residents from the province's brutal winters.[103] By 1787, modest cabins had replaced the more rudimentary dwellings. Consisting of a single chamber nearly ten feet square, the cabins were covered with a gabled log roof and included a hearth, a chimney, and a storage cellar for winter provisions.[104] While they were an improvement over their initial dwellings, Black Loyalists' homes were hardly adequate protection against torturous blizzards and blistering snowfall. "In some places," Marrant recalled, "I was obliged to lay on stools, without any blanket, when the snow was five and six feet on the earth, and sometimes in a cave on the earth itself."[105] Though at least one scholar disputes the notion that Black Loyalists in Birchtown resided in caves, Marrant's claim that he sometimes slept "in a cave on the earth itself" is deserving of consideration.[106] His narration of his visit to a cave in *Journal* discloses Africana ritual practices intended to conjure nature spirits to establish ties to the Nova Scotian landscape.

Marrant delegated administrative duties to associate ministers and church elders while he recovered in Birchtown all summer following his affliction. By fall, he was well enough to resume his itinerant preaching mission. The smallpox epidemic, however, continued to wreak havoc on Black residents in Nova Scotia. At the onset of winter in 1787, a fresh outbreak of infections prevented him from visiting Port Mouton in late November. Marrant sent his traveling company back to Birchtown, while he remained in Big Port Jolly when he learned that "the people were desirous that I should stay with them a few days." When he set out for Birchtown days later, he was thrown off course by a blizzard and got lost in the woods "by reason of the snow falling so very thick." With visibility reduced to a mere twenty yards, travel to Birchtown would be impossible, so he "went down on my knees to God, to direct me what I should do." As he prayed, his "little dog went under the rock," so Marrant "rose up ... taking my tommihawk [*sic*] in my hand, and I went in." He inspected the cave to ensure its vacancy before he resolved to stay, and after he was convinced it was empty, he settled to record the day's events in his journal and repose for the night. An hour later, he was awakened by strange sounds coming from the mouth of the cave. He later recalled:

> I heard something walk on the snow, my little dog ran away to the mouth
> of the cave. I arose up and went and met a bear at the mouth of the rock,
> but was prevented from coming in by seeing me. He drew back, and
> growled very fiercely, and continued for an hour; whilst he was raging, I
> was praying to God to encourage me and strengthen me to stand against
> him. But, I must confess to my Readers, at the first sight of the beast I
> trembled and became very faint, and had he attempted then to attack me,
> I should have fell an easy prey in his paws.[107]

The bear returned in the wee hours of morning, but Marrant was more courageous when he faced him the second time: "At half after two I had another visit from him, but met him in the name of the Lord, and with much boldness, trusting upon the promises of the Lord. He strengthened me wonderfully; he staid [*sic*] three quarters of an hour this time, and then the Lord turned him away again, and I saw him no more until half after eight in the morning on the 1st of December."

One day later, Marrant and the bear crossed paths again, "but he never growled at me," he recounted. Marrant passed by the bear unassailed, and the bear "went in my track back to his former lodging."[108] Overcome by hunger and fatigue, Marrant did not make it very far before he stopped and unloaded all his belongings except his Bible. He was so faint that he could not answer a search party's horn when he heard it blowing in the distance. His dog's barking, however, brought rescuers to his aid. Two unnamed women took him to a home where he spent three days in recovery. Once he was well enough to travel, he continued to Sable River, where he found his pupils lodging safely and the congregation awaiting his return.

Marrant's gripping narration of hunger, disorientation, and near death in the wilderness near Sable River conjures a pattern repeated throughout the Bible. When the prophet Elijah fled from Jezebel, he left his apprentice in Judah before continuing into the wilderness. He went forty days and nights without food or drink until he reached the mountain of God. At Horeb, he too found lodging in a cave, and there he was asked by God why he had come. Elijah explained that he was escaping those who sought his life. He was instructed to stand on the mountain to witness the presence of God. Instead of a blizzard, Elijah witnessed a windstorm, an earthquake, and a wildfire. When the natural disasters failed to reveal God's presence, Elijah was greeted by silence. In the silence, God again asked him why he had come. Elijah explained that he was fleeing for his life, and this time he was instructed to return through the wilderness to appoint a king.[109]

The parallels in Marrant's story and the biblical account are numerous. Elijah and Marrant both went to caves to pray in the wilderness. In both stories, natural disasters precede divine revelation that inspires each protagonist to continue his journey with renewed confidence. In Elijah's case, three natural disasters—a windstorm, an earthquake, and a wildfire—precede divine communication.[110] Marrant, on the other hand, went three days without food while lost in a snowstorm. Evidence of divine revelation was signified during his third standoff with the bear, when he faced it without trepidation before continuing to Sable River to preach. In both stories, the prophets sojourned in caves and subsequently continued their respective journeys with renewed spiritual commitment.

In Africana religious communities, caves provided domains for nature spirits that were commonly sought for fertility, prosperity, and protection. Marrant's depiction of his encounter with the bear may signify the appearance of a *simbi* spirit since in some Africana religious communities it was believed that dangerous predators guarded the souls of revered ancestors and powerful nature spirits. In low-country accounts, the *simbi* took on a variety of forms. Representations of the *simbi* as "people, animals, organic and inorganic objects . . . introduce a remarkable range of simbi forms and imply they represent something more than manifestations as particular beings or distinct physical objects."[111] When new territories were founded, village leaders were responsible for establishing and maintaining bonds with *simbi* spirits.[112] The *simbi* inhabited deep areas of the forest surrounded by water or covered by mountains. As one scholar notes, "Features of the landscape associated with *simbi* revealed additional ideas about their power. People credited the *simbi* with marking the terrain by creating ravines and chasms in hillsides while also occupying caves and other deep places. These locations provided evidence of great force that transformed solid rock, a certain indication of exceptional spiritual strength, while at the same time embodying the notions of a deep descent and darkness, the combination of both identifying a site as a locus of intense spiritual power."[113]

In times of social distress, initiation into Kimpasi societies dedicated to *simbi* spirits increased in the kingdom of Kongo. Low-country Africana communities also turned to the *simbi* for support when they were stricken by misfortune. War, the rapacity of other groups, and drought occasioned the growth of Kimpasi societies in West Central Africa in the late seventeenth and early eighteenth centuries.[114] The persistence of famine, disease, and increasing threats of reenslavement may have prompted Marrant to seek to connect with nature spirits in the caves of Nova Scotia.

In numerous biblical stories, the presence of God is encountered in caves. Additionally, the Bible contains a number of stories in which caves are selected as the final resting place of the dead. In Genesis, following the death of Sarah, his wife, Abraham requests a sepulcher to dispose of her body. He selects the cave of Machpelah belonging to Ephron as the place where Sarah's body would repose. The patriarchs of Israel (Abraham, Isaac, Jacob, and Joseph) along with their wives are also buried there when they die.[115] For Moses, the cleft of the rock on Mount Sinai is where the glory of Yahweh passed before him while Moses remained hidden. It was also, according to biblical legend, the place where Moses's body was buried.[116] Joshua, Moses's successor, entombs five opposing kings in a cave after defeating them in battle. He has a large rock placed at the entrance of the cave so that their corpses are not disturbed and cannot be rescued.[117] Placing a stone at the entrance of the tomb also prevents the army from entering the tomb to either retrieve their bodies, dress or prepare the bodies for burial, or visit the tomb to commune with the spirits of the dead. This same concern is echoed by the women who come to anoint Jesus's body when they find a stone blocking the entrance to the cave where he had been laid by Joseph of Arimathea.[118] In biblical narratives, caves were the resting place of the dead as well as the setting for dramatic encounters with God. In Elijah's story (Marrant's narrative model), the cave is the locus for divine communication.

Burial rituals, including how corpses are cared for, reveal a given society's foundational principles as well as how that society comes to terms with the passing of its members. The rituals and symbols that accompany disposal of the body disclose important beliefs about the interconnectedness between the living and the dead. As the religious studies scholar Gary Laderman explains, "The dead do not simply vanish when life is extinguished; although their final physical disposition is managed by specialists, the dead must also be accounted for in the imagination. In contrast to the relative simplicity and uniformity of the ritual activity surrounding the corpse, the life of the spirit—if it is affirmed at all—is described within a variety of symbol systems and imaginative constructs."[119] Within Black Atlantic religious thought, burial practices and tomb visitation maintained ancestral ties. Noting the "massive reinstatement" of Kongo and Angola burial traditions in North America, Robert Farris Thompson characterizes the tomb as "a charm for the persistence of the spirit." Decorative additions including bottles, shells, and trees function as "medicines of admonishment and love" and "mark a persistent cultural link between Kongo and the black New World."[120]

Additionally, in Kongo and Mbundu areas of West Central Africa, graves were the center of ancestral cults. Their adorning insignia indicated the deceased person's status in life. Tombs were often located beyond the inhabited territory and were frequently attended by surviving family members. On festive days, the deceased person's birthday, for example, offerings were made at the grave site to ensure good fortune for the living. Failure to carry out such responsibilities was believed to cause misfortune within the living community. The location of grave sites outside the inhabited territory not only was a measure of sanitary health in seventeenth- and eighteenth-century Kongo but also was intended to ensure that the soul of the deceased enjoyed maximum rest outside the clamor of the village. As one scholar notes, "The dead were carefully buried in cemeteries located in the deep woods or away from inhabited areas so that the soul could have 'maximum rest,' and would lay quietly in the grave and not bother the living."[121] Marrant's mimetic performance of the Bible's cave stories reveals not only the continuity between African and Black Atlantic religious consciousness but also a belief that nature spirits and the spirits of the deceased exist on a continuous plane with the living and were capable of offering assistance to remedy maladies of the material world.

Intergenerational Salvation

Marrant concluded *Journal* by recalling the deaths of several friends and close associates. John Lock, who lived only a short time after his conversion, was the first to be remembered. Lock died of smallpox and was lauded for his steadfastness in the face of illness. On his deathbed, he admonished his family to forsake "dancing and swearing, and following foolish diversion, and begging them to serve the Lord Jesus Christ in this world, and to forsake all the ways of sin, that they might meet in glory, to part no more." He insisted that Marrant preach at his funeral, and shortly after, he passed from this life.

In the death story of twelve-year-old Kitty Bligh, Marrant recycled a tale motif introduced in *Narrative*. Bligh, like Mary Scott, the twelve-year-old student in *Narrative*, died in an extraordinary manner. Young Kitty, a student in Marrant's school, was not considered a promising pupil. His frequent conversations with her had seemed fruitless. However, when Marrant attended her bedside just four days before she died, she told him about "the great display of God's glory that was shewn to her on the evening past." Her family and classmates gathered to hear her deathbed charge; a particularly strong admonishment was given to her mother: "[She] turned round to her mother, and said, 'O my mother, I am afraid I shall never see you any more, for you are not serving God,' said she, 'and you cannot mother deceive God, but you will deceive your own precious soul. Mother leave off backbiting God's people, and persecuting the church of God; mother God is angry with you every moment of the day.'"[122] For the next three days, Kitty continued to address all her visitors in this way. On her final day, the elders of the church, along with her family and classmates, came together "so the room was filled with small and great." They sang and prayed, and after she had bid them all farewell, she "fell asleep in Christ."

Kitty Bligh was the third twelve-year-old girl whose awe-inspiring transformation led to her mother's conversion in Marrant's writings. At the conclusion of *Narrative*, Mary Scott had also charged her family to uphold the standard of Christ from her deathbed. All those gathered to witness her transition were deeply moved by her address. In particular, according to Marrant, her mother was profoundly affected: "[Mary] shook hands with them, and bade them farewell; desiring them not to lament for her when she was dead, for she was going to that fine place where God would wipe away all tears from her eyes, and she should sing Hallelujahs to God and the Lamb for ever and ever, and where she hoped afterwards to meet them; and then turning again to me, she said— 'Farewell, and God bless you,' and then fell asleep in the arms of Jesus. This afterwards proved the conversion of her mother."[123]

The story of the awakening of a twelve-year-old girl in Green Harbor, told earlier in *Journal*, does not include the deathbed confession that preceded the mother's salvation in the other two examples. At the conclusion of a cathartic worship service, Marrant was drawn to a twelve-year-old girl who continuously "cried out so much for after the rest." When he asked why she persisted in this manner, she explained that "she was afraid she should not be able to fulfil the charge that was then given her." Marrant refused to comfort her but rather asked, was she "not afraid her soul would be lost to all eternity?" Unable to answer, "she burst out in tears" and he left her, "finding that she was not able to express her feelings." The following morning she "rose up in the time of preaching, crying out, and declaring to the congregation—that her sorrow and sighing had fled away, and she had received that peace from God, which the tongue could not express." The congregation acknowledged her confession with singing, and in the wake of the celebration, the girl's mother also "was able to testify of the love of God."[124]

The relationship between the salvation of twelve-year-old girls and adult women is established in a familiar biblical story. In the synoptic Gospels, Jairus, a leader in the synagogue, asked Jesus to heal his twelve-year-old daughter. As Jesus followed him to his home, a woman who had suffered from a blood illness for twelve years touched him and was healed. Jesus asked who touched him, the woman came forward, and he commended her faith. Then, he continued to the home of Jairus, where he found the girl lying dead. He declared that she was only sleeping and then raised her back to life.[125] The stories of the ruler's daughter and the woman with the issue of blood demonstrate the relationship between the salvation of adults and children. Jesus could not comply with Jairus's request until he first healed the adult woman because the health of the community's children was tied to the well-being of the adults. Marrant inverts the pattern each time the story is related in his writings: the daughter's salvation leads to the mother's deliverance.

In the two accounts, both adults and children are recipients of divine favor. In the biblical account, Jesus dismisses those gathered from the dead girl's home; in each of Marrant's narrations, salvation is realized only after the community is gathered. Family and friends come together to hear the tearful farewells of Mary Scott and Kitty Bligh. The unnamed daughter from Green Harbor is delivered at church during morning worship. Even the repetition of the narrative in Marrant's texts is likely founded on the trifold appearance of the story in the synoptic Gospels.

The centrality of maternal-child relationships in Marrant's stories of communal salvation also underscores the generative impact of Africana women's religiosity on his own religious outlook. Included in Marrant's congregations were former bondswomen, many of whom had been compelled to acquiesce to their status as slaves to remain connected to their children. Because of the powerful connection that existed between West African women and their children, slave traders commonly targeted children in kidnapping raids to lure mothers into captivity. The religious historian Alexis Wells-Oghoghomeh relates the account of a fifteenth-century Portuguese writer, Gomes Eanes de Zurara, who describes a young West African mother who resolved herself to the status of a slave and peacefully boarded a slave ship after kidnappers had captured her son.[126] Evidence of the influence of women's religiosity on the Nova Scotia community can also be witnessed in the designation of one of the ships in the fleet that was specially outfitted to accommodate expectant mothers. While Marrant makes no specific reference to the history of kidnapping in *Journal*, it is important to note that this experience was suffered ubiquitously among enslaved women and would come to link them together as a community. Since the loss of children was understood widely, Marrant reverses the trope—children, namely daughters, draw mothers to salvation and also facilitate communal reintegration. In Marrant's reversal of the trope, the redemption of children facilitates the redemption of mothers.

The religious rituals performed by Black Christian ministers in Nova Scotia aimed to repair communal misfortunes stemming from social injustice, lack of resources, and widespread illness. Throughout the Black Atlantic, healing included crucial social and political roles in Africana religious communities. In many cases, the minister's primary function was that of an intellectual, providing "directive, organizational, or educative" leadership. Domingos Alvares, an itinerant healer enslaved in Brazil, established healing communities and was regarded as both "a powerful healer and a potential redeemer from the cruelties and abuses of enslavement."[127] Similarly, early descriptions of West Central African Kimpasi societies note the original intention to treat the infirm or cure ailments as part of initiation into the society. Because African-descended people understood that physical ailments were manifestations of spiritual forces at work, initiation into Christian communities may have been understood as attempts to stave off hunger, lack, and disease that were so common and widespread among the Black Loyalists in Nova Scotia.[128]

The religious studies scholar Stephanie Mitchem classifies healing work as an integral component of the African American religious tradition. Mitchem's discussion encompasses a range of practices derived from throughout the African diaspora. "Healing," she explains, "offers a language through which African Americans dialogue with the world." Within the Africana religious cosmologies, healing entails "a scope expanded beyond the limits of the physical self, emphasizing connections to the community and nature and nations, as well as links with the past and future." For Black religious practitioners like Alvares and Marrant, past errors, social ills, and injustices were included as "part of the dynamics of black folk healing." Consequently, Marrant's healing work constitutes political and civic leadership and exemplifies "public expressions of a black mystical tradition."[129] Within this healing tradition, an artist or performer "functions as healer, conjuring words and emotions to cleanse or strengthen" and "indicates an artistic level of communication among African Americans that is both intellectual and healing."[130]

Marrant's allusion to biblical stories throughout *Journal* discloses important dimensions of early African American religious thought. Structural rather than theological modes of narrative analysis primarily informed black religious consciousness in the eighteenth century. The presence of African narrative forms in early black religious literature implies corresponding African meanings.[131] In Marrant's texts, the explicit religious rhetoric and symbols are Christian, but the structures by which they are made intelligible are African. They exhibit the free-flowing relationship between form and meaning that characterizes narrative expression in African diaspora communities. Marrant's *Journal* reveals a theological perspective and communal ethic common to both African and African American religious contexts. In Africana religion, ritual experience reintegrates individuals within community life via mystical, transcendent encounters with divine realities. Additionally, Marrant displays a pattern—disintegration-rejuvenation-reintegration—found in both African initiation and African American conversion experiences. This mythic community ethos is understood as a process of creation out of destruction and corresponds to the improvisational dimension of black cultural sensibilities. It also reflects the emphasis within evangelical Christianity on death and resurrection and perhaps provides an additional explanation of the frequent recurrence of the resurrection theme in Marrant's autobiographical writings.[132]

Marrant's days in Birchtown were coming to an end. When he received a letter from Halifax alerting him to the arrival of long-awaited supplies from England, he rushed to Shelburne only to learn that money sent for his relief had already been received by someone named James Earl. Earl had left word for Marrant to meet him in Halifax, but weather caused Marrant's travel to be delayed. When Marrant arrived in Halifax on December 16, James Earl was nowhere to be found. Marrant waited for Earl in Halifax for nearly two weeks, but when he did not find him, he left for Boston.

5. "As Men and as Masons"

Spiritual Genealogies and Racial Ethnogenesis in Marrant's Sermon

⫴

It took only five days to sail from Halifax, but when Marrant arrived in Boston in February 1789, he felt like he was in a "strange country, knowing nobody." With letters of recommendation in hand, he went from house to house seeking accommodations from those to whom he had been directed, but his early efforts yielded mixed results. He was initially refused by Rev. Dr. Stillman but was welcomed at the house of Samuel Bean. Stillman was unable to offer him lodging but did offer him a platform from which to launch his ministry—Marrant's first sermon was preached at Dr. Stillman's chapel. Hoping to capitalize on the remnants of the enthusiasm that had taken the New England colonies by storm just a decade earlier, Marrant announced that the appointed time had come— the long-awaited prophet was finally present.[1]

This chapter examines John Marrant's generative role in the early history of African American Freemasonry. Centering Marrant in the study of African American Freemasonry's early history renders a more expansive understanding of the temporal and geographic origins of the tradition. The "peculiar combination of modern science and ancient religion" enabled Freemasonry to captivate the imagination of many elite members of British and American society. Colonial Masons regarded their fraternal orders as means to entering public life and teaching manners and encouraging mutual love, necessary to hold society together. In the newly formed American republic, Masonic civic rituals were a key element in attempts to teach genteel behavior and promote public virtue.[2] Over the first half of the eighteenth century, Africans and their descendants encountered British forms of European Freemasonry in Africa, North America, and the Caribbean. The existence of lodges outside North America and prior to the organization of the African Lodge in Boston underscores the likelihood that Marrant encountered and began to form ideas about Freemasonry prior to his friendship with Prince Hall. While the presence of European Freemasonry provided institutional models for the organization of Black lodges, New World developments alone cannot account for the adoption of Freemasonry by persons of African descent. Striking similarities and multiple points of correspondence—including extreme secrecy and ritual progression by degrees—point to West African initiation societies as institutional predecessors to African American Freemasonry.

Chance encounters with European Freemasonry notwithstanding, Marrant's most enduring contribution to Black Freemasonry's legacy stems from *A Sermon Preached on the 24th Day of June, 1789, Being the Festival of St. John the Baptist,* the first printed formal public oration in the history of the African Lodge.[3] In the sermonic address, Marrant conjures biblical genealogies to mythologize Black racial ethnogenesis. Ritual initiation in Freemasonry, he explains, reformulates African American collective identity by restoring contemporary Black men to divine and ancestral (i.e., biblical) legacies. Marrant's *Sermon* established the foundations of an enduring template for African American male identity formation. Additionally, *Sermon* inaugurated a tradition of Masonic oration succeeded by grand masters and lodge leaders in subsequent years. In this chapter's final section, I briefly overview the lives and contributions of Prince Hall, David Walker, and Lewis Hayden—important Masonic leaders whose oratorical and rhetorical performances rely on and expand foundational principles of African American oratory articulated by Marrant.

Religion and Activism in Boston

The excitement inspired by the initial wave of revivalism waned in the wake of America's liberation from England, but religious life continued to be heavily influenced by the evangelical movement known as the Great Awakening. British revivalists John and Charles Wesley, along with the Huntingdon Connexion's own George Whitefield, soared to the heights of their popularity on the preaching circuit in Boston. Whitefield, who was noted for his extemporaneous, demonstratively powerful oratory, attracted large crowds in Boston and the surrounding towns in the years preceding the Revolutionary War. While some revivalist preachers were revered for their dynamic preaching style, many drew their share of criticism. Debates about religion were popular in Boston's print media, and revivalists were common targets for journalistic vitriol. Disputes regarding the nature of God, the rights of humanity, and the role of the church in society were popular entertainment in colonial Boston.[4] In the years after the American Revolution, revivals continued to catalyze denominational growth. Evangelical denominations (Baptists, for example) ushered in a wave of awakened Protestantism that crystallized the final dissolution of Britain's imperial hold.[5]

During the first half of the eighteenth century, Boston was the most populated town in North America, with African Americans accounting for nearly 10 percent of the total population by midcentury.[6] Though dependent on slave labor in the Caribbean and the American South, Boston itself was described as a society with slaves, rather than a slave society. Enslaved Blacks in Boston occupied a status somewhere above enslaved people on plantations in the Caribbean and the American South, but beneath white indentured servants of the Chesapeake and New England colonies. Boston slave owners rarely owned more than one slave; out of the more than fifty-five hundred Bostonians with slaves, only nine owned more than two slaves on the eve of the American Revolution.[7] Many Black Bostonians worked in domestic roles as indentured servants. Maritime industries, including fishing, whaling, and mercantile shipping, also attracted racially diverse laborers since enslaved and free Black sailors commonly enjoyed greater degrees of autonomy and equality than what was typically experienced on land. Interracial alliances, however, were frowned on and drew the ire of colonial, and later state, government officials. These suspicions included religious gatherings as well.[8] Although slaves in Massachusetts were not legally barred from baptism, marriage, or literacy, the egalitarian spirit of revival raised fears that the widespread Christianization of Blacks could fuel the rise of abolitionism. Consequently, few Blacks formed or joined Christian congregations in Boston before the eighteenth century's final decade.[9]

Nevertheless, in the aftermath of revolution, Boston was a "fertile area" for the "propagation and dissemination" of early abolitionist sentiment.[10] Both free Blacks and whites petitioned the Massachusetts state legislature for general emancipation, while enslaved people contested the legality of their enslavement in the courts. In 1781, Elizabeth "Mum Bett" Freeman, an enslaved woman in Sheffield, Massachusetts, became the first person to be freed after the adoption of the Massachusetts constitution in 1780. Two years later, an enslaved man in Boston, Quok Walker, was freed when Chief Justice William Cushing ruled that the peculiar institution undermined the constitution of Massachusetts, effectively ending slavery in the Bay State. The end of slavery in the state was owed, in large part, to the organizing efforts of early abolitionists during the previous decade.[11] In 1777, Prince Hall, a prominent leader in Boston's fledgling abolitionist movement, had submitted multiple petitions to the court for individual manumissions and the abolition of slavery in Massachusetts. Hall, along with fourteen other free Black men, founded the African Lodge of Free and Accepted Masons in Boston. Their activism paved the way for the legal victories enjoyed in succeeding years by Freeman, Walker, and numerous other enslaved Black people whose political fate they helped radically alter. Members of the African Lodge sought to foster racial solidarity for Black Bostonians in the new republic. As the religious studies scholar Chernoh Sesay has noted, "Abolition steeled Black Masonic leadership, and Masonry provided an institutional frame for antislavery organizing."[12]

The ambiguities of emancipation in New England and the mid-Atlantic states helped to crystallize notions of racial solidarity for Black Freemasons. In several northern states, gradual and conditional emancipation was applied unevenly and did not always improve Black people's lived experience in the ways that their altered political status implied. Although constitutionally held as an inalienable right to which all men were entitled, many white Boston abolitionists believed that Black people had to earn their freedom.[13] Free Blacks in Boston were "subject to compulsory labor and discriminated against in employment."[14] Black Freemasons' belief, by contrast, that freedom was the universal right of every human being compounded their increasing frustration with gradual abolition. Excluded from both Masonic fellowship and participation in civic institutions, members of the African Lodge developed elaborate public demonstrations—funeral services, parades, and festive celebrations—that exhibited the bonds of Masonic brotherhood. The combination of activism and public demonstrations appealed to Black non-Masons and helped establish the African Lodge as a leading institution in Boston's African American community.

Prince Hall and the Diasporic Context for African American Freemasonry

Marrant's fame spread quickly through Boston in the weeks following his first sermon at Dr. Stillman's chapel. Soon, he would find himself preaching before "a large concourse of people" multiple times per week. However, not everyone who attended the meetings found his sermons edifying. On one occasion in late February on Boston's West End, a gang of nearly forty men "came prepared that evening with swords and clubs, and other instruments, to put an end to my life," he recalled.[15] Marrant was warned of the approaching danger by a companion, however, and was able to slip past his would-be captors unharmed. When the men realized he had eluded them, they went to where he was staying and threw stones through the window. Dr. Bean came out and dispersed the mob, and the next morning the neighborhood was abuzz with news of the previous night's drama.

In Boston, mob violence was "a familiar tool of political protest," and interracial fellowships were a common denominator in many instances. In the 1740s, an assembly of "Foreign Seamen, Servants, Negroes, and Other Persons of a Mean and Vile Condition" took to the streets in protest of British impressment of sailors and laborers in Boston.[16] Both John Wesley and George Whitefield were mocked, attacked, and frequently assaulted during the years of their respective itinerancies.[17] Many in Boston's high society were especially alarmed by fervent, extemporaneous preaching by Black ministers in revival settings.[18] When the assailants who ambushed Marrant were apprehended and brought to court, they confessed that they targeted his interracial fellowship because "we used to see our girls, and when we came to their houses, we always found they were gone to meeting, and we were determined to put an end to the meeting."[19] The perpetrators were assessed a fine, and Marrant "was never disturbed by them any more."

Episodes of racially motivated violence like the one described by Marrant may explain why he sought refuge at the residence of Prince Hall, described as "one of the most respectable characters in Boston," and his wife in Boston's North End. Though census records do not confirm the practice of boarding until the mid-nineteenth century, Black households in Boston commonly included non-family members. Boarding gave new arrivals an opportunity to be acclimated to life in Boston more smoothly; through hosts, boarders were introduced to social groups, churches, and employment opportunities. By 1860, two out of every five Black Boston households included boarders.[20]

The close bond that commonly developed between boarders and their hosts may explain why Marrant rose so quickly through the ranks of leadership within the African Lodge.

Marrant and Hall quickly developed a close friendship in early 1789. Over the course of the spring months, they likely spent countless hours exchanging war stories over tea. Hall, on the edge of his seat, may have nodded in sympathy and shook his head in disbelief as Marrant described "the engagement with the Dutch off the Dogger bank, on board the Princess-Amelia, of eighty-four guns."[21] In return, Hall perhaps gave a blow-by-blow account of the Revolution in Boston, filling in important gaps on the death of Crispus Attucks, the early conflicts at Lexington and Concord, the bloody Battle of Bunker Hill, and the evacuation of wealthy Loyalists with their slaves to Nova Scotia that had all but depleted Boston's Black population by war's end. He certainly included details of his own encounter with the British military just weeks before the initial skirmishes of the war. Hall, along with fourteen other free Black men, had been initiated by an outfit of Irish Freemasons, members of Army Lodge Number 441, into the Ancient and Accepted Order of Freemasons on March 6, 1775, at Bunker Hill. The two men also may have shared their thoughts on slavery—Hall's firsthand perspective in Barbados, and Marrant's eyewitness account in South Carolina—and discovered a mutual disdain for the peculiar institution. They probably finished each other's sentences as they discovered a shared Africana vocabulary of ritual, symbolism, and mythology underlying their respective expressions of Christianity and Freemasonry. Hall also undoubtedly took note of Marrant's international associations with Selina Hastings and George Whitefield through the Huntingdon Connexion. Those same connections, Hall remembered, had introduced Phillis Wheatley, Boston's most renowned Black writer, to a larger transatlantic audience more than a decade earlier.[22] Hall seemingly hoped to join an international dialogue in which Black authors imagined the future of African diaspora communities. In an undated letter to Hastings, Hall thanked her for her support of Marrant. In the past year, Marrant had been made a member and chaplain of the African Lodge, an association, Hall assured, that would "be a great help to him in his travels, and may do a great deal of good to society."[23] Marrant's familiarity with Africana initiation rituals and his quick ascendancy through the ranks of the African Lodge suggest a generative role alongside Prince Hall in translating the rituals of Freemasonry into cultural formations that signified African American civic and political inclusion and refuted notions of Black inferiority.

Official histories of African American Freemasonry cite the initiation of Prince Hall and fourteen others by an Irish military sergeant, John Batt, in

1775, as the founding narrative and central point of institutional origin. Free-mason lodges, like Anglican and Protestant churches, dotted the Atlantic land-scape and were central to perpetuating ideological networks and emotional connections to the British Empire. Fraternal membership granted access to global networks of individuals and lodges that "helped men adjust to strange surroundings, find fellowship in new environments, and secure employment and assistance when in need." Boston, a major hub in the eighteenth-century transatlantic nexus of exchange, was a "fertile area for the propagation and dis-semination" of ideas and ideologies contributing to the "cosmopolitan atmo-sphere" that enabled Freemasonry to flourish among many of the city's African American elite.[24]

In 1779, John Rowe, grand master of the Grand Lodge of Massachusetts, granted a provisional charter to Black Freemasons in Boston. The charter en-abled members of the African Lodge to gather publicly to observe Masonic festivals and to perform funerals, but they were expressly prohibited from initiating new members. The inability to initiate new members limited insti-tutional growth during the early years of African American Freemasonry. Mem-bers of the African Lodge, mostly excluded from fraternal fellowship by white Masons, unsuccessfully sought to secure a full charter from the Grand Lodge of Massachusetts. However, when their "fraternal overtures" were rebuffed, Black Masons turned again to the British. In 1787, the African Lodge was granted a charter from the English Modern Lodge in London that certified its complete recognition as a Masonic body. The founding of African Lodge 459 in Boston constituted the formal beginnings of African American Freemasonry. As the religious historian Corey Walker reminds us, however, it may be more illumi-nating to consider "the founding narrative of African American Freemasonry" not as one having "a singular point of origin, but as a cultural formation embed-ded in a wider geography" of "zones of cultural contact of Africans and their descendants confronting European Masonic activity in the emerging spaces of the African diaspora."[25]

The intellectual and cultural history of African American Freemasonry is complex and draws on multiple institutional and cultural predecessors. In New England, Pinkster and Election Day celebrations established cultural prece-dents that gradually gave way to Masonic ritual performances. Masonic rituals and funeral ceremonies emerged alongside, and eventually replaced, Pinkster and Election Day celebrations as central communal events around which Blacks "could coalesce in celebration of . . . the values and coherence of their community."[26] For some, the shift in cultural forms signaled transitions in African American political leadership. Leadership roles once filled by Pinkster kings and

Election Day governors were increasingly assumed by Freemasons and marked an important pivot in the "changing black politics of public presentation and abolition."[27] Election Day and Pinkster ceremonies demonstrate a "dynamic process of cultural transformations and revisions" that enabled Freemasonry to take root among African Americans in Boston.[28]

Other theories about the origins of African American Freemasonry point to West African initiation societies as institutional forerunners. In their precolonial contexts, Poro and Bundu societies in West Africa functioned more like government agencies, administering aid to families and individuals in crisis and also helping to resolve diplomatic and commercial differences between villages and independent territories. Responsible also for the administration of the formal education of young people as well as the rituals of adult formation, these organizations were utilized for representational government in political contexts and were vital to the functioning of society.[29] Leaders within these societies regulated communal standards of behavior and were expected to exemplify the highest character and moral standing. Additionally, membership in some West African initiation societies was characterized by degrees of progression through which initiates rose by mastery of esoteric knowledge.[30] While religious symbolism and ritual ceremonies of European Freemasonry may have differed from the traditional initiation societies such as Poro, principles of the Craft—secrecy regarding organizational affairs, social services for constituents, a hierarchical membership structure based on degrees of progression in relation to various levels of knowledge, and extreme loyalty to the ideals and leaders of the organization—were likely understood by Freemasons of African descent long before their initiation into the lodge.[31]

Throughout the African Atlantic diaspora, Africans and their descendants had ample opportunities to encounter European Freemasonry. As early as the 1730s, Blacks in New York were alleged to have had "the Impudence to assume the Stile and Title of FREEMASONS, in Imitation of a Society" of white Freemasons.[32] This early display of African American Freemasonry, notes Corey Walker, acknowledged a Black presence within European Freemasonry, several decades prior to Hall's initiation in Massachusetts. While not included in formal, institutional histories of Prince Hall Freemasonry, this early account of "black participation in and adoption of the characters and symbols of Freemasonry" exemplifies how African Americans "recreated the fraternity in *their* own image."[33] In addition to the New York display, numerous Freemason lodges on the west coast of Africa afforded persons of African descent opportunities to become at least passively familiar with the Craft. A Freemason lodge at James Fort on the river Gambia was established in 1735 at a "crossroads of commerce, culture, and capital in the rapidly expanding Atlantic world." In the Caribbean, the expanded reach of European Freemasonry in the Atlantic world is rendered more salient. Lodges in British-controlled territories, including Jamaica and Antigua, were established by the mid-eighteenth century. In Barbados, the alleged homeland of Prince Hall, a lodge reportedly was established in 1740. The global networks connecting European Freemasonry and people of African descent are also implied by the backgrounds of other charter initiates from the African Lodge in Boston. The names of at least two initiates, Cuff Bufform and Cato Speain, suggest points of origin outside North America—Akan for the former, and a possible Cuban derivation for the latter.[34]

The expansive temporal and geographic reach of European Freemasonry throughout the Atlantic world underscores that multiple individual and cultural sources can be credited with generative contributions to the origins of African American Freemasonry. Within a nexus of transoceanic exchange, religious and cultural reserves "played a crucial role in aiding Africans and their descendants" in translating "the experiences and conditions of diaspora" into the forms and symbols of Freemasonry.[35] Cultural elements inherited from West African initiation societies and New England and mid-Atlantic Pinkster and Election Day ceremonies raise speculative questions regarding John Marrant's generative role in helping to create African American Freemasonry's institutional culture. Marrant was born in New York, the site of the earliest emergence of an African American presence within European Freemasonry. In South Carolina and in Nova Scotia, he underwent and officiated rites and ceremonies derived from many of the same West and West Central African initiation societies that contributed to the formation of African American Freemasonry lodges. His understanding of Africana initiatory forms and corresponding symbols of transformation enabled him to quickly ascend to the ranks of leadership of the African Lodge.

A Grand Tradition of Masonic Oration

Within early African American communities, oratory was an essential tool for organizing political and social life. Community and political leaders utilized public oration to voice group interests and mobilize collective action.[36] Within early African American Freemasonry, Marrant's generative role comes to the fore most saliently in his *Sermon* for the Festival of Saint John the Baptist. Alongside funeral processions and public processions, festival days in honor of Saint John were among the most important celebrations in Masonic temporality.[37] It is noteworthy that Marrant was selected to deliver the foundational address that announced the presence of the African Lodge to the broader Atlantic world. As noted previously, Marrant's institutional connections to international patrons likely prompted Hall to trust him with such an important responsibility; his gift of oration and his familiarity with meanings associated with Masonic rituals and symbols may have also encouraged Hall's decision. In their numerous exchanges, Marrant had ample opportunities to demonstrate his keen understanding of meanings associated with the public presentation of Masonic bodies. Dressed in full Masonic regalia as they paraded through the streets of Boston, African American Freemasons aimed to reproduce Black manhood "distinguished in every physical aspect from the racist images of 'typical' black men in eighteenth-century runaway slave advertisements."[38] Marrant had also once utilized bodily adornment to signify transformation. When he returned to his family in Savannah dressed "purely in the Indian style" of a Creek warrior, his bodily adornment—"a long pendant down my back, a sash round my middle, without breeches, and a tomohawk [sic] by my side"—signaled a more profound transformation and revealed new dimensions of an expanded identity.[39] As one scholar notes, "Marrant undergoes a complete change of identity, the fullness of his rebirth signified by his assuming the wardrobe" of an Indian elite.[40] Taking into account Marrant's preexisting familiarity with the rituals and symbols that undergirded Black Freemasonry, one can imagine his influential role in aiding Prince Hall to transform the rituals of Freemasonry into rituals of race.

Within the broader context of Masonic oratory, ritual aspects of Marrant's *Sermon* during the Festival of Saint John the Baptist are more readily discernible. As Corey Walker explains, Masonic public demonstrations intended to reveal the communal foundation of Freemasonry that distinguished its members from non-Masons. Members of Euro-American lodges immersed themselves in the sanctifying virtues and values of Freemasonry so that they could be purified to "then act for the betterment of society with a purity of intentions and motives." Public orations were part of the ritual culture designed to represent the highest ideals of Freemasonry to both members of the Craft and external audiences.[41] Because Black Freemasons' rhetorical performance inherently called into question the integrity of Euro-American Freemasonry, it is not only a Masonic ritual but also a ritual of race. Rituals of race, Walker explains, were codified performances of Masonic rituals that signified, gave meaning to, or offered commentary on political and religious meanings shaped by the phenomenon of race in America. For example, when Prince Hall founded the African Lodge along with the original fourteen members, he enacted "the cultural practice of Freemasonry on the same ideals as his European American counterparts." However, their articulation of universal fraternity and mutual support was unique because of the legal and extralegal racial prohibitions that excluded them from universal fellowship. Members of the African Lodge appropriated Masonic rituals (including but not limited to oration, ceremonial processions, and public demonstration) to underscore the irony of their exclusion from interracial Masonic bodies and the civic institutions in Boston. Euro-American Freemasonry succumbed to the racist ordering of American society and established racialized difference within the continuity of Freemasonry. "This difference," notes Walker, "transformed the rituals of Freemasonry into the rituals of race."[42]

Rituals of race, according to Walker, were most salient in the performance of African American Masonic oratory. In his 1789 *Sermon* for the Festival of Saint John the Baptist, Marrant extolled the egalitarian principles of Freemasonry and utilized the Bible's mythic history to (re)position African Americans squarely within the ancient Masonic tradition and, by extension, within the civic and social institutions of American society. Addressing "a great number of people" that included some of the most prominent men in Boston, he narrated a tale of racial and Masonic origins that drew from several early chapters of Genesis. Through his account of origins, he traced the spiritual lineage of Black Americans through a genealogy of biblical figures tied to African geographies. He also contended that the history of Freemasonry traces its origins to African-descended kings and prophets from biblical lore. In his final summation, the African legacy of Black Americans enabled Black Freemasons to stand with "the greatest kings on the earth, as Men and as Masons," thus undermining the logic of race-based exclusion supported by myths of inherent Black inferiority. Marrant's oratorical performance and rhetorical strategy would be succeeded by a long succession of Masonic leaders extending into the period of Reconstruction.

In both *Narrative* and *Journal*, Marrant's reading of biblical narratives is relayed through autobiographical storytelling. In *Sermon*, however, his storytelling assumes a mythical, rather than autobiographical, form. The shift from autobiographical to mythical storytelling enables him to establish the African Lodge's legitimate claim to the ancient legacy of Freemasonry. The origins of Freemasonry could be traced to the creation of the world by God. The Genesis account of creation explained the divine, or ideal, arrangement of the social order.[43] Marrant's retelling of the Genesis creation myth aimed to demonstrate the symbolic ordering of Freemasonry through which Black collective self-understanding could be remade.[44] Utilizing the esoteric knowledge of Freemasonry, the Grand Architect "framed the heavens for beauty and delight" and "set the sun, moon and stars in the firmament of heaven."[45] Freemasonry, Marrant explains, was taught to men by God: in the Garden of Eden, the mythical point of origin for biblical creation, Adam learned this secret knowledge when he was commanded to "employ his mind as well as exercise his body" and "to contemplate and study God's works." Knowledge of the Craft was then passed down through a succession of patrilineal lineage from Adam to his son Cain that continued through the lineage of Solomon. Black Freemasons' Masonic ancestors included "Nimrod the son of Cush, the son of Ham," who "first founded the Babylonian monarchy, and kept possession of the plains, and founded the first great empire at Babylon, and became grand master of all Masons." Through Nimrod, Freemasonry also spread into Egypt, where the "descendants of Abram" were "trained up to the building with stone and brick, in order to make them expert Masons before they possessed the promised land." The biblical legacy of Masonic succession descended from African ancestors, Marrant emphasized, thus establishing the nobility of African heritage and undermining arguments in favor of Africans' exclusion from civic society.[46]

Comparative analysis of West African creation myths reveals structural parallels to the Genesis-inspired account Marrant narrates in *Sermon*. In the Dogon creation myth relayed by the cultural anthropologist Marcel Griaule, the earth was created when "the stars came from pellets of earth flung out into space by the God Amma, the one God." The sun and the moon were created by "the art of pottery."[47] Pottery, the creative force of God, would be critical to symbolic expressions of Dogon cosmology. A celestial granary allegorized the divine order of Amma. It consisted of a "woven basket with a circular opening and a square base." The sides of the base were eight cubits long and formed a flat roof; the height was ten cubits. The frame was covered with puddled clay, and in the center of each side of the square, stairways of ten steps each faced each of the cardinal directions. At the sixth step of the north staircase, there was a door giving access to the interior, which contained eight chambers arranged on two floors.[48]

The granary replicated the divine order of the cosmos. Each of the eight compartments on the two floors was designated for a different species of the earth's creatures: the north for men and fish; the south for domestic animals, the east for birds; and the west for wild animals, vegetables, and insects. The model granary symbolized the human body and "was therefore a picture of the world-system of the new order." The eight compartments represented "the eight principal organs of the Spirit of water which are comparable to the organs of men."[49] The granary made by pottery, the creative force of Amma, proclaimed the ancient mysteries of the cosmos.

The ancient progenitors of the African Lodge also utilized divine creative force—"the art of freemasonry," according to Marrant—to build structures to express their cosmology myths. Within Masonic lore, the construction of the

Temple of Solomon was hailed as a crowning achievement of ancient Freemasons. The temple's construction included the contributions of diverse laborers from "different nations and different colours, yet were they in perfect harmony among themselves, and strongly cemented in brotherly love and friendship."[50] The contributions of Sidonians, Canaanites, and Phoenicians laboring in their various roles as stone setters, timber cutters, bricklayers, and builders underscore the egalitarian collaboration on which the Craft was founded.

The temple also signified meaning beyond its physical structure. "Solomon, as grand master, and Hiram as his deputy, carried on and finished that great work of the temple of the living God," Marrant explains, "the inside work of which, in many instances as well as the tabernacle, resembles men's bodies; but this is better explained in a well filled lodge."[51] Within African American Freemasonry, corresponding symbolic meanings were associated with the structure of the African Lodge. The literary and cultural historian Maurice Wallace notes, "The Masonic lodge room as artifact and edifice expresses black masculine-Masonic ideality." Master Masons like Marrant, who possessed "the full knowledge of how to construct black masculine selfhood," hoped to inspire "the interior adjustment of the fractured life of black manhood to the promise of cohesiveness" reflected in the structure of the African Lodge and the mutuality of fraternalism.[52]

Marrant's previous employment as a carpenter likely aided him as he applied the principles of architecture to the ritualistic and reflective work of self-creation. American Freemasonry championed the artisan who "embodied such values as masculine labor, capitalist production, economic independence, and masculine self-sufficiency." The artisanal background was also central to conceptions of African American masculinity; thus Freemasonry's symbolic grammar was well suited to the "social, psychological, and political ambitions of early race men" like Prince Hall and John Marrant, "who tended to share a labor history in craft work." Marrant utilized the rituals and rhetoric of Freemasonry to "transform black men into symbolic artisans, and thus citizens of the masculine body politic." While white Masons pursued similar strategies via fraternal association, the unique and particular history of American slavery distinguishes such attempts by African Americans.[53] According to Wallace, "Although the idea of 'self-creation through labor' might also signify the dialectics of white Masonic identity, I submit that black Freemasonry distinguishes itself because the artisanal consciousness Freemasonry encourages is anticipated by a historical consciousness of structure and design that black men have shared as artisans in slavery and freedom. It is by this consciousness, which informs and is informed by what one might call a 'work aesthetic,' that black men in

America have self-reflexively 'built' the black masculine into their labor as men and Masons."[54]

The walls of the African Lodge provided both a structural and a social sanctuary for Black Freemasons' self-construction. The association of architectural construction with inner self-construction was well supported by biblical precedence as well. As Marrant reminded his audience, "Our blessed Saviour compared his sacred body to a temple, when he said, John ii. 19. Destroy this temple and I will raise it up again in three days; and the Apostle, I Peter, i. 44 says, that shortly he should put off this tabernacle." The African Lodge would "build" Black men whose interior lives had been ravaged by the destructive forces of racism and slavery. The "one grand end and design of Masonry," explained Marrant, "is to build up the temple that Adam destroyed in Paradise."[55]

Like creation myths in numerous religious contexts, the Bible's creation story included the rupture of divine order caused by transgression. Marrant traces the origins of racial strife to the murder of Abel by his brother Cain—the progeny of humanity's first union. The example of fratricide in the creation myth explains the breach of fraternal fellowship on the part of white Freemasons in Boston. "What was it," Marrant asked rhetorically, "but [envy and pride] that made Cain murder his brother, whence is it but from these that our modern Cains call us Africans the sons of Cain?"[56] The contemporary problem of race in America, argues Marrant, was explained by the Bible's ancient mythology of fratricide. Consequently, race prejudice constituted a spiritual, and not merely a political or social, crisis.

The crisis brought about by fratricide was dire but not beyond repair. "Bad as Cain was," states Marrant, "yet God took not from him his faculty of studying architecture, arts and sciences." Despite his transgression, Cain retained knowledge of Freemasonry, which he learned from his father, Adam. Marrant imagines that the sons of Cain "also were endued with the same spirit, and in some convenient place no doubt they met and communed with each other for instruction." The knowledge of Freemasonry, he argues, enabled Cain's family to "divert their minds from musing on their father's murder and the woful curse God had pronounced on him."[57] The transmission of the secret rites and understanding of Freemasonry restored Cain's lineage in the aftermath of transgression.

Freemasonry, according to Marrant's rendering of the mythical transgression, was essential for restoring legacies disrupted by fratricide. In the Dogon cosmology narrative told to Griaule, Amma, the supreme deity, "took a lump of clay, squeezed it in his hand and flung it from him, as he had done with the stars."

When the clay fell and stretched in the four cardinal directions and formed the earth, the earth took the shape of a body, and "Amma, being lonely and desirous of intercourse with this creature, approached it. That was the occasion of the first breach of the order of the universe."[58] Order is restored, however, by Amma's progeny. The twin spirits of Nummo are born of the same divine essence as Amma, and they represent the ideal unit. When they descend to earth, they bring heavenly plant fibers full of divine essence to restore the creation. The plant fibers, which enable communication between Amma and the earth's creatures, are the vehicle through which the Nummo restore the world.

In both the Dogon and the Genesis creation stories, offspring bear the gifts that redeem past transgressions. The twin spirits of Nummo bring the heavenly plant fibers to earth to reconcile the creation with its creator. Similarly, in the Genesis account told by Marrant, Cain's restoration is facilitated by his children, who learn and practice the mysteries of the Craft. In both stories, the transmission of divine knowledge (symbolized by the plant fibers and the teachings of Freemasonry, respectively) enables the restoration of the cosmos. As Marrant's *Sermon* explains, the chaotic nature of the cosmos that results from transgression is not irreversible; through the Craft of Freemasonry, redemption is possible.

The *Sermon* would be Marrant's last printed work. Shortly after the Festival of Saint John the Baptist ended, he spent several weeks in the communities on the outskirts of Boston "preaching the gospel twice every day" and experiencing "much of the out-pouring of God's spirit."[59] He returned to Boston in the second week of July, and for the remainder of the year, he "continued to keep school and to preach" alongside Prince Hall at the African Lodge. Shortly after the beginning of the new year, he began to seriously ponder returning to England. His letters to the Countess of Huntingdon had gone unanswered. He had written to her for aid while he battled smallpox in Nova Scotia. "I am now getting a little better," he reported. His illness, he implied, had exhausted his resources, and it was "with a view of obtaining such comfort that I write to your Ladyship."[60] When he had still received no correspondence by mid-January, he "thought it best to come to England, to know what her Ladyship intended to do."[61] He sailed to London in early March and fully intended to pursue his gospel calling, but the accumulation of injuries suffered during the war and years spent battling the harsh Nova Scotia winters was a heavy toll for a body that had been ravaged by disease. Marrant died shortly after returning to England at the age of thirty-five. His contributions to Black Freemasonry's legacy of advocacy, however, would have a profound impact on Masonic leaders in future generations.

Prince Hall's Charges

It would be a full three years before the African Lodge would publish another publicly delivered oration. During the Festival of Saint John the Baptist in 1792, Prince Hall addressed an audience of Black Freemasons in the Boston neighborhood of Charlestown. Hall told his audience that his formal public address, or *Charge*, would only add to the foundation established by Marrant three years earlier.[62] While "it is requisite that we should on these public days, and when we appear in form, give some reason as a foundation for our so doing," Hall stated, "this has been already done, in a discourse delivered in substance by our late Reverend Brother *John Marrant*, now in print."[63] Hall's address reiterated the primary duties of a Mason—belief in a supreme deity, regular lodge attendance, and mutual support of fellow Masons and those in distress. Like Marrant, he utilized biblical narratives—"a few instances ... from Holy Writ"—to illustrate and substantiate the validity of Masonic ideals. Old Testament prophets like Abraham and Elisha provided highly esteemed models of benevolence, while Jesus's parable of the Good Samaritan upheld the New Testament's requirement for aid to strangers in need.[64]

Also like Marrant, in *Charge*, Hall included an appeal to ancient African legacies to validate African American demands for full inclusion in the civic and social life of the new American republic and to refute doctrines of racial inferiority. The generative contributions of African church fathers—"Tertullian who defended the Christians against their heathen false accusations," "Cyprian ... that he would rather suffer death than betray his trust and the truth of the gospel," along with Augustine and Fulgentius—evinced moral exemplars whose faith and integrity were worthy of imitation. Additionally, these "reverend fathers" established the antiquity of Christianity in Africa, thus undermining support for race-based exclusion of persons of African descent from participation in American civic life.[65]

Hall's concern for the validation of African ancestry is also demonstrated by his insistence that their lodge be known by its proper title, the African Lodge, rather than "Saint Black's Lodge," as had been derisively reported in Boston's *Independent Ledger* in 1782. "With due submission to the public," Hall wrote in his correction to the printers, "our title is not Saint Black's Lodge, neither do we aspire after high titles."[66] His emphasis on the correct title, African Lodge, linked their performance of Freemasonry to other African American institutions identified by the same title throughout New England and the mid-Atlantic states.[67] The designation "African" marked emerging African American institutions with "layered images and meanings" that underscored "global dimensions of the experience and conditions of diaspora [that] were at the heart of the African American encounter with Euro Freemasonry" and wider patterns of acculturation in African American history.[68] The universal and transnational ideals of Freemasonry undergirded Hall's demand for African American inclusion. The character and conduct exhibited by members of the African Lodge qualified them for what Corey Walker calls "supranational citizenship"—one that simultaneously embraces and transcends US citizenship.[69] Consequently, it resituated Black identity from outside the boundaries of legal personhood (i.e., slave, criminal), to firmly within the boundaries of legality. White Masons unwilling to acknowledge the equal standing of African Americans as brother Masons jeopardized the legitimacy of Euro-American Freemasonry on the basis of their racism.

As he closed his address, Hall admonished lodge members to "make it your study to live up to the precepts" they dearly espoused and to "let it be known this day to the spectators, that you have not been to a feast of Bacchus, but to a refreshment with Masons." He also acknowledged the "dear brethren of Providence, who are at a distance from, and cannot attend the Lodge" but were able to utilize the extensive networks of exchange afforded by African Americans' emerging presence in Atlantic print culture.[70] The far-reaching influence of African American Freemasonry's rhetorical tradition was also noted by white Masons who were threatened by the potential spread of Black lodges. Jeremy Belknap, a Boston-based minister, carried on extensive correspondence with his colleague from Virginia, St. George Tucker, on the activities of the African Lodge in Boston.[71] A handwritten inscription on the inside cover of a pamphlet publication of Prince Hall's 1792 *Charge* provided important surveillance on members of the fraternity. In particular, Belknap noted the leadership of the late John Marrant: "This Marrant was a native of New York—went to England at the conclusion of the Revolution War [*sic*]. Got a kind of education in a school of the Late Countess of Huntington [*sic*] and was sent out as a Methodist Preacher to the blacks in Nova Scotia from whence he came to Boston and was made a member of African Lodge—he is since dead."[72]

The inscription, dated some six years after Marrant's death, underscores his enduring legacy within the African Lodge. Since Marrant had died several years earlier, Belknap's assessment could not have been informed by a firsthand interaction with Marrant, nor could he have merely read Marrant's 1789 *Sermon* since the biographical details referenced in his correspondence to Tucker are not included in Marrant's Masonic address. Rather, he must have learned of Marrant's influence from his observations of and interactions with lodge members in Boston. Seemingly, in the years after his death, Marrant's memory lived on in the hearts and minds of his Masonic brethren. The oral and print culture traditions he inaugurated would have a lasting influence on the development of abolitionist thought and methods of political organizing within African American Freemasonry.

David Walker: Black Masonic Oratory in Print Culture

As the gradual swell of abolitionism increased to a more steady flow in the early decades of the nineteenth century, Black Masonic leaders continued to utilize print culture to direct community politics and social organizing. Boston resident and African Lodge member David Walker helped advance a national debate on the abolition of slavery. Walker, who was born in North Carolina, arrived in Boston during the mid-1820s after spending part of his early life in Charleston, where he was likely acquainted with Denmark Vesey, a local artisan and alleged conspirator. As a writer for *Freedom's Journal*, the oldest Black national newspaper, Walker emerged as a leading voice in the anticolonization and abolitionist movements. On July 28, 1826, he was initiated into the first degree of Prince Hall Freemasonry, and several weeks later, he was elevated to the status of Master Mason in Boston's African Lodge.[73] His inflammatory *Appeal to the Colored Citizens of the World* (1829) decried the unjust treatment of African Americans and promoted visions of global citizenship, Black solidarity, and racial uplift that typified the ideas of Black political thinkers during the early years of the antebellum era.[74] Walker's rhetorical style drew from a tradition of Black preachers who, like Marrant, utilized dynamic oratory to galvanize their audiences. As one scholar notes, the *Appeal* "has its roots in an oral, not a print, culture" and reflects the tradition of extemporaneous preaching that was central to African American public life: "Walker intended the *Appeal* to be read aloud to groups, not quietly to oneself, as he made clear at numerous points in the work. Its principal function was a public, not a private, one. It was structured like an enthusiastically preached extemporaneous sermon intended to excite and inspire the audience to support some general ideas and plans—not like a formal discursive work whose goal was to demonstrate the validity of some proposition or interpretation of the Bible."[75]

Walker's call to action also bore the ideological imprint of Masonic predecessors. He deploys the rhetorical structure of conjure narratives to depict Black people's suffering. Conjure narratives, as may be recalled, "nearly always focus on some sort of human suffering, and they inevitably articulate a link between conflict and supernaturally induced misfortune" intended to alleviate or eliminate suffering.[76] As Walker describes:

I have known tyrants or usurpers of human liberty in different parts of this country to take their fellow creatures, the coloured people, and beat them until they would scarcely leave life in them; what for? Why they say "The black devils had the audacity to be found *making prayers and supplications to the God who made them*!!!!" Yes, I have known small collections of coloured people to have convened together, for no other purpose than to worship God Almighty, in spirit and in truth, to the best of their knowledge; when tyrants, calling themselves *patrols*, would also convene and wait almost in breathless silence for the poor coloured people to commence singing and praying to the Lord our God, as soon as they had commenced, the wretches would burst in upon them and drag them out and commence beating them as they would rattle-snakes—many of whom, they would beat so unmercifully, that they would hardly be able to crawl for weeks and sometimes for months.[77]

The hypothetical scene described in Walker's *Appeal* is similar to the one relayed in Marrant's *Narrative*. In Marrant's account, Mr. Jenkins, along with his overseer, assaulted enslaved people as they worshipped in the woods of the Carolina low country. Their closely aligned accounts are a reminder that free Blacks in Charleston and the South Carolina countryside were profoundly impacted by the horrific violence of slavery, even if they experienced it indirectly. The assault at Jenkins's plantation may have lived in the local lore of Charleston's free Black community, or perhaps Walker learned of it directly by reading Marrant's *Narrative*. While it is nearly impossible to establish precisely the myriad of sources that influenced Walker's thought, comparisons between his and Marrant's respective approaches yield important connections within the institutional and intellectual legacy of Black Freemasonry.

Lewis Hayden and Masonic Militancy

In the decade prior to the Civil War, the banner of militancy and activism bequeathed by David Walker was taken up by the African Lodge under the leadership of Lewis Hayden during his tenure as Most Worshipful Grand Master from 1852 to 1855 and again from 1857 to 1858. Hayden was born enslaved in Kentucky around 1811. While enslaved, he married Esther Harvey, and the couple had two daughters. Esther and one of the children were purchased and subsequently sold by Kentucky statesman Henry Clay. Hayden never saw his wife and child again, and his other daughter died in Kentucky. Hayden remarried, and with the aid of white abolitionists Calvin Fairbank of Ohio and Delia

Webster of Vermont, he and his second wife, Harriet, escaped to Canada posing as a white lady and a gentleman. They settled in Detroit, where Lewis helped organize the Colored Methodist Society, which in 1849 was incorporated as the Bethel African Methodist Episcopal Church. The couple was soon drawn to Boston, the national center of abolitionist activism, where Lewis (in the tradition of David Walker) quickly found work as a clothing dealer, while Harriet transformed their house at 66 Southac Street into a boardinghouse for Black migrants. With a cache of weapons hidden securely beneath the front steps, the Haydens' house was one of the most important stops on the Underground Railroad.[78]

As the nation marched down the path toward war, Hayden emerged as one of Boston's most prominent leaders. He was a founding member of the Boston Vigilance Committee, an interracial group of abolitionists that provided aid to fugitive slaves. He also hosted John Brown during his visit to the city and helped raise money for Brown's foiled raid on Harpers Ferry. During the Civil War, his leadership was instrumental in helping to recruit and enlist Black soldiers for the Union army's famed Fifty-Fourth Massachusetts Regiment.

In the years following the war, Hayden believed that Freemasonry would be essential for restoring the confidence of former slaves emerging from the state of oppression. Consequently, he, along with other Masonic leaders, would play a crucial role in Reconstruction-era politics. As Prince Hall had done almost a century earlier, Hayden sought fellowship with white Masons to bolster African Americans' demands for social equality and civic inclusion. The Civil War had thoroughly delegitimized proslavery sentiment as a political position. The destruction of racial caste, Hayden believed, was the test of true Masonry. In 1868, Hayden, along with other Black Masons from Boston, petitioned the Grand Lodge of Massachusetts for recognition. White Masons who dismissed the fraternal overtures of their Black brethren were accused by Hayden of "working against the emancipating spirit of the age and of the nation."[79] By casting white Masons who refused interracial fellowship as "enemies of the victorious Union," Hayden equated the conflicts within the Masonic order to those of national politics.[80]

Some white Masons found support for notions of racial caste by insisting that initiates must be "free born," and not simply "free men," a qualification that had been clarified by the Grand Lodge of England in 1847 following the abolition of slavery in British imperial territories.[81] Hayden drew on the foundational principles of Masonry, established by the earliest orators within the tradition, to refute claims of their illegitimacy. Like John Marrant and Prince Hall before him, he reiterated the mythical genealogy of Black Freemasonry in which the secrets of the Craft had been passed down from God through Moses to King Solomon. "Israelites, a people doomed to perpetual slavery," he indicated, "were Masons."[82] The invocation of the Jewish origins of Freemasonry underscored the historical association of African American slavery with Israel's slavery in the biblical story of Exodus and consequently connected the struggles of African American Freemasons to the struggles of African Americans more generally. Additionally, it reinforced their claim that modern African Americans were descendants and inheritors of cultures and civilizations that originated in Egypt and Ethiopia, then subsequently spread throughout the Western world.

The rhetorical strategy employed by the earliest orators within the Craft would guide Black Masonic leaders through the end of Reconstruction. However, as the nineteenth century drew to a close, Black Freemasons were "less compelled to take on the freeborn qualification as an issue," and when they did, it was "often on grounds that relied more on procedural or secular arguments than on romantic and religious analogizing of the historical experiences of Jews and blacks."[83] Some African American Freemasons invoked the Declaration of Independence to insist on the basic equality of all people, but "the absence of reference to Old Testament Jews may have signaled . . . a reluctance to invoke the actual history of African American slavery."[84] Nevertheless, the rhetorical strategy established by John Marrant and Prince Hall at the nation's founding would be echoed by their Masonic successors nearly a century later at the critical moment of the nation's rebirth.

Marrant's application of the metaphoric language of building to his role as chaplain of the African Lodge is likely at least partly inspired by his former employment as a carpenter on the Jenkins's plantation in South Carolina. John Saillant argues that Marrant's *Sermon* is the first part of a three-part series of addresses that outline Masonic ideology. Both Marrant and Prince Hall, founder of the African Lodge, explain complementary foundational aspects of Freemasonry that mimic an initiate's progression through the lodge. Marrant's *Sermon* lays the foundation or most basic understanding of Prince Hall's Freemasonry. Hall's subsequent addresses, delivered in 1792 and 1797, respectively, build on the foundation that Marrant establishes in his 1789 address.[85] Joanna Brooks also notes how these three sermons function "as steps in a building process" that correlate to the elements of the Masonic motto, "Wisdom, Strength, Beauty."[86] Additionally, she speculates that the three lectures are designed to initiate new members in preparation for the lodge's three symbolic degrees: Apprentice, Fellow Craft, and Master. Marrant's *Sermon* of 1789, argues Brooks, provided a foundation of "anciency," while Hall's *Charge* of 1792 introduced the pillar of civic duty, and his later *Charge* of 1797 established the second pillar of sympathy, or racial solidarity. Within the symbolism of Freemasonry, the pillars represented the two columns in the porch at the Temple of Solomon through which one entered under the scrutiny of brother Freemasons, in a ritual enactment of the passage from the profane world of slavery and humiliation to the sacred world of fraternal inclusion and mutuality. As Brooks surmises, "Perhaps Prince Hall and his fellows saw in this ritual configuration of space and symbol a semblance of their own passage through the profane logic of racial formation into the more sacred realm of community. From outside to inside, from confusion to understanding, from bondage to freedom, from death to life—the initiations and rituals of Freemasonry allowed the African Lodge to sacralize their bond as black people."[87]

For Hall and Marrant, public oration substituted for the construction of a physical edifice and inaugurated the creation of a new society. Their teachings aimed to help form the spiritual body that their physical meeting place symbolized. By re-creating the ritual structure, they mimicked the original act of creation that ordered the material world from the cosmic, primordial world.[88] Their lectures disclose the meaning of narrative symbols and the realities their Masonic rituals signify.

Brooks's and Saillant's insights concerning the dialogical relationship between Marrant's and Hall's texts raise questions regarding the relationship of Marrant's *Sermon* to his other writings. *Sermon* is not just a symbolic text for the primary phase of Masonic ritual initiation; it is also a capstone for Marrant's own written corpus. The third of his published works, *Sermon* reveals the communal covenant announced in the prophet's public ministry. As Saillant notes, the covenant community underscores a distinctly African influence in Marrant's consciousness:

> One of the uniquely Africanist elements of Marrant's theology was his merger of an orthodox notion of conversion with a notion of the covenanted community, which had faded out of late eighteenth-century Calvinism but was still convincing to the dispossessed Blacks of Nova Scotia. Had Marrant merely used the sentimentalist language of the New Divinity—affection, benevolence, charity, and the like—he would have established himself as a theologian of the Black community, a theoretician of the way in which conversion integrated Blacks into a community of believers. But Marrant added to New Divinity sentimentalism an older notion of the covenanted community—in his formulation a Black community in a particular covenant with God to pass through suffering to a Zion.[89]

The formation of the covenanted community culminates Marrant's prophetic journey. In *Narrative*, his first text, his prophetic identity is established through the narration of his call and prophetic initiation. *Narrative* is structured on the pattern of the Old Testament's principal story, the Exodus. *Journal* mimics the prophetic ministry of Jesus, the central character of the New Testament. His prophetic authority is demonstrated via parabolic reports of miraculous deliverances and healings and stories of personal transformation. In *Journal*, Marrant initiates Nova Scotia's Black worshippers into a covenanted community seeking restoration and political autonomy. *Sermon* explains the contours of Marrant's covenant ministry in the expository style of the New Testament's epistles. It is his most explicitly articulated vision for a new society based on his understanding of the order of the cosmos. He expounds the message of the gospel by retelling the Bible's creation story according to the narrative principles of the Black Atlantic storytelling tradition. *Sermon* is the foundation of the series on Freemasonry with Prince Hall's contributions, but it is also the culmination of Marrant's own written corpus. Marrant's three texts mimic the central narratives and components of the Bible, the foundational text in American religious consciousness. His body of work signifies the Bible and thus completes his construction of Black prophetic identity even as it opens the way for a new social order founded on the principles of Freemasonry.

Epilogue

The rain fell hard the evening of October 26, 1791, as more than three hundred Black settlers crowded into the chapel in Birchtown. Broadsides advertising a "Free Settlement on the Coast of Africa" had been circulating throughout Nova Scotia's Black settlements since late summer. Those gathered were eager to hear the Sierra Leone Company's proposal. As company spokesman John Clarkson stood to address those in attendance, he was struck by the possibility that "perhaps the future welfare and happiness, nay the very lives," of the poor souls there before him "might depend . . . upon the words which [he] should deliver." Black settlers would be regarded as equal to whites in every regard, and "the civil, military, personal and commercial rights and duties" of the respective races were to be "secured in the same manner."[1] Additionally, every free Black man would receive twenty acres of land for himself, ten acres for his wife, and an additional five for each of his children. The Sierra Leone Company would enable them to establish a free society in which they could worship and govern themselves as they saw fit.[2]

Several prominent church leaders were present to hear Clarkson present the Sierra Leone Company's proposal. Among them were Boston King, who had escaped from his owner in South Carolina with his wife, Violet, during the war; Moses Wilkinson, the Wesleyan minister with whom Marrant had earlier feuded; David George, the Baptist minister from Virginia; and Cato Perkins, who had escaped from Virginia and had been installed as Marrant's successor to lead the Huntingdon congregation. The Africana rituals and rites that John Marrant had undergone, and through which he had guided many of the Huntingdon congregants, were handed down to Perkins in succession. Perkins and the other ministers weighed Clarkson's proposal, but if they took their cue from the response of the congregation, they knew the matter had already been decided. "Cries and shouts of joy and exultation" were heard throughout the meetinghouse. By the time Clarkson had concluded his address, he knew that "they were unanimous in their desire for embarking for Africa."[3]

Over the next three days, 514 names were added to the list of prospective emigrants. A variety of geographic, family, and communal relationships underscored how the covenant theology was being lived out in the community in Marrant's absence. Of the nearly twelve hundred Black voyagers, almost half were from Birchtown.[4] Between 30 and 35 percent had been enslaved in Virginia or South Carolina. The presence of Christian ministers from these states at the meeting in Birchtown perhaps explains the high concentration from these states and is suggestive of a broad, extensive "network of connections in the emigration." Black settlers from other states (Georgia, New York, Maryland, etc.) did not participate in the emigration in such large numbers.[5]

Church membership also seemingly played a role in the decision to emigrate. In Preston, where Black evangelists had established vibrant, autonomous congregations, the decision to stay or leave was contemplated collectively. Nearly all of Black Preston was determined to make the voyage to Africa. About fifty families participated in the expedition, including "David George's Baptist congregation, virtually intact, Cato Perkins' Huntingdonians and most of Moses Wilkinson's Methodists." The emigration to Sierra Leone so depleted Preston's Black population that the Society for the Propagation of the Gospel in Foreign Parts closed the school and mission there, since "the Blacks are all gone from Preston."[6]

Family connections also factored prominently in the decision to emigrate. Only three men (one of whom was eighty years old) emigrated without families.

Many of the prospective émigrés insisted that they must go for the sake of their children, for whom they desired better opportunities unencumbered by the threat of slavery. John Clarkson remarked that the family ties among the Black Loyalists surpassed those of their British counterparts and included loved ones for whom no formal bonds of kinship existed. Black parents, he noted, would raise the children of family, community, and church members without distinguishing between adopted and biological kin. When lingering debt threatened to prevent some applicants in Birchtown from making the journey, neighbors sold their property to assist them so that their community might not be broken up. Family customs like the ones described were "widely obtained in black American slave society," but they have "been traced to West African pre-slave origins." The provision of aid and concern for mutual welfare of family and neighbors underscore how deeply Black preachers' gospel message had influenced the Black Loyalists.[7]

However, not everyone in Nova Scotia supported the plans for emigration. Black settlers had become a reliable source of cheap labor, and many white landowners were vehemently opposed to losing the services on which their fortunes depended. Rumors that the Sierra Leone Company agents hoped to sell them for profit were circulated throughout Preston, Birchtown, and Digby to discourage emigration. One attack, published pseudonymously in the Halifax newspaper, warned that some émigrés would be sold as slaves when they reached West Africa, while most would succumb to illness within a year. Those who survived would be subject to quitrents, which threatened to reduce them to slavery.[8]

Shelburne officials tried to entice Black settlers to stay by offering free livestock—a sheep and a cow—to those willing to remain in Nova Scotia. Only fifty people took them up on this offer. Shelburne nobles also proposed to jump-start the town's flailing economy by opening its port to American trade. For Black settlers, however, this proposal only conjured visions of reunions with former masters eager to lead them "back to Virginia and the Carolinas in chains." When economic incentives failed, some white Nova Scotians turned to violence to try to dissuade Blacks from emigrating. David George received threats of violence when it was learned that he planned to take the whole of his Baptist congregation to Sierra Leone. He warned John Clarkson to exercise caution, especially in the areas surrounding Digby and Annapolis, as "it appeared probable that we might be waylaid by some of these violent people."[9]

Despite the campaign to dissuade them, many Black settlers were resolved to quit their settlements in Nova Scotia. When their fleet left Halifax harbor the morning of January 9, 1792, fifteen ships transported a convoy of nearly "2,000 tons, carrying 1,196 people, 383 of them young children." Forty Black captains, distributed among the ships, were authorized as supervisors and empowered to resolve disputes and judicial matters during the voyage. Lists of rules were given to each of the captains with detailed instructions on the rationing of food and on schedules for daily cleaning. Company agents were careful to avoid anything in the voyage that might conjure memories of the Middle Passage.[10] One of the larger ships was designated as the fleet hospital and housed the majority of elderly migrants, while the *Morning Star* had been specially fitted for expectant mothers.[11]

When the Black pilgrims finally arrived in Sierra Leone in early March, they quickly erected a tent as a temporary edifice to house their worship. A hymn "from Lady Huntingdon's book" was selected because it captured "the marvel of their arrival." There was plenty of reason to rejoice. Three of the pregnant women had delivered healthy babies and were doing well by the time the Sierra Leone Company's "inter-racial, floating Christian republic" pulled into the harbor at Freetown.[12] There was also reason to mourn. Sixty of the passengers, mostly from among the old, the sick, and the very young, were lost during the voyage. Another forty died within the first few weeks of their arrival. By the middle of summer in 1792, nearly 20 percent of the Black Loyalists had perished. Although "they sang of a new day," the settlers had discovered that "the realities of Freetown were hard to bear."[13]

After a year in Sierra Leone, some of the hardships they encountered began to echo familiar patterns from their previous experiences in Nova Scotia. Paternalistic attitudes, for example, continued to undermine Black autonomy. Settlers had hoped to form their democracy without the interference of European authority, but company directives had strictly forbidden all-Black governance. White settlers, appointed by the company, occupied prominent leadership roles in the colony's government. And there were also issues with the land.[14]

Because they had arrived at the height of the rainy season, the distribution of farmland was delayed. Nearly a year later, not only had most settlers still not received their allotments, but the surveyor had not even finished laying them all out. Forthcoming allotments, they learned, would be far less than what they originally had been promised. Moreover, the lands were not good for farming. It would be nearly impossible to raise a sustainable crop from the "mountainous, barren and rocky" soil in which they had been planted. Worst of all, perhaps, was that the Sierra Leone Company sought to impose quitrents, a tax on settlers' land that, while not exactly reenslavement, was historically tied to "European traditions of lordship and bondage."[15]

Resistance to the proposed tax and general dissatisfaction regarding life in the colony were most demonstrably visible in the church. In fact, political leadership generally rested on the shoulders of church ministers. According to the colony's founding charter, each head of household could vote to elect "tithingmen." One tithingman was elected for every ten households. "Hundredors" were elected initially to represent ten tithingmen, but this number was later changed to five.[16] In 1793, thirty-one assembled hundredors and tithingmen selected Cato Perkins to travel to London to present a petition of grievances to the directors of the Sierra Leone Company on their behalf. Perkins had been selected and installed by Marrant to lead the Huntingdon Methodists in his absence shortly before he departed for Boston in 1788. He was accompanied by Isaac Anderson, a free carpenter from Charleston and a Loyalist veteran of the War of Independence, who had also made the sojourn from Halifax. Together, they listed the complaints of the Freetown settlers, including the delayed land allotments, the shortage of supplies, decreased representation in local government, and, of course, the abhorred quitrent.[17]

Though their complaints fell on deaf ears in London, Perkins and Anderson returned to Freetown more determined than defeated. On their return, Perkins's New Light meetinghouse was a center of political activity. All the visible markers of political campaigns could be observed around Freetown. "Posters and placards were nailed up outside shops and houses," and impromptu meetings were held both in public and in private homes. Passionate speeches were delivered from church pulpits; tithingmen and hundredors also preached, ensuring that "congregations in churches and chapels heard campaign rhetoric as well as psalms."[18]

Although the Black Nova Scotian settlers implemented a radical democracy, religion remained "the foundation of their society, and its most distinctive trait." The Africana rituals and practices that John Marrant had instituted in Charleston and in Nova Scotia helped condition "their attitudes towards themselves and towards other people." Marrant's teaching had "bound them together as a select all-Black group against the encroachments of outsiders" and "influenced their political outlook, which was anti-establishment and anti-authoritarian, and made them fearful that state power would somehow interfere with the independence that guaranteed their living a Christian life."[19] This political outlook inspired a militancy among the Huntington Connexion that was not found among the Baptists. When the proposed quitrents were finally due in the summer of 1797, the Baptists, led by David George, rendered the requisite tribute. The Methodists, led by Anderson and Perkins and by far the larger group, did not.[20]

In 1798, the settlers proposed a resolution to the company governor calling for a self-governing legislature composed of two houses: one made up of hundredors and the other made up of tithingmen. Invoking statutory precedents from the North American colonies, they proposed "a road tax of six days' work per year, equivalent to and in place of the quitrent."[21] The following summer, 150 settlers, led by Perkins and Anderson, assembled at the New Light meetinghouse and declared their independence from the Sierra Leone Company. Concerned simply with establishing just laws that reflected their sense of Christian piety and presumption of sovereignty, their legal code was "conspicuously free of highfaluting expressions of political theory."[22] Their plainness of speech, however, was not to be mistaken for lack of political sophistication. In little more than a decade after winning their freedom, this colony of former slaves had brought Black religion and democratic rebellion to the shores of Africa.[23]

This study has sought to redress the failure on the part of some Atlantic scholars to consider transatlantic religious and intellectual histories from perspectives other than European and American. My inclusion of conjure as an Africana episteme highlights the impact of African-derived ideas and institutions on the making of the Americas.[24] While Christian interpretive models can provide useful frameworks for understanding Black religion, they leave many expressions of Black religion unexplored, ultimately obscuring more than revealing Black religious phenomena. Additionally, the constitutive impact of traditional African and other non-Christian religious influences remains undervalued. My aim has been to render visible the substantial contribution of Africana religious cultures to John Marrant's religious development and to religious consciousness in the broader Black Atlantic world.

My analysis of Marrant's religious consciousness has sought to enhance the understanding of Black religion and rhetoric, and their ties to Africana forms, rituals, and ways of knowing within Anglo-Protestant colonial North America. The examples of Black Christian communities in Nova Scotia and the African Lodge in Boston demonstrate how early Black Americans adopted and appropriated Euro-American institutional forms of social and religious organization. But, importantly, these processes of adaptation utilized Africana religious symbols, rituals, and ways of knowing to conjure biblical texts. For Marrant and other early Black Christian religious leaders in Nova Scotia, the Bible was a source for the Africana rituals that enabled disparate groups of ethnically and culturally diverse former slaves to be formed into free Black Christian communities. Conjure was not only a mechanism for religious performance but also a theoretical lens through which early Black Christians read and redeployed the vocabularies of Protestantism in North America.

John Marrant's message of Black self-determination and collective destiny utilized the rhetoric and symbolism of Methodist perfectionism. Through his writings and preaching, he allegorized rituals of regeneration and provided a sacred interpretation of Black people's shared experiences of loss and displacement. Though he would not live to see its fulfillment, Marrant's followers embarked on a journey across the Atlantic in pursuit of an autonomous African homeland, settling in Sierra Leone in 1792. As Joanna Brooks notes, Marrant's ministry demonstrated his belief in his own prophetic identity and his communities' messianic role in the redemption of African descended people:

> As an emissary of the Huntingdon Connexion, he was sent to Nova Scotia to preach the Connexion's brand of evangelical Calvinism, do battle against "free-thinkers" and Wesleyan Arminians, and serve the province's indigenous and black populations. The Huntingdon Connexion—and especially the late George Whitefield—had long demonstrated an interest in the religious welfare of the blacks and Indians. Publicly, the ordination of John Marrant was a commitment to this end. Privately, Marrant was not motivated by patronistic or charitable but rather by more radical views: he believed himself a prophet, sent to Nova Scotia to initiate the redemption of scattered Africa.[25]

While Marrant's understanding of the messianic role of African Americans comes to the fore during his ministry in Nova Scotia, the formation of this aspect of his consciousness likely began at a much earlier stage in his life. This survey of Marrant's life has emphasized the generative impact of his residency in New York, St. Augustine, Savannah, and Charleston, highlighting the presence of Africana religious culture in the respective locales.

Marrant was likely aware that his adoption of Christianity and Freemasonry potentially included some social and political benefits. His leadership in Christian and Masonic communities helped establish a collective vision for Black Americans in the early republic. The religious and fraternal institutions established by African American Christians in the eighteenth century would not endure intact but would, in fact, be reshaped and reconfigured in subsequent generations as material needs shifted in response to changes in the broader social world. However, Black messianism—the belief in a collective, salvific destiny for Black people—continued into the nineteenth century as exhibited by his literary successors. Marrant's texts and those of his contemporaries and successors uncover a hitherto unexplored tradition of biblical and social criticism within Black religion. *The Gospel of John Marrant* has emphasized that the narratives composed by Black Atlantic writers and their North American successors utilized the Bible as a storytelling model. Consequently, early Black American autobiographies illustrate a tradition of criticism in that their narratives reveal how they read the Bible. The intertextual dialogue that exists within this tradition describes and discloses a conversation that is as much about how the Bible should be read and understood as it is about how Black people should live in the New World.

The narratives of John Marrant and his successors also exhibit the development of Africana religion in North America. Marrant's texts disclose early Black Christian expressions of Protestant Christianity in colonial North America as not merely simple recapitulations of orthodox European doctrine but rather the intellectual product of integrated theological reflection and Africana ritual practice. Black Christian practitioners modified their religious practices to accommodate their involuntary presence in the New World. Marrant and early Black writers credit their direct experience with God rather than the doctrinal tenets of Protestantism as being responsible for their participation in Christian communities. In Marrant's case, the "Lord's wonderful dealings" include the narrative and ritual cultures of the African diaspora that contextualized his religious formation prior to, and after, his meeting with the famed evangelist George Whitefield in Charleston. At the moment that he was apprehended by the overwhelming presence of the divine, Marrant also apprehended the authority to speak in the public sphere, thus signifying cross-cultural exchange. Moreover, the structural pattern of his call narrative and the subsequent development of his ministry in Nova Scotia and Boston unfolded along a parallel trajectory to the pattern of ritual initiation in traditional African religion. The representation of initiation throughout his writings suggests that his religious consciousness remained rooted in traditional African modes of thought even while it was modified by Christian rhetoric and symbolism.

Notes

INTRODUCTION

1   Raboteau describes brush arbors, also known as hush harbors, as "secluded places—
woods, gullies, ravines, and thickets" which enslaved people utilized "to avoid detection
of their meetings." See Albert J. Raboteau, *Slave Religion: The "Invisible Institution" in
the Antebellum South* (New York: Oxford University Press, 2004), 215. The religious
studies scholar Alonzo Johnson contends that brush arbors constituted the formative
grounds in which enslaved Blacks fashioned their distinct vision of Christianity. "The
spirituality that was forged in the brush arbors," notes Johnson, "coupled with the folk
traditions that were forged in the religious meetings in the slave quarters, provided
the impetus for the formation of the pray's [*sic*] house spirit and later the independent
black churches in the South Carolina Lowcountry." See Alonzo Johnson, "'Pray's House
Spirit': The Institutional Structure and Spiritual Core of an African American Folk
Tradition," in *Ain't Gonna Lay My 'ligion Down: African American Religion in the
South*, ed. Alonzo Johnson and Paul Jersild (Columbia: University of South Carolina
Press, 1999), 8–38. See also Janet Cornelius, *Slave Missions and the Black Church in the
Antebellum South* (Columbia: University of South Carolina Press, 1999); Christopher
Hunter, "The African American Church House: A Phenomenological Inquiry of an
Afrocentric Sacred Space," *Religions* 13, no. 3 (2022): 246, https://doi.org/10.3390
/rel13030246.

2   In his depiction of Marrant's spiritual transformation in the narrative poem *The Negro
Convert*, the English poet Samuel Whitchurch relates that his portrayal was informed by
Marrant's oral narration at "his ordination, at the Countess of Huntingdon's chapel, in
Bath, on Sunday the 15th of May, 1785." See Samuel Whitchurch, *The Negro Convert,
a Poem, Being the Substance of the Experience of Mr. John Marrant, a Negro* (Bath: S.
Hazard, 1785); in *Eighteenth Century Collections Online* (Detroit, MI: Gale Group,
2003–), a resource available to subscribers. Lemuel Haynes, the Congregational minister
who pastored churches in Connecticut and Vermont, was the son of a Black father and
white mother in West Hartford, Connecticut. According to Haynes's biographer, the
nineteenth-century Massachusetts minister Timothy Mather Cooley, "the ordination of
Mr. Haynes was solemnized November 9th, 1785." See Timothy Mather Cooley, *Sketches
of the Life and Character of the Rev. Lemuel Haynes, A.M., for Many Years Pastor of a
Church in Rutland, Vt., and Late in Granville, New York* (1837) (New York: Negro

Universities Press, 1969), 71. Richard Allen, the founding bishop of the African Methodist Episcopal Church, was officially ordained in the ministry of the Methodist Episcopal Church in 1799. See John Saillant, "Richard Allen," in *The Concise Oxford Companion to African American Literature,* eds. William L. Andrews, Frances Smith Foster, and Trudier Harris (New York: Oxford University Press, 1992), 2–3.

3 For the *Narrative,* see chapters 1, 2, and 3; for the *Journal,* see chapters 3 and 4; for the *Sermon,* see chapter 5. Publication details are provided in the chapters and in the selected bibliography.

4 Joanna Brooks and John Saillant, eds., *"Face Zion Forward": First Writers of the Black Atlantic, 1785–1798* (Boston: Northeastern University Press, 2002).

5 Theophus H. Smith, *Conjuring Culture: Biblical Formations of Black America,* facsimile (New York: Oxford University Press, 1994), 6.

6 See Brooks and Saillant, *"Face Zion Forward,"* 25.

7 Josiah Ulysses Young III, "Dogged Strength within the Veil: African-American Spirituality as a Literary Tradition," *Journal of Religious Thought* 55–56 (1999): 87–107.

8 Frances Smith Foster, *Witnessing Slavery: The Development of Ante-Bellum Slave Narratives* (Westport, CT: Greenwood Press, 1979), 85.

9 Smith, *Conjuring Culture,* 26–27.

10 Lawrence W. Levine, *Black Culture and Black Consciousness: Afro-American Folk Thought from Slavery to Freedom* (Oxford: Oxford University Press, 1978), 88.

11 Levine, *Black Culture and Black Consciousness,* 92–95.

12 Smith, *Conjuring Culture,* 209.

13 Sylvia R. Frey, *Come Shouting to Zion: African American Protestantism in the American South and British Caribbean to 1830* (Chapel Hill: University of North Carolina Press, 1998).

14 A broad analytical lens that considers data throughout the Black transatlantic world is particularly instructive for recognizing Africana elements in Black religious phenomena. For works on eighteenth-century African Atlantic religion, see Jon F. Sensbach, *Rebecca's Revival: Creating Black Christianity in the Atlantic World* (Cambridge, MA: Harvard University Press, 2006); James H. Sweet, *Domingos Alvares: Afro-American Folk Thought from Slavery to Freedom* (Oxford: Oxford University Press, 1978); David T. Shannon Sr., Julia Frazier White, and Deborah Van Broekhoven, *George Liele's Life and Legacy: An Unsung Hero* (Macon, GA: Mercer University Press, 2013); Vincent Carretta and Ty M. Reese, eds., *The Life and Letters of Philip Quaque, the First African Anglican Missionary* (Athens: University of Georgia Press, 2010); Rita Roberts, *Evangelicalism and the Politics of Reform in Northern Black Thought, 1776–1863* (Baton Rouge: Louisiana State University Press, 2011); Cécile Fromont, *The Art of Conversion: Christian Visual Culture in the Kingdom of Kongo* (Chapel Hill: University of North Carolina Press, 2014); Katharine Gerbner, *Christian Slavery: Conversion and Race in the Protestant Atlantic World* (Philadelphia: University of Pennsylvania Press, 2018); Kathryn M. Luna, "Sounding the African Atlantic," *William and Mary Quarterly* 78, no. 4 (2021): 581–616.

15 Ras Michael Brown, *African-Atlantic Cultures and the South Carolina Lowcountry* (Cambridge: Cambridge University Press, 2012), 218.

16 Nat Turner, *The Confessions of Nat Turner*, in *The Confessions of Nat Turner and Related Documents*, ed. Kenneth S. Greenberg (Boston: Bedford, 1996), 46.

CHAPTER 1. *"No Continuing City": Colonial Black Religion during Marrant's Early Life*

1 John Marrant, *A Narrative of the Lord's Wonderful Dealings with John Marrant, a Black (Now Going to Preach the Gospel in Novia-Scotia)*, 4th ed., in Brooks and Saillant, *"Face Zion Forward,"* 49. All quotations from *Narrative*, first published in London in 1785, are taken from the fourth edition, reprinted in Brooks and Saillant, *"Face Zion Forward,"* 47–75.

2 James Noel refers to Black peoples' collective experience of exclusion and uncertainty as the "nothingness" from which Black religious consciousness emerges. Noel should not be misunderstood to mean that Black consciousness, culture, and identity literally emerge from nothing. In fact, he makes strong arguments about the continuity of African material cognition within African American New World religious and cultural formations. Rather, what he refers to is the instability of Black people's collective and individual existence(s) in the New World and the culture and identity produced from this particular view of the world. See James A. Noel, *Black Religion and the Imagination of Matter in the Atlantic World* (New York: Palgrave Macmillan, 2009).

3 On silence as an epistemological foundation of Black religious experience, see Charles H. Long, *Significations: Signs, Symbols, and Images in the Interpretation of Religion*, 2nd ed. (Aurora, CO: Davies Group, 1999), 63–69; Noel, *Black Religion and the Imagination of Matter*, 135–37; Barbara A. Holmes, *Joy Unspeakable: Contemplative Practices of the Black Church* (Minneapolis, MN: Fortress, 2004), 20–21.

4 Marrant's ability to pinpoint the time and place of his birth distinguished him from many of his fellow Black Atlantic writers since most were enslaved and their birth records were not meticulously maintained. Frederick Douglass, for example, could only approximate the year of his birth since the slave and African American births frequently passed without record.

5 Thelma Wills Foote, *Black and White Manhattan: The History of Racial Formation in Colonial New York City* (Oxford: Oxford University Press, 2004), 141.

6 Thelma Foote notes, "Importantly the racially segregated cemetery became an incubator for the retribalization of diverse African peoples who were brought together by the externally imposed and shared experience of forced migration and enslavement in a foreign land. Put differently, the semi-autonomous space of colonial New York City's Negros [sic] Burial Ground became the site for the formation of racial blackness, a process that involved a dialectic inclusion and exclusion, centripetal and centrifugal forces in counterpoint to the formation of racial whiteness." Foote, *Black and White Manhattan*, 141.

7 Foote, *Black and White Manhattan*, 143; Graham Russell Hodges, *Root and Branch: African Americans in New York and East Jersey, 1613–1863* (Chapel Hill: University of North Carolina Press, 1999), 104–5.

8 Hodges, *Root and Branch*, 39–40.

9 Hodges, *Root and Branch*, 54.

10 W. Jeffrey Bolster, *Black Jacks: African American Seamen in the Age of Sail* (Cambridge, MA: Harvard University Press, 1998), 108.

11 Sterling Stuckey, *Slave Culture: Nationalist Theory and the Foundations of Black America* (New York: Oxford University Press, 1988), 142–43.

12 Hodges, *Root and Branch*, 88.

13 Hodges, *Root and Branch*, 87.

14 Hodges, *Root and Branch*, 87.

15 Hodges, *Root and Branch*, 88.

16 Hodges, *Root and Branch*, 24.

17 Jeroen Dewulf, *The Pinkster King: The Forgotten History of America's Dutch-Owned Slaves* (Jackson: University Press of Mississippi, 2017), 99.

18 Dewulf, *Pinkster King*, 113.

19 Stuckey, *Slave Culture*, 25, 30, 35.

20 Hodges, *Root and Branch*, 86.

21 Hodges, *Root and Branch*, 87.

22 Foote, *Black and White Manhattan*, 92.

23 Foote, *Black and White Manhattan*, 93.

24 Hodges, *Root and Branch*, 57–58.

25 Foote, *Black and White Manhattan*, 129.

26 Hodges, *Root and Branch*, 60, 62.

27 Hodges, *Root and Branch*, 121.

28 Hodges, *Root and Branch*, 84.

29 Hodges, *Root and Branch*, 33.

30 Robert Nelson Anderson, "The Quilombo of Palmares: A New Overview of a Maroon State in Seventeenth-Century Brazil," *Journal of Latin American* 38, no. 3 (1996): 545–66.

31 Hodges, *Root and Branch*, 17–18. Thelma Foote cites a dearth of documentary references as a reason for the scant scholarly treatment of Black brotherhoods of colonial New York City in comparison to their counterparts in Brazil. According to Foote, "The studies indicate that the black brotherhoods in the cities of Brazil date back to the eighteenth century and that these confraternities organized the burial of slaves and free blacks, as well as other mutual aid activities for colonial Brazil's black urban communities." See Foote, *Black and White Manhattan*, 277n13.

32 See Michael A. Gomez, *Exchanging Our Country Marks: The Transformation of African Identities in the Colonial and Antebellum South* (Chapel Hill: University of North Carolina Press, 1998).

33 Hodges, *Root and Branch*, 35.

34 Hodges, *Root and Branch*, 49.

35 Hodges, *Root and Branch*, 48.

36 Hodges, *Root and Branch*, 48.

37 Foote, *Black and White Manhattan*, 132.

38 Foote, *Black and White Manhattan*, 132.

39 Hodges, *Root and Branch*, 65.

40 Hodges, *Root and Branch*, 65.

41 Hodges, *Root and Branch*, 67.

42 Hodges, *Root and Branch*, 312n20.

43 Daniel Horsmanden, *The New York Conspiracy, or A History of the Negro Plot, with the Journal of the Proceedings against the Conspirators at New York in the Years 1741–2* (New York: Southwick and Pelsue, 1810), 27.

44 Horsmanden, *New York Conspiracy*, 29.

45 Horsmanden, *New York Conspiracy*, 32.

46 Horsmanden, *New York Conspiracy*, 32–33.

47 Hodges, *Root and Branch*, 103.

48 Foote, *Black and White Manhattan*, 150.

49 Foote, *Black and White Manhattan*, 274n141.

50 Foote, *Black and White Manhattan*, 156.

51 Jane Landers, *Black Society in Spanish Florida* (Champaign: University of Illinois Press, 1999), 1–2.

52 Landers, *Black Society in Spanish Florida*, 2.

53 Landers, *Black Society in Spanish Florida*, 4, 16–17.

54 See, for example, Jason Young, *Rituals of Resistance: African Atlantic Religion in Kongo and the Lowcountry South in the Era of Slavery* (Baton Rouge: Louisiana State University Press, 2011), 69; Landers, *Black Society in Spanish Florida*, 34; Herbert Aptheker, *American Negro Slave Revolts* (New York: International Publishers, 1963).

55 Landers, *Black Society in Spanish Florida*, 29–32, 113.

56 Watson W. Jennison, *Cultivating Race: The Expansion of Slavery in Georgia, 1750–1860* (Lexington: University Press of Kentucky, 2012), 14–15, 20.

57 Jennison, *Cultivating Race*, 16–20.

58 Jennison, *Cultivating Race*, 20–24.

59 Paul M. Pressly, *On the Rim of the Caribbean: Colonial Georgia and the British Atlantic World* (Athens: University of Georgia Press, 2013), 69.

60 Pressly, *On the Rim of the Caribbean*, 76–78.

61 Pressly, *On the Rim of the Caribbean*, 80, 87.

62 Young, *Rituals of Resistance*, 45.

CHAPTER 2. *"Prepare to Meet Thy God"*: *Conjuring Initiation in Marrant's* Narrative

1   Marrant, *Narrative*, 49–50.

2   Victor Witter Turner, *The Forest of Symbols: Aspects of Ndembu Ritual* (Ithaca, NY: Cornell University Press, 1967), quoted in Laurenti Magesa, *African Religion: The Moral Traditions of Abundant Life* (Maryknoll, NY: Orbis, 1997), 95.

3   Brown, *African-Atlantic Cultures*, 218.

4   Marrant, *Narrative*, 51.

5   Marrant, *Narrative*, 51.

6   Brown, *African-Atlantic Cultures*, 91–94.

7   Zora Neale Hurston, *The Sanctified Church: The Folklore Writings of Zora Neale Hurston* (Berkeley, CA: Turtle Island Foundation, 1981), 91.

8 Sheila Walker, *Ceremonial Spirit Possession in Africa and Afro-America: Forms, Meanings, and Functional Significance for Individuals and Social Groups* (Leiden: Brill, 1972), 53.

9 Marrant, *Narrative*, 52–53.

10 Hurston, *Sanctified Church*, 85.

11 Hurston, *Sanctified Church*, 86.

12 See Exodus 3:10; Isaiah 6:5.

13 Marrant, *Narrative*, 53.

14 James Albert Ukawsaw Gronniosaw, *A Narrative of the Most Remarkable Particulars in the Life of James Albert Ukawsaw Gronniosaw, an African Prince* (1770), in *Unchained Voices: An Anthology of Black Authors in the English-Speaking World of the Eighteenth Century*, ed. Vincent Carretta (Lexington: University Press of Kentucky, 1996), 35.

15 See Mark 3:20–27.

16 See Genesis 37:9–11.

17 Marrant, *Narrative*, 56.

18 Hurston, *Sanctified Church*, 85.

19 Ras Michael Brown, "'Walk in the Feenda': West-Central Africans and the Forest in the South Carolina–Georgia Lowcountry," in *Central Africans and Cultural Transformations in the American Diaspora*, ed. Linda M. Heywood (Cambridge: Cambridge University Press, 2002), 290.

20 Brown, *African-Atlantic Cultures*, 3.

21 Brown, *African-Atlantic Cultures*, 199.

22 Young, *Rituals of Resistance*, 79; see also Brown, *African-Atlantic Cultures*, 219.

23 Holmes, *Joy Unspeakable*, 58.

24 Magesa, *African Religion*, 86.

25 Abraham A. Akrong argues that new forms of traditional African spirituality began to emerge within West African Christianity when European missionary activity increased, and consequently, the concerns of African Christians were marginalized to the periphery of missionary theology during the nineteenth century. The movement of West African Christianity signaled a "shift in hermeneutics which initiated this process of transforming scripture into a coherent indigenous African Christianity [that] was a radical departure from missionary theology." African American Christians in the low country similarly exhibit "the creative dynamism of African spirituality" that nurtures new forms of Africana Christianity. See Abraham A. Akrong, "African Traditional Religion and Christianity: Continuities and Discontinuities," in *Reclaiming the Human Sciences and the Humanities through African Perspectives*, ed. Helen Lauer and Kofi Anyidoho (Accra: Sub-Saharan, 2012), 1:307–20.

26 Marrant, *Narrative*, 57–58.

27 Marrant, *Narrative*, 56.

28 Marrant, *Narrative*, 58.

29 Marrant, *Narrative*, 58–59.

30 Walker, *Ceremonial Spirit Possession*, 52.

31 Brown, "'Walk in the Feenda,'" 309–11. Andrew Philips Adega notes, "In the pre-colonial time, every person in Mende society—male and female—was in

principle initiated into the appropriate school of puberty. A non-initiate was simply not considered as a mature person, whatever the age. The initiation in the bush school which could last as many as seven years was based on gender roles." See Andrew Philips Adega, "Secret Societies: Fraternities, Witches, Wizards, and Sorcerers," in *The Palgrave Handbook of African Traditional Religion*, ed. Ibigbolade S. Aderibigbe and Toyin Falola (Cham: Springer International, 2022), 207–17.

32 Brown, "'Walk in the Feenda,'" 314.

33 Marrant, *Narrative*, 58.

34 Marrant, *Narrative*, 59.

35 Marrant, *Narrative*, 59.

36 Gary Zellar, *African Creeks: Estelvste and the Creek Nation* (Norman: University of Oklahoma Press, 2007), xvii.

37 Margaret Creel, *"A Peculiar People": Slave Religion and Community-Culture among the Gullahs* (New York: New York University Press, 1988), 290–92.

38 Tiya Miles contends that Indian Removal ruptured tribal well-being and "created a legacy of detachment between Cherokees and blacks that would lessen potential for cross-racial alliances" and inhibit the possibility of undermining racial hierarchies. "Removal," she notes, "separated Cherokees and blacks from the ground where they first encountered one another and developed bonds, and thus it damaged ties of connection that were inscribed and reinforced in the landscape." See Tiya Miles, *The Ties That Bind: The Story of an Afro-Cherokee Family in Slavery and Freedom,* 2nd ed. (Berkeley: University of California Press, 2015), 157.

39 Marrant, *Narrative*, 60–61 (emphasis added).

40 Gomez, *Exchanging Our Country Marks*, 98.

41 Magesa, *African Religion*, 101.

42 Olaudah Equiano, *The Interesting Narrative of the Life of Olaudah Equiano, or Gustavus Vassa, the African* (1789), in *Unchained Voices: An Anthology of Black Authors in the English-Speaking World of the Eighteenth Century*, expanded edition, ed. Vincent Carretta (Lexington: University Press of Kentucky, 2004), 202–3. Vincent Carretta raises compelling questions regarding the veracity of Equiano's account of his birth and childhood in Africa. He cites naval and baptismal records that indicate Equiano was born in South Carolina rather than West Africa. See Vincent Carretta, *Equiano, the African: Biography of a Self-Made Man* (Athens: University of Georgia Press, 2005), 1–16.

43 Gronniosaw, *Narrative*, 35, 37.

44 Marrant, *Narrative*, 61.

45 Marrant, *Narrative*, 62–63.

46 Marrant, *Narrative*, 64.

47 Marrant, *Narrative*, 64–65.

48 Tiya Miles, "'His Kingdom for a Kiss': Indians and Intimacy in the Narrative of John Marrant," in *Haunted by Empire: Race and Colonial Intimacies in North American History*, ed. Ann Laura Stoler (Durham, NC: Duke University Press, 2006), 163–88.

49 Clara Sue Kidwell, "What Would Pocahontas Think Now?: Women and Cultural Persistence," *Callaloo* 17, no. 1 (1994): 149–59.

50 Rudia Haliburton, *Red over Black: Black Slavery among the Cherokee Indians* (Westport, CT: Greenwood, 1977), 5–12; Kidwell, "What Would Pocahontas Think Now?," 155.

51 Hodges, *Root and Branch*, 87.

52 Marrant, *Narrative*, 65.

53 Marrant, *Narrative*, 66.

54 See Acts 12:1–19.

55 Marrant, *Narrative*, 67.

56 Gronniosaw, *Narrative*, 36.

57 Equiano, *Interesting Narrative*, 198.

58 Marrant, *Narrative*, 67.

59 Marrant, *Narrative*, 73.

60 Holmes, *Joy Unspeakable*, 39.

CHAPTER 3. *Exodus: Conjuring Retaliation in Marrant's* Narrative

1 For treatments of Exodus themes in Black religion and Black literature, see J. Laurence Cohen, *Excavating Exodus: Biblical Typology and Racial Solidarity in African American Literature* (Clemson, SC: Clemson University Press, 2021); Herbert Robinson Marbury, *Pillars of Cloud and Fire: The Politics of Exodus in African American Biblical Interpretation* (New York: New York University Press, 2015); Eddie S. Glaude Jr., *Exodus! Race, Religion, and Nation in Early Nineteenth-Century Black America* (Chicago: University of Chicago Press, 2000).

2 Marrant, *Narrative*, 70.

3 Turner, *Confessions*, 46.

4 See Genesis 12:10–13:1.

5 Marrant, *Narrative*, 68.

6 Marrant, *Narrative*, 69.

7 See Exodus 7:14–24.

8 Marrant, *Narrative*, 70.

9 *The Confessions of Nat Turner* is the most widely utilized source for knowledge of the Southampton slave rebellion in 1831. As Kenneth Greenberg points out, Turner was not an author in a conventional sense, and *Confessions* should be carefully regarded as "a joint production—with many of the major decisions in the hands of local lawyer and slave owner Thomas R. Gray." See Kenneth S. Greenberg, "The Confessions of Nat Turner: Text and Context," in *The Confessions of Nat Turner and Related Documents*, ed. Kenneth S. Greenberg (Boston: Bedford, 1996), 8. While *Confessions* is part of the official court documents, an understanding of Gray's motives in publishing Turner's *Confessions* enables more astute analysis. Concerning Gray's motives for publishing Turner's *Confessions*, Vanessa Holden notes, "Gray published the document for profit, hoping to cash in on the fast-growing legend of America's most famous rebellious enslaved person." See Vanessa M. Holden, *Surviving Southampton: African American Women and Resistance in Nat Turner's Community* (Urbana: University of Illinois Press, 2021), 83.

10 Turner, *Confessions*, 46–47. On spiritual seasons of Kimpasi ritual initiation, see Young, *Rituals of Resistance*, 79–80, 95; Brown, *African-Atlantic Cultures*, 95.

11 Turner, *Confessions*, 46.

12 Turner, *Confessions*, 47 (emphasis added).

13 Turner, *Confessions*, 47.

14 Samson Adetunji Fatokun, "The Concept of Expiatory Sacrifice in the Early Church and in African Indigenous Religious Traditions," in *African Traditions in the Study of Religion, Diaspora and Gendered Societies*, ed. Afe Adogame, Ezra Chitando, and Balaji Bateye (Burlington, VT: Ashgate, 2012), 71–84.

15 Lucas Nandih Shamala, "Approaches to Peacemaking in Africa: *Obuntu* Perspectives from Western Kenya," in *African Traditions in the Study of Religion, Diaspora and Gendered Societies*, ed. Afe Adogame, Ezra Chitando, and Balaji Bateye (Burlington, VT: Ashgate, 2012), 20.

16 C. L. R. James, *The Black Jacobins: Toussaint L'Ouverture and the San Domingo Revolution*, 2nd ed. (New York: Vintage, 1963), 87; see also Michael A. Gomez, *Reversing Sail: A History of the African Diaspora* (Cambridge: Cambridge University Press, 2005), 136.

17 Fatokun, "Concept of Expiatory Sacrifice," 79–80.

18 Frederick Douglass, *Narrative of the Life of Frederick Douglass, an American Slave. Written by Himself* (Boston: Anti-Slavery Office, 1845), 67 (emphasis added), https://docsouth.unc.edu/neh/douglass/douglass.html.

19 Douglass, *Narrative*, 71–72.

20 Yvonne Chireau, *Black Magic: Religion and the African American Conjuring Tradition* (Berkeley: University of California Press, 2003), 59–60.

21 Tim Lockley, "David Margrett: A Black Missionary in the Revolutionary Atlantic," *Journal of American Studies* 46, no. 3 (2012): 729–45; see also Joseph Rezek, "Early Black Evangelical Writing and the Radical Limitations of Print," in *African American Literature in Transition, 1750–1800*, ed. Rhondda Thomas (Cambridge: Cambridge University Press, 2022), 17–41.

22 The quoted text is from a partial transcription of Margrett's sermon written by John Edwards, a Charleston slave owner and associate of the Huntingdon Connexion. In a letter to William Piercy, Edwards explains that Margrett's sermon was given to him by Colonel Stephen Bull, a delegate at the First Provincial Congress of South Carolina. The transcribed excerpt in Edwards's letter is all that remains of Margrett's sermon. See Rezek, "Early Black Evangelical Writing," 30.

23 This statement is attributed to Margrett in a letter from William Piercy to Selina Hastings. See Rezek, "Early Black Evangelical Writing," 34.

24 The quoted text is from William Piercy's letter to Selina Hastings. See Lockley, "David Margrett," 740.

25 See Lockley, "David Margrett," 740.

26 Marrant, *Narrative*, 69.

27 Rezek, "Early Black Evangelical Writing," 34.

28 Alexis Wells-Oghoghomeh, *The Souls of Womenfolk: The Religious Cultures of Enslaved Women in the Lower South* (Chapel Hill: University of North Carolina Press, 2021), 31–32.

29 See Pernille Ipsen, *Daughters of the Trade* (Philadelphia: University of Pennsylvania Press, 2015), 6–8.

30 Wells-Oghoghomeh, *Souls of Womenfolk*, 33.

31 Chireau, *Black Magic*, 66. The scholarship contributing to the debate surrounding the Denmark Vesey trial and related conspiracy is contentious. In Michael P. Johnson's "Denmark Vesey and His Co-Conspirators," the author states his belief that historians adhering to the prevailing opinion regarding Vesey "have been wrong about the conspiracy." Citing inconsistencies in various recordings of court proceedings and trial records, he contends that "the court, for its own reasons, colluded with a handful of intimidated witnesses to collect testimony about an insurrection that, in fact, was not about to happen." Historians who persist in retaining what Johnson termed the "heroic interpretation of Vesey" run the risk of following in the lead of predecessors who "failed to exercise due caution in reading the testimony of witnesses recorded by the conspiracy court" and had thereby become "unwitting co-conspirators with the court in the making of the Vesey conspiracy." My use of quotes attributed to Rolla Bennett in this text aims neither to confirm nor to deny the existence of a conspiracy of rebellion—a matter well beyond the scope of this book. Even if Vesey did not lead a conspiracy to overthrow slavery, allusions to his alleged expositions of Exodus illumine much regarding "the perception of Black Charlestonians," especially pertaining to their understanding of biblical prophecy and divine retribution. As James Sidbury (one of several respondents to Johnson) notes, "That Denmark Vesey's antislavery scriptural interpretation 'belonged' in an imagined slave insurrection tells us almost as much about the role of Christianity and the African Methodist Episcopal Church in black Charlestonians' resistance to white oppression as we would know if we could prove that the conspiracy existed exactly as portrayed in the records." See Michael Johnson, "Denmark Vesey and His Co-Conspirators," *William and Mary Quarterly* 58, no. 4 (2021): 915–76. For James Sidbury's response, see "Plausible Stories and Varnished Truths," *William and Mary Quarterly* 58, no. 1 (2022): 179–84.

32 Walter C. Rucker, *Gold Coast Diasporas: Identity, Culture, and Power* (Bloomington: Indiana University Press, 2015), 91–92 (emphasis added).

33 On the ubiquity of oathing throughout West and West Central Africa, Rucker posits that "loyalty oaths may have been universally employed throughout Atlantic Africa— particularly in regions with expansionist states that needed the security of inviolable contracts to lengthen their political and commercial reach. Whether or not loyalty oaths can be categorized as uniquely Akan-speaking practices that spread to other language cohorts through military conquests and political domination is probably unknowable." See Rucker, *Gold Coast Diasporas*, 92.

34 Chireau, *Black Magic*, 68–70.

35 Chireau, *Black Magic*, 73.

36 Bolster, *Black Jacks*, 31.

37 Bolster, *Black Jacks*, 32.

38 Marrant, *Narrative*, 72.

39 Bolster, *Black Jacks*, 34.

40 See Carretta, *Unchained Voices*, 130–31n47.

41   Marrant, *Narrative*, 72.

42   Marrant, *Narrative*, 72–73.

43   Marrant, *Narrative*, 73.

44   For sources on Selina Hastings, see Alan Harding, *The Countess of Huntingdon's Connexion* (Oxford: Oxford University Press, 2003); Edwin Welch, *Spiritual Pilgrim: A Reassessment of the Life of the Countess of Huntingdon* (Cardiff: University of Wales Press, 1995).

45   Harding, *Countess of Huntingdon's Connexion*, 59.

46   Harding, *Countess of Huntingdon's Connexion*, 67–78, 96–150.

47   Simon Schama, *Rough Crossings: Britain, the Slaves and the American Revolution* (London: BBC, 2005), 69.

48   James St. G. Walker notes, "Estimates of the number of slaves who found their way to the British lines range up to 100,000, or one-fifth the total black American population. Even if this is an exaggeration it seems certain that slaves fled their American masters in tens of thousands. Thomas Jefferson declared that Virginia alone lost 30,000, though there is no indication that they all went over to the British after deserting their erstwhile owners." See James W. St. G. Walker, *The Black Loyalists: The Search for a Promised Land in Nova Scotia and Sierra Leone, 1783–1870* (London: Longman, 1976), 1, 6–7; Schama, *Rough Crossings*, 75–76, 135.

49   Schama, *Rough Crossings*, 156.

50   John Marrant, *A Journal of the Rev. John Marrant from August the 18th, 1785, to the 16th of March, 1790*, in Brooks and Saillant, *"Face Zion Forward,"* 93–160.

51   Marrant, *Journal*, 98–99.

52   Bolster, *Black Jacks*, 63.

53   Bolster, *Black Jacks*, 49.

54   Brown, *African-Atlantic Cultures*, 3.

55   Brown, *African-Atlantic Cultures*, 92.

56   Equiano, *Interesting Narrative*, 209–10.

57   Boston King and Olaudah Equiano also narrate that their spiritual fervor wanes while at sea. W. Jeffrey Bolster writes, "Black sailors historically found it difficult to practice meaningful religion in a predominantly white, and largely skeptical, community of sailors." See Bolster, *Black Jacks*, 122.

58   Marrant, *Journal*, 98.

59   Marrant, *Journal*, 99–100.

60   Long, *Significations*, 197.

61   Hurston, *Sanctified Church*, 69.

62   Hurston, *Sanctified Church*, 71–72.

63   Marrant, *Journal*, 100.

CHAPTER 4. *"My Travels in Nova Scotia": Ritual Healing and Communal Restoration in Marrant's* Journal

1   Schama, *Rough Crossings*, 231; see also Alan Gilbert, *Black Patriots and Loyalists: Fighting for Emancipation in the War for Independence* (Chicago: University of Chicago Press, 2012), 207.

2   Gilbert, *Black Patriots and Loyalists*, 209, 213; see also Walker, *Black Loyalists*, 19.

3   Schama, *Rough Crossings*, 4; see also Gilbert, *Black Patriots and Loyalists*, 208–9; Walker, *Black Loyalists*, 23–24.

4   Walker, *Black Loyalists*, 28.

5   Gilbert, *Black Patriots and Loyalists*, 209–10; see also Walker, *Black Loyalists*, 22; Schama, *Rough Crossings*, 236.

6   Gilbert, *Black Patriots and Loyalists*, 207; see also Walker, *Black Loyalists*, 22.

7   Walker, *Black Loyalists*, 64.

8   Walker, *Black Loyalists*, 73–74.

9   Walker, *Black Loyalists*, 76.

10 Walker, *Black Loyalists*, 79.

11 Walker, *Black Loyalists*, 77.

12 Walker, *Black Loyalists*, 64.

13 Walker, *Black Loyalists*, 79.

14 Walker, *Black Loyalists*, 64, 66, 73–74, 76–77, 79.

15 See Adam Potkay and Sandra Burr, "About John Marrant," in *Black Atlantic Writers of the Eighteenth Century: Living the New Exodus in England and the Americas* (New York: St. Martin's, 1995), 67–74; Jack C. Whytock, "The Huntingdonian Mission to Nova Scotia, 1782–1791: A Study in Calvinistic Methodism," *Historical Papers: Canadian Society of Church History* (2003), 149–70, https://doi.org/10.25071/0848 -1563.39292. Although some scholars contend that Furmage was Black and that he accompanied Marrant on the journey from London to Halifax, correspondence from Furmage in Nova Scotia to Selina Hastings predates Marrant's arrival in 1785. Furthermore, early biographies of Selina Hastings maintain that Marrant was the first Black minister ordained in the Huntingdon Connexion. The letters of credential that accompany Furmage's signature confirm his ordination, so it seems that he was acquainted with Marrant from the college but was not Black.

16 See Marrant, *Journal*, 102.

17 Marrant, *Journal*, 104. Marrant's sermon text, Acts 3:22–23, reads, "For Moses truly said unto the fathers, a prophet shall the Lord your God raise up unto you of your brethren, like unto me; him shall ye hear in all things whatsoever he shall say unto you. And it shall come to pass, that every soul, which will not hear that prophet, shall be destroyed from among the people."

18 Marrant, *Journal*, 104. Marrant's sermon text is John 5:28–29, which reads, "Marvel not at this: for the hour is coming, in the which all that are in the graves shall hear his voice, And shall come forth, they that have done good, unto the resurrection of life; and they that have done evil, unto the resurrection of damnation."

19 Stuckey, *Slave Culture*, 12–13, 17.

20 Stuckey, *Slave Culture*, 20.

21 W. E. B. Du Bois describes the "frenzy of a Negro revival" as the moment when the Spirit of the Lord causes the devotee to become "made with supernatural joy." The frenzy, according to Du Bois, is "the last essential of Negro religion and the one more devoutly believed in than all the rest." See W. E. B. Du Bois, *The Souls of Black Folk: Essays and Sketches* (Greenwich, CT: Fawcett, 1967), 196–97.

22 For a discussion of the religious and historical contexts of Brer Rabbit and of trickster-heroes in human society, see Ruth A. Leslie, "Brer Rabbit, a Play of the Human Spirit: Recreating Black Culture through Brer Rabbit Stories," *International Journal of Sociology and Social Policy* 17, no. 6 (1997): 59–83, https://doi.org/10.1108/eb013312.

23 Boston King, *Memoirs of the Life of Boston King, a Black Preacher, Written by Himself, during His Residence at Kingswood-School*, in Brooks and Saillant, *"Face Zion Forward,"* 226–27.

24 King, *Memoirs*, 210.

25 Gomez, *Exchanging Our Country Marks*, 22.

26 Sylviane Diouf, *Servants of Allah: African Muslims Enslaved in the Americas* (New York: New York University Press, 1998), 69.

27 Schama, *Rough Crossings*, 235.

28 David George, *An Account of the Life of Mr. David George*, in Brooks and Saillant, *"Face Zion Forward,"* 183.

29 King, *Memoirs*, 224.

30 Marrant, *Journal*, 101.

31 See Joshua 6.

32 Marrant, *Journal*, 104–5.

33 See Marrant, *Journal*, 105–6. Marrant's sermon text is Mark 16:16, which reads, "He that believeth and is baptized shall be saved; but he that believeth not shall be damned."

34 Marrant, *Journal*, 105–6. Marrant's sermon text is John 1:19, which reads, "And this is the record of John when the Jews sent priests and Levites from Jerusalem to ask him, Who are thou?" Marrant specifies that his emphasis was on "the latter part of the nineteenth verse."

35 Marrant's sermon texts include Acts 2:38, which reads, "Then Peter said unto them, Repent and be baptized every one of you in the name of Jesus Christ for the remission of sins, and ye shall receive the gift of the Holy Ghost"; and Mark 6:12, which reads, "And they went out, and preached that men should repent."

36 Marrant, *Journal*, 106. Marrant's sermon text is Genesis 1:2, which reads, "And the earth was without form, and void; and darkness was upon the face of the deep. And the Spirit of God moved upon the face of the waters."

37 Marrant, *Journal*, 108. Marrant's sermon text is Romans 2:7, which reads, "To them who by patient continuance in well doing seek for glory and honor and immortality, eternal life."

38 Marrant, *Journal*, 108. Marrant's sermon text is Romans 6:3, which reads, "Know ye not, that so many of us who were baptized into Jesus Christ were baptized into his death."

39 Marrant, *Journal*, 109. Marrant's sermon text is Matthew 28:19–20, which reads, "Go ye therefore, and teach all nations, baptizing them in the name of the Father and of the Son, and of the Holy Ghost: teaching them to observe all things whatsoever I have commanded you: and, lo, I am with you always, even unto the end of the world."

40 Marrant, *Journal*, 109.

41 Marrant's inclusion of adults and children underscores the communal nature of baptism in early Black Christian communities. As Ras Michael Brown explains, "The rite of baptism was entirely communal, as large groups of initiates gathered along with many family members and friends along with numerous other observers." See Brown, *African-Atlantic Cultures*, 216.

42 See Betty M. Kuyk, *African Voices in the African American Heritage* (Bloomington: Indiana University Press, 2003), 83.

43 See Young, *Rituals of Resistance*, 77–78. Young explains that water immersion rites informed the conversion experience of African slaves in the American South. The gravitation toward Protestant denominations that practiced water immersion is explained by West and West Central African predispositions to similar rituals in Africa. Water baptism conformed to the cycles of death-resurrection-reintegration common in many African religious communities. As Young explains,

> Noting the varied rituals of water immersion in Africa and the deep reverence for river priests on the continent, Melville Herskovits argued that slaves came to the Americas with strong traditions of water immersion rites that they transmuted onto Christian baptism in the New World. Certain Christian symbols, as in the river Jordan, for example, were symbolic representations of both an ostensibly Christian, yet deeply African spiritual meaning. The prevalence of the imagery of the river Jordan in the musical traditions of slaves further emphasized this connection. That is, the river Jordan reflected a multitude of African rituals of water immersion in the Americas.

See Young, *Rituals of Resistance*, 77.

44 The Reverend William Walter, an Anglican minister from Shelburne, baptized seventy Blacks, adults and children, in November 1783 and another seventy-nine in 1784. Though the numbers waned and were mostly confined to children for the remainder of the decade, "several hundred Birchtown blacks were admitted to the Church of England" over a ten-year period. See Walker, *Black Loyalists*, 69.

45 Walker, *Black Loyalists*, 66–68.

46 On white rage, see Carol A. Anderson, *White Rage: The Unspoken Truth of Our Racial Divide* (New York: Bloomsbury, 2016).

47 George, *Account*, 185.

48 See Walker, *Black Loyalists*, 76.

49 Brown, *African-Atlantic Cultures*, 95.

50 Ras Michael Brown notes, "With this last water rite, the initiate completed the process of spiritual transformation that satisfied both the model of the older Kongo institutions and that of the new Lowcountry Christian church." See Brown, *African-Atlantic Cultures*, 247–48.

51 Dianne M. Stewart, *Three Eyes for the Journey: African Dimensions of the Jamaican Religious Experience* (New York: Oxford University Press, 2005), 129.

52 George, *Account*, 183.

53 George Leile, *An Account of Several Baptist Churches*, in Carretta, *Unchained Voices*, 327.

54 George, *Account*, 184, 186.

55 Brown, *African-Atlantic Cultures*, 217.

56 Regarding the need to establish ties to nature spirits in new territories, Brown explains, "No ancestors in the new land meant no graves, and no graves meant no access to the land of the dead. This represented a serious crisis as the internment of ancestors in the soil provided sacred sites that served as shrines for descendants and as markers of the spiritual sanction for the living to inhabit the territory." See Brown, *African-Atlantic Cultures*, 91.

57 See Marrant, *Narrative*, 72–73.

58 Brown, *African-Atlantic Cultures*, 246–47.

59 Walker, *Black Loyalists*, 79.

60 George, *Account*, 185.

61 King, *Memoirs*, 218.

62 Named for Dutch Reformed theologian Jacobus Arminius (1560–1609), Arminianism, a branch of Protestant theology, arose in the late sixteenth century in opposition to the followers of Calvinism, named for French theologian John Calvin (1509–64). Arminius and his followers (known as Remonstrants) rejected Calvinist doctrines of atonement only for a predestined select few, arguing instead for a theology of universal atonement through the salvific work of Christ. While Arminius believed that human effort accompanied divine grace to yield salvation, Calvinists emphasized divine sovereignty—that is, since God has predetermined who will be saved, humans can do nothing to alter their fate. Some scholars have suggested that the Calvinist emphasis on divine rather than human authority has enabled followers to resist unjust state power. Conversely, the Arminian doctrine of human cooperation with divine grace has resulted at times in uncritical acquiescence to the state. See Alan P. F. Sell, *The Great Debate: Calvinism, Arminianism, and Salvation* (Grand Rapids, MI: Baker, 1983); Alan C. Clifford, *Atonement and Justification: Evangelical Theology 1640–1790: An Evaluation* (Oxford: Oxford University Press, 1990); "Arminianism," in *The Concise Oxford Companion to American Literature*, ed. James D. Hart, Wendy Martin, and Danielle Hinrichs (Oxford: Oxford University Press, 2021).

63 Marrant, *Journal*, 121. Marrant's sermon text is John 7:37–38.

64 See Marrant, *Journal*, 121.

65 Marrant, *Journal*, 122.

66 Marrant, *Journal*, 123–24.

67 Marrant, *Journal*, 124.

68 Marrant, *Journal*, 124–25.

69 Marrant, *Journal*, 125–26.

70 Marrant, *Journal*, 126.

71 Freeborn Garretson, "The Journal of Mr. Freeborn Garretson," *Arminian Magazine Consisting of Extracts and Original Treatises on Universal Redemption, Jan. 1778– Dec. 1797* 17, no. 10 (1794): 505–11.

72 Marrant, *Journal*, 127.

73 Schama, *Rough Crossings*, 243; Gilbert, *Black Loyalists and Patriots*, 211.

74 Schama, *Rough Crossings*, 221.

75 King, *Memoirs*, 223.

76 Schama, *Rough Crossings*, 245.

77   Schama, *Rough Crossings*, 281.

78   Schama, *Rough Crossings*, 245.

79   Schama, *Rough Crossings*, 246.

80   Schama, *Rough Crossings*, 244–45.

81   See Bolster, *Black Jacks*, 166. On the prevalence of brothels and establishments support-ing prostitution in port communities, see Sowande Mustakeem, *Slavery at Sea: Terror, Sex, and Sickness in the Middle Passage* (Urbana: University of Illinois Press, 2016), 83–84.

82   Wells-Oghoghomeh, *Souls of Womenfolk*, 41. On enslaved women's experiences of sexual violence at sea during the transatlantic slave trade, see Jennifer L. Morgan, *Reckoning with Slavery: Gender, Kinship, and Capitalism in Early Modern America* (Durham, NC: Duke University Press, 2021); Mustakeem, *Slavery at Sea*, 84–90; Karen Cook Bell, *Running from Bondage: Enslaved Women and the Remarkable Fight for Freedom in Revolutionary America* (Cambridge: Cambridge University Press, 2021).

83   Alexander Falconbridge, *An Account of the Slave Trade on the Coast of Africa* (London: J. Phillips, 1788), 23; https://www.gutenberg.org/cache/epub/69178/pg69178-images .html.

84   Marrant, *Journal*, 111.

85   Marrant, *Journal*, 112.

86   Marrant, *Journal*, 112–13.

87   Marrant, *Journal*, 113–14.

88   Marrant, *Journal*, 114–15.

89   George, *Account*, 187.

90   See Matthew 9:1–8; Mark 2:1–12.

91   Young, *Rituals of Resistance*, 100.

92   Young, *Rituals of Resistance*, 100.

93   Schools, like churches, enabled Black settlers to develop identities independent of their white counterparts in Loyalist Nova Scotia. Though established and supported by English philanthropic organizations, administrative and teaching responsibilities were left to the Black Loyalists themselves. In the school headed by Marrant, the curriculum included "spelling, reading and the Anglican catechism, with knitting and sewing for the girls." See Walker, *Black Loyalists*, 80–84.

94   Marrant, *Journal*, 131–32.

95   Gilbert, *Black Loyalists and Patriots*, 211; Schama, *Rough Crossings*, 250.

96   See George, *Account*, 184.

97   King, *Memoirs*, 223.

98   For descriptions of Marrant's illness, see Marrant, *Journal*, 128–34.

99   See Elizabeth A. Finn, *Pox Americana: The Great Smallpox Epidemic of 1775–82* (New York: Hill and Wang, 2001).

100 Marrant, *Journal*, 134.

101 Marrant, *Journal*, 141.

102 See Matthew 9:20–22; Mark 5:25–34; Luke 8:43–48.

103 Schama, *Rough Crossings*, 243.

104 Schama, *Rough Crossings*, 243; Ruth Whitehead, *Black Loyalists: Southern Settlers of Nova Scotia's First Free Black Communities* (Halifax: Nimbus, 2013), 159–64.

105 Marrant, *Journal*, 132.

106 Simon Schama contends that "Birchtown was hardly a Come Counties village, but nor was it a place where, as subsequent myth had it, the settlers were forced to live in 'caves.'" See Schama, *Rough Crossings*, 249.

107 Marrant, *Journal*, 145.

108 Marrant, *Journal*, 146.

109 See 1 Kings 19:1–18.

110 On African American seeking rituals, see Hurston, *Sanctified Church*.

111 Brown, *African-Atlantic Cultures*, 113.

112 Brown, *African-Atlantic Cultures*, 125.

113 Brown, *African-Atlantic Cultures*, 121.

114 Brown, *African-Atlantic Cultures*, 127–28.

115 See Genesis 23:9–19; 25:9; 49:30; 50:13.

116 See Exodus 33:18–33; Deuteronomy 34:6.

117 See Joshua 10:15–27.

118 See Matthew 27:57–61; Mark 15:42–16:3.

119 Gary Laderman, *The Sacred Remains: American Attitudes toward Death, 1799–1883* (New Haven, CT: Yale University Press, 1996), 3–4.

120 See Robert Farris Thompson, *Flash of the Spirit: African and Afro-American Art and Philosophy* (New York: Vintage, 1984), 132–45.

121 John K. Thornton, *The Kongolese Saint Anthony: Dona Beatriz Kimpa Vita and the Antonian Movement, 1684–1706* (New York: Cambridge University Press, 1998), 79–80. In late sixteenth-century Havana, people of African descent expressed a clear desire to be buried next to members of their own families and ethnic groups in churches. For a comparative analysis of African-derived burial practices in the Spanish Caribbean, see Pablo Gomez, *The Experiential Caribbean: Creating Knowledge and Healing in the Early Modern Atlantic* (Chapel Hill: University of North Carolina Press, 2017), 32–39.

122 Marrant, *Journal*, 154.

123 Marrant, *Narrative*, 72.

124 Marrant, *Journal*, 108–10.

125 See Matthew 9:18–26; Mark 5:21–43.

126 See Wells-Oghoghomeh, *Souls of Womenfolk*, 4, 55. Regarding captured African women, the Atlantic historian Jennifer Morgan notes that "the use of children as a lure, the recognition that their identity as women and mothers changed the strategies that slavecatchers used to capture them" were constituent factors that "confirmed the outlines of their enslavement." See Morgan, *Reckoning with Slavery*, 141. For a discussion of expressions of grief and the evolving grieving practices of enslaved women, see Sasha Turner, "The Nameless and the Forgotten: Maternal Grief, Sacred Protection, and the Archive of Slavery," *Slavery and Abolition* 38, no. 2 (2017): 232–50.

127 Sweet, *Domingos Alvares*, 6, 76.

128 Brown, *African-Atlantic Cultures*, 220.

129 Stephanie Y. Mitchem, *African American Folk Healing* (New York: New York University Press, 2007), 100.

130 Mitchem, *African American Folk Healing*, 101.

131 Donald H. Matthews, *Honoring the Ancestors: An African Cultural Interpretation of Black Religion and Literature* (New York: Oxford University Press, 1998), 15.

132 Matthews, *Honoring the Ancestors*, 114–16.

CHAPTER 5. *"As Men and as Masons": Spiritual Genealogies and Racial Ethnogenesis in Marrant's* Sermon

1 Marrant, *Journal*, 149. Marrant's sermon text, Acts 3:22–23, reads, "For Moses truly said unto the fathers, a prophet shall the Lord your God raise up unto you of your brethren, like unto me; him shall ye hear in all things whatsoever he shall say unto you. And it shall come to pass, that every soul, which will not hear that prophet, shall be destroyed from among the people."

2 Steven C. Bullock, *Revolutionary Brotherhood: Freemasonry and the Transformation of the American Social Order, 1730–1840* (Chapel Hill: University of North Carolina Press, 1996), 4–10.

3 John Marrant, *A Sermon Preached on the 24th Day of June 1789, Being the Festival of St. John the Baptist at the Request of the Right Worshipful the Grand Master Prince Hall, and the Rest of the Brethren of the African Lodge of the Honorable Society of Free and Accepted Masons in Boston*, in Brooks and Saillant, *"Face Zion Forward,"* 77–92.

4 Vincent Carretta, *Phillis Wheatley: Biography of a Genius in Bondage* (Athens: University of Georgia Press, 2011), 42.

5 Katherine Carté employs awakened Protestantism to describe the various brands of evangelical Christianity that emerged during and after the revival movement of the late eighteenth century. The rise of awakened Protestant denominations, argues Carté, signaled the crumbling of transatlantic networks that tied American Protestant institutions to British Protestantism. See Katherine Carté, *Religion and the American Revolution: An Imperial History* (Chapel Hill: University of North Carolina Press, 2021), 6n7, 288–89.

6 James Oliver Horton and Lois E. Horton, *Black Bostonians: Family Life and Community Struggle in the Antebellum North*, rev. ed. (New York: Holmes and Meier, 1999), xiv. By 1750, Rhode Island boasted the highest concentration of enslaved people; nearly 10 percent of Rhode Island's population was enslaved compared with only 3 percent in Massachusetts. Additionally, Rhode Island trafficked almost 60 percent of the North American trade in African slaves. On slavery in Rhode Island, see Christy Clark-Pujara, *Dark Work: The Business of Slavery in Rhode Island* (New York: New York University Press, 2016).

7 Carretta, *Phillis Wheatley*, 18.

8 Horton and Horton, *Black Bostonians*, xv–xvi.

9 Vincent Carretta notes the deleterious effect of the Seven Years' War on transatlantic trade and, consequently, on population growth in Boston. The number of free and enslaved Blacks had greatly declined (as had Boston's population generally) by the time of Marrant's birth in 1755. See Carretta, *Phillis Wheatley*, 4–6, 11, 15; James Oliver Horton and Lois E. Horton, *In Hope of Liberty: Culture, Community and Protest among Northern Free Blacks, 1700–1860* (New York: Oxford University Press, 1997), 42.

10   Corey D. B. Walker, *A Noble Fight: African American Freemasonry and the Struggle for Democracy in America* (Champaign: University of Illinois Press, 2008), 52. Gary Nash points out that students at Harvard regularly debated the morality of American slavery, with positions on both sides having adequate representation. Gary Nash, *The Forgotten Fifth: African Americans in the Age of Revolution* (Cambridge, MA: Harvard University Press, 2006), 16–17.

11   Gloria McCahon Whiting argues that a 1783 judicial interpretation of the state's 1780 constitution did little to meaningfully alter the reality of slavery in Massachusetts, but rather that emancipation "resulted from internal negotiations within slaveholding households and changes in attitudes towards slavery." See Gloria McCahon Whiting, "Emancipation without the Courts or Constitution: The Case of Revolutionary Massachusetts," *Slavery and Abolition* 41, no. 3 (2020): 458–78, https://doi.org/10.1080/0144039X.2019.1693484. Chernoh Sesay notes a number of petitions filed by enslaved people in Massachusetts in the decade leading to the adoption of the state's constitution. Black activism during the 1770s, he argues, not only sought to end slavery but also aimed to define the meanings and conditions of freedom throughout the nineteenth century. See Chernoh M. Sesay Jr., "The Revolutionary Black Roots of Slavery's Abolition in Massachusetts," *New England Quarterly* 87, no. 1 (2014): 99–131.

12   Chernoh M. Sesay Jr., "Emancipation and the Social Origins of Black Freemasonry," in *All Men Free and Brethren: Essays on the History of African American Freemasonry*, ed. Peter Hinks and Stephen Kantrowitz (Ithaca, NY: Cornell University Press, 2013), 26.

13   Sesay, "Emancipation and the Social Origins of Black Freemasonry," 26.

14   Carretta, *Phillis Wheatley*, 20.

15   Marrant, *Journal*, 149.

16   Horton and Horton, *Black Bostonians*, xvi.

17   Carretta, *Phillis Wheatley*, 25.

18   Horton and Horton, *Black Bostonians*, xvi.

19   Marrant, *Journal*, 150.

20   Horton and Horton, *Black Bostonians*, 16–18.

21   Marrant, *Narrative*, 73.

22   Carretta, *Phillis Wheatley*, 33.

23   Prince Hall to Countess of Huntingdon, reprinted in *Prince Hall's Letter Book* (1900), ed. William H. Upton, 7, quoted in Sesay, "Emancipation and the Social Origins of Black Freemasonry," 33–34.

24   Walker, *Noble Fight*, 51–53.

25   Walker, *Noble Fight*, 54.

26   Sesay, "Emancipation and the Social Origins of Black Freemasonry," 21.

27   Sesay, "Emancipation and the Social Origins of Black Freemasonry," 21–22.

28   Walker, *Noble Fight*, 52.

29   Gomez, *Exchanging Our Country Marks*, 95.

30   Gomez, *Exchanging Our Country Marks*, 101.

31   Gomez, *Exchanging our Country Marks*, 101.

32   See Winthrop D. Jordan, *White over Black: American Attitudes toward the Negro, 1550–1812* (Chapel Hill: University of North Carolina Press, 1968), 130.

33   Walker, *Noble Fight*, 55.

34   Michael A. Gomez, *Black Crescent: The Experience and Legacy of African Muslims in the Americas* (Cambridge: Cambridge University Press, 2005), 242. On names as markers of African ethnic identity, see John C. Inscoe, "Carolina Slave Names: An Index to Acculturation," *Journal of Southern History* 49 (1983): 527–34; Cheryll Ann Cody, "There Was No 'Absalom' on the Ball Plantations: Slave-Naming Practices in the South Carolina Low Country, 1720–1865," *American Historical Review* 92 (1987): 563–96.

35   Walker, *Noble Fight*, 53; 49.

36   Philip S. Foner and Robert J. Branham, eds., *Lift Every Voice: African American Oratory, 1787–1900* (Tuscaloosa: University of Alabama Press, 1998), 1.

37   See "Appendix B," in *All Men Free and Brethren: Essays on the History of African American Freemasonry*, ed. Peter P. Hinks and Stephen Kantrowitz (Ithaca, NY: Cornell University Press, 2013), 186.

38   Maurice Wallace, "'Are We Men?': Prince Hall, Martin Delany, and the Masculine Ideal in Black Freemasonry, 1775–1865," *American Literary History* 9, no. 3 (1997): 403.

39   Marrant, *Narrative*, 65.

40   Benilde Montgomery, "Recapturing John Marrant," in *A Mixed Race: Ethnicity in Early America*, ed. Frank Shuffelton (New York: Oxford University Press, 1993), 109.

41   Walker, *Noble Fight*, 63.

42   Walker, *Noble Fight*, 64.

43   In African religious thought, cosmology narratives explain not only how the world comes to be but also the purpose and nature of human existence. See Benjamin C. Ray, *African Religions: Symbol, Ritual, and Community* (Englewood Cliffs, NJ: Prentice-Hall, 1976), 29.

44   On creation myths and mythical thinking, see Charles H. Long, *Alpha: The Myths of Creation* (New York: George Braziller, 1963), 11–15.

45   "Grand Architect of the Universe" is a Masonic name for God. See "Appendix B," 184.

46   See Marrant, *Sermon*, 82–84.

47   Marcel Griaule, *Conversations with Ogotemmêli: An Introduction to Dogon Religious Ideas* (New York: Oxford University Press for International African Institute, 1970), 17.

48   Griaule, *Conversations with Ogotemmêli*, 31–32.

49   Griaule, *Conversations with Ogotemmêli*, 39.

50   Marrant, *Sermon*, 86.

51   Marrant, *Sermon*, 86.

52   Wallace, "'Are We Men?,'" 408.

53   See Wallace, "'Are We Men?,'" 405–6.

54   Wallace, "'Are We Men?,'" 407.

55   Marrant, *Sermon*, 86.

56   Marrant, *Sermon*, 82. Cain was believed to be the father of the African race. This belief was attributed to his accursed status represented by a mark on his skin. See Genesis 4:15. The association of Cain with African-descended people was popular in eighteenth-century Black literary culture. In her noted poem "On Being Brought from Africa to America," the Boston poet Phillis Wheatley writes, "Remember, Christians,

Negroes, Black as Cain / May be refin'd, and join th' angelic train." See Wheatley, "On Being Brought from Africa to America," in *The Norton Anthology of African American Literature*, ed. Henry Louis Gates Jr. and Valerie A. Smith (New York: W. W. Norton, 2014), 143–44.

57 Marrant, *Sermon*, 82.

58 Griaule, *Conversations with Ogotemmêli*, 17.

59 Marrant, *Journal*, 151.

60 John Marrant, "Copy of a Letter from the Rev. Mr. Marrant, to Lady Huntingdon, dated North America, Nov. 24, 1788," in Brooks and Saillant, *"Face Zion Forward,"* 158–59.

61 Marrant, *Journal*, 151.

62 Prince Hall, *A Charge Delivered to the Brethren of the African Lodge on the 25th of June, 1792. At the Hall of Brother William Smith, in Charlestown*, in Brooks and Saillant, *"Face Zion Forward,"* 191–98.

63 Hall, *Charge . . . 1792*, 192

64 Hall, *Charge . . . 1792*, 192–93.

65 Hall, *Charge . . . 1792*, 195–96.

66 Prince Hall, quoted in Joanna Brooks, "Prince Hall, Freemasonry, and Genealogy," *African American Review* 34, no. 2 (2000): 197–216, https://doi.org/10.2307/2901249, 199.

67 James Horton and Lois Horton note, "Throughout the first generation of the nineteenth century, the names of most black churches, schools, social and mutual aid societies, and intellectual associations included the designation 'African.'" See Horton and Horton, *In Hope of Liberty*, 178.

68 Walker, *Noble Fight*, 73, 83.

69 Walker, *Noble Fight*, 48.

70 Hall, *Charge . . . 1792*, 197–98.

71 St. George Tucker was a Virginia-based lawyer and one of the most influential jurists in America during the years of the early republic. In 1796, he published *A Dissertation on Slavery*, described by Corey Walker as "his tragically flawed plan for gradual emancipation." See Walker, *Noble Fight*, 98; Leonard W. Levy, "Tucker, St. George (1751–1827)," in *Encyclopedia of the American Constitution*, 2nd ed., ed. Leonard W. Levy and Kenneth L. Karst (New York: Macmillan Reference USA, 2000), 6:2737.

72 Quoted in Walker, *Noble Fight*, 98.

73 Peter Hinks, *To Awaken My Afflicted Brethren: David Walker and the Problem of Antebellum Slave Resistance* (University Park: Pennsylvania State University Press, 2000), 70.

74 David Walker, *Walker's Appeal, in Four Articles; Together with a Preamble, to the Coloured Citizens of the World, but in Particular, and Very Expressly, to Those of the United States of America, Written in Boston, State of Massachusetts, September 29, 1829* (1830), Documenting the American South, University Library, University of North Carolina at Chapel Hill, https://docsouth.unc.edu/nc/walker/walker.html.

75 Hinks, *To Awaken My Afflicted Brethren*, 193–94.

76 Chireau, *Black Magic*, 59–60.

77 Walker, *Walker's Appeal*, 42.

78 See Horton and Horton, *Black Bostonians*, 58–59; Kerri Greenidge, *Boston's Abolitionists* (Beverly, MA: Commonwealth, 2006), 31–34.

79 Stephen Kantrowitz, "Brotherhood Denied: Black Freemasonry and the Limits of Reconstruction," in *All Men Free and Brethren: Essays on the History of African American Freemasonry*, ed. Peter Hinks and Stephen Kantrowitz (Ithaca, NY: Cornell University Press, 2013), 107.

80 On "enemies of the victorious Union," see Kantrowitz, "Brotherhood Denied," 112.

81 As Martin Summers notes, African American Freemasons argued that "the original intent behind this proscription was to exclude from the order those individuals who voluntarily became servants and those who were subjected to servitude as a result of criminal punishment. This did not preclude the enslaved African American, the 'kindred brother in humanity . . . with panting aspirations for liberty,' from joining the craft [*sic*] once he was freed because of either abolition or his own initiative." See Martin Summers, "'Arguing for Our Race': The Politics of Non-Recognition and the Public Nature of the Black Masonic Archive," in Hinks and Kantrowitz, *All Men Free and Brethren*, 159; Kantrowitz, "Brotherhood Denied," 111.

82 Hayden quoted in "Masonic, Odd Fellow and Other Items from the Anglo-African," *Pacific Appeal*, August 23, 1862, cited in Summers, "Arguing for Our Race," 159.

83 Summers, "Arguing for Our Race," 162.

84 Summers, "Arguing for Our Race," 163.

85 See Hall, *Charge . . . 1792*, and Prince Hall, *A Charge, Delivered to the African Lodge, June 24, 1797, at Menotomy*, in Brooks and Saillant, *"Face Zion Forward,"* 191–208.

86 Joanna Brooks, *American Lazarus: Religion and the Rise of African-American and Native American Literatures* (New York: Oxford University Press, 2003), 146.

87 Brooks, *American Lazarus*, 146–47.

88 Mircea Eliade explains the relationship between territory, ritual, and conquest in his discussion of ancient civilizations and their cosmological narratives. The cosmological myth of creation is ritually reenacted when space is consecrated. Ancient civilizations believed that space was differentiated by theophany, or a revelation of a god in a particular location. For Eliade, the differentiation of space is critical to understanding how religious humanity apprehends sacred reality. The manifestation of sacred space establishes an ontological point of origin within the mythic world because orientation implies a fixed point; the center is constructed at the place of sacred manifestation—"real living" is made possible as a result. See Mircea Eliade, *The Sacred and the Profane: The Nature of Religion* (New York: Harcourt Brace Jovanovich, 1987).

89 John Saillant, "'Wipe Away All Tears from Their Eyes': John Marrant's Theology in the Black Atlantic, 1785–1808," *Journal of Millennial Studies* 1, no. 2 (Winter 1999): 18–41.

EPILOGUE

1 Gilbert, *Black Patriots and Loyalists*, 270.

2 Gilbert, *Black Patriots and Loyalists*, 220–21; Schama, *Rough Crossings*, 277.

3 Schama, *Rough Crossings*, 289, 290.

4   Gilbert, *Black Patriots and Loyalists*, 224.

5   Gilbert, *Black Patriots and Loyalists*, 223.

6   Walker, *Black Loyalists*, 121–23; see also Schama, *Rough Crossings*, 294; Gilbert, *Black Patriots and Loyalists*, 221.

7   Walker, *Black Loyalists*, 85–86; see also Schama, *Rough Crossings*, 300–302; Gilbert, *Black Patriots and Loyalists*, 224.

8   Schama, *Rough Crossings*, 286–87, 293.

9   Schama, *Rough Crossings*, 287.

10 At the insistence of company agents, Black emigrants were to be regarded as "passengers who have paid the price demanded by the Owners for their accommodation." By policy, the Sierra Leone Company specified that each passenger would be allotted a space that was "at least five feet wide and that on double-decked ships there should also be at least five feet of good clearance between decks." Moreover, Black passengers were not to be subjected to "ill language and disrespect." When the fleet of ships arrived at Freetown, none of the Blacks complained of ill-treatment by white sailors. The company's hopes that "the crossing from Halifax to Sierra Leone would be a reversal of slave-ship passages in more than just geographical direction seemed, astonishingly, to have been fulfilled." See Schama, *Rough Crossings*, 295, 307, 310–11.

11 Schama, *Rough Crossings*, 309, 322.

12 Schama, *Rough Crossings*, 308, 321.

13 Gilbert, *Black Patriots and Loyalists*, 229.

14 Walker, *Black Loyalists*, 149–52. Black Loyalist settlers also unknowingly entered an ongoing dispute between the Sierra Leone Company and the neighboring Temne people led by King Jimmy regarding the territory occupied by the settlers. Although these disputes predated the arrival of Black settlers from Nova Scotia, Temne attacks on the colony were a continuous threat to their safety during the early years of their arrival. Raids, kidnappings, and acts of warfare were a constant cause for settlers' concern. On settler conflicts with the Temne, see Walker, *Black Loyalists*, 169–71.

15 Gilbert, *Black Patriots and Loyalists*, 230–31.

16 Because women constituted more than one-third of all heads of household, they were allowed to vote in Sierra Leone's earliest democratic elections, held near the end of 1792. As Simon Schama explains, "Female voting was something that even the French Revolution in its most radical phase had not been able to contemplate. Indeed, the Jacobins were hostile to the idea. It was momentous, then, that the first women to cast their votes for any kind of public office anywhere in the world were black, liberated slaves who had chosen British freedom; women such as Mary Perth from Norfolk, Virginia, and Martha Hazeley from Charleston, South Carolina." See Schama, *Rough Crossings*, 374.

17 Schama, *Rough Crossings*, 375.

18 Schama, *Rough Crossings*, 374–75; see also Gilbert, *Black Patriots and Loyalists*, 231, 239.

19 Walker, *Black Loyalists*, 86.

20 Gilbert, *Black Patriots and Loyalists*, 231.

21 Gilbert, *Black Patriots and Loyalists*, 240; see also Schama, *Rough Crossings*, 388–89.

22 Schama, *Rough Crossings*, 392; see also Gilbert, *Black Patriots and Loyalists*, 241.

23 The Sierra Leone Company authorities dealt with the Freetown Huntingdonians harshly. A violent standoff between Black settlers and maroon refugees from Halifax (who fought on behalf of the company) ensued. In the end, the rebellion was put down, the settlers' church building was destroyed, and Isaac Anderson was hanged. See Schama, *Rough Crossings*, 394–95.

24 See Sweet, *Domingos Alvares*, 4–5.

25 Brooks, *American Lazarus*, 87.

Selected Bibliography

PRIMARY SOURCES

Douglass, Frederick. *Narrative of the Life of Frederick Douglass, an American Slave. Written by Himself.* Boston: Anti-Slavery Office, 1845. http://docsouth.unc.edu/neh/douglass/douglass.html.

Equiano, Olaudah. *The Interesting Narrative of the Life of Olaudah Equiano, or Gustavus Vassa, the African.* [1789.] In *Unchained Voices: An Anthology of Black Authors in the English-Speaking World of the Eighteenth Century,* edited by Vincent Carretta, 185–318. Lexington: University Press of Kentucky, 1996.

Falconbridge, Alexander. *An Account of the Slave Trade on the Coast of Africa.* London: J. Phillips, 1788. https://www.gutenberg.org/cache/epub/69178/pg69178-images.html.

George, David *An Account of the Life of Mr. David George.* [1793.] In *"Face Zion Forward": First Writers of the Black Atlantic, 1785–1798,* edited by Joanna Brooks and John Saillant, 177–90. Boston: Northeastern University Press, 2002.

Gronniosaw, James Albert Ukawsaw. *A Narrative of the Most Remarkable Particulars in the Life of James Albert Ukawsaw Gronniosaw, an African Prince.* [1770.] In *Unchained Voices: An Anthology of Black Authors in the English-Speaking World of the Eighteenth Century,* edited by Vincent Carretta, 32–58. Lexington: University Press of Kentucky, 1996.

Hall, Prince, William White, R. Holt, Byrus Forbes, George Middleton, Peter Mantone, Primus Hall, et al. "Documents Relating to Negro Masonry in America." *Journal of Negro History* 21, no. 4 (1936): 411–32. https://doi.org/10.2307/2714334.

Hastings, Selina. *The Countess of Huntingdon's Connexion Hymn Book. Prepared by Authority of the Conference.* London: Knight, 1880.

Horsmanden, Daniel. *The New York Conspiracy, or A History of the Negro Plot, with the Journal Proceedings against the Conspirators at New York in the Years 1741–2.* New York: Southwick and Pelsue, 1810.

King, Boston. *Memoirs of the Life of Boston King, a Black Preacher, Written by Himself, during His Residence at Kingswood-School.* [1798.] In *"Face Zion Forward": First Writers of the Black Atlantic, 1785–1798,* edited by Joanna Brooks and John Saillant, 209–32. Boston: Northeastern University Press, 2002.

Leile, George. *An Account of Several Baptist Churches.* [1793.] In *Unchained Voices: An Anthology of Black Authors in the English-Speaking World of the Eighteenth Century,* edited by Vincent Carretta, 325–32. Lexington: University Press of Kentucky, 1996.

Marrant, John. *A Journal of the Rev. John Marrant, from August the 18th, 1785, to the 16th of March, 1790.* [1790.] In *"Face Zion Forward": First Writers of the Black Atlantic, 1785–1798*, edited by Joanna Brooks and John Saillant, 93–160. Boston: Northeastern University Press, 2002.

Marrant, John. *A Narrative of the Lord's Wonderful Dealings with John Marrant, a Black, (Now Going to Preach the Gospel in Nova-Scotia).* 4th ed. [1785.] In *"Face Zion Forward": First Writers of the Black Atlantic, 1785–1798*, edited by Joanna Brooks and John Saillant, 47–75. Boston: Northeastern University Press, 2002.

Marrant, John. *A Sermon Preached on the 24th Day of June 1789, Being the Festival of St. John the Baptist, at the Request of the Right Worshipful the Grand Master Prince Hall, and the Rest of the Brethren of the African Lodge of the Honorable Society of Free and Accepted Masons in Boston.* [1789.] In *"Face Zion Forward": First Writers of the Black Atlantic, 1785–1798*, edited by Joanna Brooks and John Saillant, 77–92. Boston: Northeastern University Press, 2002.

Turner, Nat. *The Confessions of Nat Turner.* [1831.] In *The Confessions of Nat Turner and Related Documents*, edited by Kenneth S. Greenberg, 37–58. Boston: Bedford, 1996.

SECONDARY SOURCES

Adega, Andrew Philips. "Secret Societies: Fraternities, Witches, Wizards, and Sorcerers." In *The Palgrave Handbook of African Traditional Religion*, edited by Ibigbolade S. Aderibigbe and Toyin Falola, 207–17. Cham: Palgrave Macmillan and Springer International, 2022.

Akrong, Abraham A. "African Traditional Religion and Christianity: Continuities and Discontinuities." In *Reclaiming the Human Sciences and the Humanities through African Perspectives*, edited by Helen Lauer and Kofi Anyidoho, 1:307–20. Accra: Sub-Saharan, 2012.

Albanese, Catherine L. *America: Religions and Religion.* 4th ed. Belmont, CA: Wadsworth, 2006.

Anderson, Carol A. *White Rage: The Unspoken Truth of Our Racial Divide.* New York: Bloomsbury, 2016.

Anderson, Robert Nelson. "The Quilombo of Palmares: A New Overview of a Maroon State in Seventeenth-Century Brazil." *Journal of Latin American Studies* 38, no. 3 (1996): 545–66.

Andrews, William L. *Sisters of the Spirit: Three Black Women's Autobiographies of the Nineteenth Century.* Bloomington: Indiana University Press, 1986.

Andrews, William L. *To Tell a Free Story: The First Century of Afro-American Autobiography, 1760–1865.* Urbana: University of Illinois Press, 1986.

Aptheker, Herbert. *American Negro Slave Revolts.* New York: International, 1963.

Armah, Ayi Kwei. *The Healers: An Historical Novel.* Nairobi: East African, 1978.

Baker, Margaret P. "The Rabbit as Trickster." *Journal of Popular Culture* 28, no. 2 (1994): 149–58.

Baraka, Amiri. *Blues People: Negro Music in White America.* New York: William Morrow, 1963.

Barrett, Leonard E. *Soul-Force: African Heritage in Afro-American Religion.* Garden City, NY: Anchor, 1974.

Bassard, Katherine Clay. *Transforming Scriptures: African American Women Writers and the Bible.* Athens: University of Georgia Press, 2010.

Beard, Rick, and Leslie Berlowitz. *Greenwich Village: Culture and Counterculture.* New Brunswick, NJ: Rutgers University Press, 1993.

Bell, Karen Cook. *Running from Bondage: Enslaved Women and the Remarkable Fight for Freedom in Revolutionary America.* Cambridge: Cambridge University Press, 2021.

Bennett, Herman L. "The Subject in the Plot: National Boundaries and the 'History' of the Black Atlantic." *African Studies Review* 43, no. 1 (2000): 101–24.

Bolster, W. Jeffrey. *Black Jacks: African American Seamen in the Age of Sail.* Cambridge, MA: Harvard University Press, 1998.

Breen, Louise A., ed. *Converging Worlds: Communities and Cultures in Colonial America.* New York: Routledge, 2012.

Brooks, Joanna. *American Lazarus: Religion and the Rise of African-American and Native American Literatures.* New York: Oxford University Press, 2003.

Brooks, Joanna. "Prince Hall, Freemasonry, and Genealogy." *African American Review* 34, no. 2 (2000): 197–216. https://doi.org/10.2307/2901249.

Brooks, Joanna, and John Saillant. *"Face Zion Forward": First Writers of the Black Atlantic, 1785–1798.* Boston: Northeastern University Press, 2002.

Brooks De Vita, Alexis. "Escaped Tricksters: Runaway Narratives as Trickster Tales." *Griot: Official Journal of the Southern Conference on Afro American Studies* 17 (1998): 1–10.

Brooks De Vita, Alexis. "Waking on the Road: Quests, Deities, and Tricksters in African American Storytelling." *Griot: Official Journal of the Southern Conference on Afro American Studies* 18 (1999): 50.

Brown, Ras Michael. *African-Atlantic Cultures and the South Carolina Lowcountry.* Cambridge: Cambridge University Press, 2012.

Brown, Ras Michael. "'Walk in the Feenda': West-Central Africans and the Forest in the South Carolina–Georgia Lowcountry." In *Central Africans and Cultural Transformations in the American Diaspora,* edited by Linda M. Heywood, 289–317. New York: Cambridge University Press, 2002.

Bullock, Steven C. *Revolutionary Brotherhood: Freemasonry and the Transformation of the American Social Order, 1730–1840.* Chapel Hill: University of North Carolina Press, 1996.

Burkett, Randall K. *Garveyism as a Religious Movement.* Metuchen, NJ: Scarecrow, 1978.

Carney, Judith Ann. *In the Shadow of Slavery: Africa's Botanical Legacy in the Atlantic World.* Berkeley: University of California Press, 2009.

Carretta, Vincent. *Equiano, the African: Biography of a Self-Made Man.* Athens: University of Georgia Press, 2005.

Carretta, Vincent. *Phillis Wheatley: Biography of a Genius in Bondage.* Athens: University of Georgia Press, 2011.

Carretta, Vincent, ed. *Unchained Voices: An Anthology of Black Authors in the English-Speaking World of the Eighteenth Century.* Expanded ed. Lexington: University Press of Kentucky, 2004.

Carretta, Vincent, and Ty M. Reese, eds. *The Life and Letters of Philip Quaque, the First African Anglican Missionary*. Athens: University of Georgia Press, 2010.

Carté, Katherine. *Religion and the American Revolution: An Imperial History*. Chapel Hill: University of North Carolina Press, 2021.

Chireau, Yvonne P. *Black Magic: Religion and the African American Conjuring Tradition*. Berkeley: University of California Press, 2003.

Christian, Barbara. "The Race for Theory." *Cultural Critique* 6 (1987): 51–63.

Clark-Pujara, Christy, *Dark Work: The Business of Slavery in Rhode Island*. New York: New York University Press, 2016.

Clifford, Alan C. *Atonement and Justification: Evangelical Theology 1640–1790: An Evaluation*. Oxford: Oxford University Press, 1990.

Clifford, Mary Louise. *From Slavery to Freetown: Black Loyalists after the American Revolution*. Jefferson, NC: McFarland, 1999.

Cody, Cheryll Ann. "There Was No 'Absalom' on the Ball Plantations: Slave-Naming Practices in the South Carolina Low Country, 1720–1865." *American Historical Review* 92, no. 3 (1987): 563–96. https://doi.org/10.2307/1869910.

Cone, James H. *Black Theology and Black Power*. New York: Seabury, 1969.

Creel, Margaret. *"A Peculiar People": Slave Religion and Community-Culture among the Gullahs*. New York: New York University Press, 1988.

Crook, Zeba A. *Reconceptualising Conversion: Patronage, Loyalty, and Conversion in the Religions of the Ancient Mediterranean*. Berlin: De Gruyter, 2004.

Deagan, Kathleen A., and Darcie A. Macmahon. *Fort Mose: Colonial America's Black Fortress of Freedom*. Gainesville: University Press of Florida, 1995.

DeLombard, Jeannine Marie. *In the Shadow of the Gallows: Race, Crime, and American Civic Identity*. Philadelphia: University of Pennsylvania Press, 2012.

DeLombard, Jeannine Marie. "Turning Back the Clock: Black Atlantic Literary Studies." *New England Quarterly* 75, no. 4 (2002): 647–55.

Dewulf, Jeroen. *The Pinkster King: The Forgotten History of America's Dutch-Owned Slaves*. Jackson: University Press of Mississippi, 2017.

Dillon, Elizabeth Maddock. "John Marrant Blows the French: Print, Performance, and the Making of Publics in Early African American Literature." In *Early African American Print Culture*, edited by Jordan Alexander Stein and Lara Langer Cohen, 318–39. Philadelphia: University of Pennsylvania Press, 2012.

Diouf, Sylviane. *Servants of Allah: African Muslims Enslaved in the Americas*. New York: New York University Press, 1998.

Dorsey, Peter A. *Sacred Estrangement: The Rhetoric of Conversion in Modern American Autobiography*. University Park: Pennsylvania State University Press, 1993.

Du Bois, W. E. B. *The Souls of Black Folk: Essays and Sketches*. Greenwich, CT: Fawcett, 1967.

Dundes, Alan. *Mother Wit from the Laughing Barrel: Readings in the Interpretation of Afro-American Folklore*. Jackson: University Press of Mississippi, 1990.

Eliade, Mircea. *The Sacred and the Profane: The Nature of Religion*. Translated by Willard R. Trask. New York: Harcourt Brace Jovanovich, 1987.

Evans, Curtis J. *The Burden of Black Religion*. New York: Oxford University Press, 2008.

Fatokun, Samson Adetunji. "The Concept of Expiatory Sacrifice in the Early Church and in African Indigenous Religious Traditions." In *African Traditions in the Study of Religion, Diaspora and Gendered Societies*, edited by Afe Adogame, Ezra Chitando, and Balaji Bateye, 71–81. Burlington, VT: Ashgate, 2012.

Fennell, Christopher C. *Crossroads and Cosmologies: Diasporas and Ethnogenesis in the New World*. Gainesville: University Press of Florida, 2010.

Fett, Sharla M. *Working Cures: Healing, Health, and Power on Southern Slave Plantations*. Chapel Hill: University of North Carolina Press, 2002.

Finn, Elizabeth A. *Pox Americana: The Great Smallpox Epidemic of 1775–82*. New York: Hill and Wang, 2001.

Foner, Philip Sheldon, and Robert J. Branham. *Lift Every Voice: African American Oratory, 1787–1900*. Tuscaloosa: University of Alabama Press, 1998.

Foote, Thelma Wills. *Black and White Manhattan: The History of Racial Formation in Colonial New York City*. Oxford: Oxford University Press, 2004.

Foote, Thelma Wills. "Crossroads or Settlement? The Black Freedmen's Community in Historic Greenwich Village, 1644–1855." In *Greenwich Village: Culture and Counterculture*, edited by Rick Beard and Leslie Berlowitz, 120–33. New Brunswick, NJ: Rutgers University Press, 1993.

Foster, Frances Smith. *Witnessing Slavery: The Development of Ante-Bellum Slave Narratives*. Westport, CT: Greenwood, 1979.

Fradkin, Arlene. "Cherokee Folk Zoology: The Animal World of a Native American People, 1700–1838." PhD diss., University of Florida, 1990.

Frey, Sylvia R. *Come Shouting to Zion: African American Protestantism in the American South and British Caribbean to 1830*. Chapel Hill: University of North Carolina Press, 1998.

Frey, Sylvia R. "The Visible Church: Historiography of African American Religion since Raboteau." *Slavery and Abolition* 29, no. 1 (2008): 83–110.

Fromont, Cécile. *The Art of Conversion: Christian Visual Culture in the Kingdom of Kongo*. Chapel Hill: University of North Carolina Press, 2014.

Garretson, Freeborn. "The Journal of Mr. Freeborn Garretson." *Arminian Magazine Consisting of Extracts and Original Treatises on Universal Redemption, Jan. 1778–Dec. 1797* 17, no. 10 (1794): 505–11.

Garrett, J. T. *Medicine of the Cherokee: The Way of Right Relationship*. Santa Fe, NM: Bear, 1996.

Gates, Henry Louis, Jr. *Figures in Black: Words, Signs, and the "Racial" Self*. New York: Oxford University Press, 1987.

Gates, Henry Louis, Jr. *The Signifying Monkey: A Theory of African-American Literary Criticism*. Oxford: Oxford University Press, 1989.

Gates, Henry Louis, Jr. *Tradition and the Black Atlantic: Critical Theory in the African Diaspora*. New York: BasicCivitas, 2010.

Gates, Henry Louis, Jr., and William L. Andrews, eds. *Pioneers of the Black Atlantic: Five Slave Narratives from the Enlightenment, 1772–1815*. Washington, DC: Civitas, 1998.

Gayle, Addison. *The Black Aesthetic*. Garden City, NY: Doubleday, 1971.

Gerbner, Katherine. *Christian Slavery: Conversion and Race in the Protestant Atlantic World*. Philadelphia: University of Pennsylvania Press, 2018.

Gilbert, Alan. *Black Patriots and Loyalists: Fighting for Emancipation in the War for Independence*. Chicago: University of Chicago Press, 2012.

Glaude, Eddie S., Jr. *Exodus! Religion, Race, and Nation in Early Nineteenth-Century Black America*. Chicago: University of Chicago Press, 2000.

Gomez, Michael A. *Black Crescent: The Experience and Legacy of African Muslims in the Americas*. Cambridge: Cambridge University Press, 2005.

Gomez, Michael A. *Exchanging Our Country Marks: The Transformation of African Identities in the Colonial and Antebellum South*. Chapel Hill: University of North Carolina Press, 1998.

Gomez, Michael A. *Reversing Sail: A History of the African Diaspora*. Cambridge: Cambridge University Press, 2005.

Gomez, Pablo. *The Experiential Caribbean: Creating Knowledge and Healing in the Early Modern Atlantic*. Chapel Hill: University of North Carolina Press, 2017.

Gould, Philip. "Free Carpenter, Venture Capitalist: Reading the Lives of the Early Black Atlantic." *American Literary History* 12, no. 4 (2000): 659–84.

Greenberg, Kenneth S. "The Confessions of Nat Turner: Text and Context." In *The Confessions of Nat Turner and Related Documents*, edited by Kenneth S. Greenberg, 1–36. Boston: Bedford, 1996.

Greene, Lorenzo J. (Lorenzo Johnston). *The Negro in Colonial New England*. New York: Atheneum, 1968.

Greenidge, Kerri. *Boston's Abolitionists*. Beverly, MA: Commonwealth, 2006.

Griaule, Marcel. *Conversations with Ogotemmêli: An Introduction to Dogon Religious Ideas*. New York: Oxford University Press for International African Institute, 1970.

Haliburton, Rudia. *Red over Black: Black Slavery among the Cherokee Indians*. Westport, CT: Greenwood, 1977.

Harding, Alan. *The Countess of Huntingdon's Connexion*. Oxford: Oxford University Press, 2003.

Harris, Leslie M. *In the Shadow of Slavery: African Americans in New York City, 1626–1863*. Chicago: University of Chicago Press, 2003.

Harrison, Paul Carter. *The Drama of Nommo*. New York: Grove, 1972.

Harrison, Paul Carter, Victor Leo Walker II, and Gus Edwards, eds. *Black Theatre: Ritual Performance in the African Diaspora*. Philadelphia: Temple University Press, 2002.

Harvey, Marcus. "'Life Is War': African Grammars of Knowing and the Interpretation of Black Religious Experience." PhD diss., Emory University, 2012.

Hewatt, Alexander. *An Historical Account of the Rise and Progress of the Colonies of South Carolina and Georgia*. London: Printed for A. Donaldson, 1779.

Hinks, Peter P. *To Awaken My Afflicted Brethren: David Walker and the Problem of Antebellum Slave Resistance*. University Park: Pennsylvania State University Press, 1997.

Hinks, Peter P., and Stephen Kantrowitz, eds. *All Men Free and Brethren: Essays on the History of African American Freemasonry*. Ithaca, NY: Cornell University Press, 2013.

Hodges, Graham Russell. *Root and Branch: African Americans in New York and East Jersey, 1613–1863*. Chapel Hill: University of North Carolina Press, 1999.

Holden, Vanessa M. *Surviving Southampton: African American Women and Resistance in Nat Turner's Community*. Urbana: University of Illinois Press, 2021.

Holmes, Barbara A. *Joy Unspeakable: Contemplative Practices of the Black Church*. Minneapolis: Fortress, 2004.

Horton, James Oliver, and Lois E. Horton. *Black Bostonians: Family Life and Community Struggle in the Antebellum North*. Rev. ed. New York: Holmes and Meier, 1999.

Horton, James Oliver, and Lois E. Horton. *In Hope of Liberty: Culture, Community and Protest among Northern Free Blacks, 1700–1860*. New York: Oxford University Press, 1997.

Howard-Pitney, David. *The African American Jeremiad: Appeals for Justice in America*. Philadelphia: Temple University Press, 2005.

Hucks, Tracey E. *Yoruba Traditions and African American Religious Nationalism*. Albuquerque: University of New Mexico Press, 2012.

Hunter, Christopher. "The African American Church House: A Phenomenological Inquiry of an Afrocentric Sacred Space." *Religions* 13, no. 3 (2022): 246. https://doi.org/10.3390/rel13030246.

Hurston, Zora Neale. *Mules and Men*. New York: Perennial, 1990.

Hurston, Zora Neale. *The Sanctified Church: The Folklore Writings of Zora Neale Hurston*. Berkeley, CA: Turtle Island Foundation, 1981.

Husserl, Edmund. *Cartesian Meditations: An Introduction to Phenomenology*. Translated by Dorion Cairns. The Hague: M. Nijhoff, 1960.

Hyde, Lewis. *Trickster Makes This World: Mischief, Myth, and Art*. New York: Farrar, Straus and Giroux, 1999.

Inscoe, John C. "Carolina Slave Names: An Index to Acculturation." *Journal of Southern History* 49, no. 4 (1983): 527–54. https://doi.org/10.2307/2208675.

Ipsen, Pernille. *Daughters of the Trade*. Philadelphia: University of Pennsylvania Press, 2015.

Jacobs, Donald M., ed. *Courage and Conscience: Black and White Abolitionists in Boston*. Bloomington: Indiana University Press, 1993.

James, C. L. R. *The Black Jacobins: Toussaint L'Ouverture and the San Domingo Revolution*. 2nd ed. New York: Vintage, 1963.

Jennison, Watson W. *Cultivating Race: The Expansion of Slavery in Georgia, 1750–1860*. Lexington: University Press of Kentucky, 2012.

Johnson, Alonzo. "'Pray's House Spirit': The Institutional Structure and Spiritual Core of an African American Folk Tradition." In *"Ain't Gonna Lay My 'ligion Down": African American Religion in the South*, edited by Alonzo Johnson and Paul Jersild, 8–38. Columbia: University of South Carolina Press, 1999.

Johnson, Clifton H. *God Struck Me Dead: Religious Conversion Experiences and Autobiographies of Ex-Slaves*. Philadelphia: Pilgrim, 1969.

Johnson, Michael. "Denmark Vesey and His Co-Conspirators." *William and Mary Quarterly* 58, no. 4 (2021): 915–76.

Johnson, Sylvester A. *The Myth of Ham in Nineteenth-Century American Christianity: Race, Heathens, and the People of God*. New York: Palgrave Macmillan, 2004.

Jordan, Winthrop D. *White over Black: American Attitudes toward the Negro, 1550–1812*. Chapel Hill: University of North Carolina Press, 1968.

Kidwell, Clara Sue. "What Would Pocahontas Think Now? Women and Cultural Persistence." *Callaloo* 17, no. 1 (1994): 149–59.

Koger, Larry. *Black Slaveowners: Free Black Slave Masters in South Carolina, 1790–1860.* Columbia: University of South Carolina Press, 1995.

Kuyk, Betty M. *African Voices in the African American Heritage.* Bloomington: Indiana University Press, 2003.

Laderman, Gary. *The Sacred Remains: American Attitudes toward Death, 1799–1883.* New Haven, CT: Yale University Press, 1996.

Landers, Jane. *Black Society in Spanish Florida.* Champaign: University of Illinois Press, 1999.

Landers, Jane. "Traditions of African American Freedom and Community in Spanish Colonial Florida." In *The African American Heritage of Florida,* edited by David R. Colburn and Jane Landers, 17–41. Gainesville: University Press of Florida, 1995.

Langley, April C. E. *The Black Aesthetic Unbound: Theorizing the Dilemma of Eighteenth-Century African American Literature.* Columbus: Ohio State University Press, 2008.

Leslie, Ruth A. "Brer Rabbit, a Play of the Human Spirit: Recreating Black Culture through Brer Rabbit Stories." *International Journal of Sociology and Social Policy* 17, no. 6 (1997): 59–83. https://doi.org/10.1108/eb013312.

Levine, Lawrence W. *Black Culture and Black Consciousness: Afro-American Folk Thought from Slavery to Freedom.* Oxford: Oxford University Press, 1978.

Littlefield, Daniel F. *Africans and Creeks: From the Colonial Period to the Civil War.* Westport, CT: Greenwood, 1979.

Lockley, Tim. "David Margrett: A Black Missionary in the Revolutionary Atlantic." *Journal of American Studies* 46, no. 3 (2012): 729–45.

Long, Charles H. "African American Religion in the United States of America: An Interpretative Essay." *Nova Religio* 7, no. 1 (2003): 11–27.

Long, Charles H. *Alpha: The Myths of Creation.* New York: George Braziller, 1963.

Long, Charles H. *Significations: Signs, Symbols, and Images in the Interpretation of Religion.* 2nd ed. Aurora, CO: Davies, 1999.

Lovejoy, Paul E., and David Vincent Trotman. *Trans-Atlantic Dimensions of Ethnicity in the African Diaspora.* London: Continuum, 2003.

Lowther, Kevin. *The African American Odyssey of John Kizell: A South Carolina Slave Returns to Fight the Slave Trade in His African Homeland.* Columbia: University of South Carolina Press, 2011.

Luna, Kathryn M. "Sounding the African Atlantic." *William and Mary Quarterly* 78, no. 4 (2021): 581–616.

Magesa, Laurenti. *African Religion: The Moral Traditions of Abundant Life.* Maryknoll, NY: Orbis, 1997.

Malone, Henry Thompson. "Cherokee Civilization in the Lower Appalachians, Especially in North Georgia, before 1830." MA thesis, Emory University, 1949.

Matory, J. Lorand. *Black Atlantic Religion: Tradition, Transnationalism, and Matriarchy in the Afro-Brazilian Candomble.* Princeton, NJ: Princeton University Press, 2005.

Matthews, Donald H. *Honoring the Ancestors: An African Cultural Interpretation of Black Religion and Literature.* New York: Oxford University Press, 1998.

May, Cedrick. *Evangelism and Resistance in the Black Atlantic, 1760–1835.* Athens: University of Georgia Press, 2008.

Mays, Benjamin E. *The Negro's God: As Reflected in His Literature*. Boston: Chapman and Grimes, 1938.

M'Baye, Babacar. *The Trickster Comes West: Pan-African Influence in Early Black Diasporan Narratives*. Jackson: University Press of Mississippi, 2009.

McLoughlin, William Gerald. *The Cherokees and Christianity, 1794–1870: Essays on Acculturation and Cultural Persistence*. Athens: University of Georgia Press, 1994.

Merleau-Ponty, Maurice. *The Visible and the Invisible*. Evanston, IL: Northwestern University Press, 1968.

Miles, Tiya A. "'His Kingdom for a Kiss': Indians and Intimacy in the Narrative of John Marrant." In *Haunted by Empire: Race and Colonial Intimacies in North American History*, edited by Ann Laura Stoler, 163–88. Durham, NC: Duke University Press, 2006.

Miles, Tiya A. *Ties That Bind: The Story of an Afro-Cherokee Family in Slavery and Freedom*. 2nd ed. Berkeley: University of California Press, 2015.

Mitchem, Stephanie. *African American Folk Healing*. New York: New York University Press, 2007.

Montgomery, Benilde. "Recapturing John Marrant." In *A Mixed Race Ethnicity in Early America*, edited by Frank Shuffelton, 105–15. New York: Oxford University Press, 1993.

Moody, Joycelyn. *Sentimental Confessions: Spiritual Narratives of Nineteenth-Century Black Women*. Athens: University of Georgia Press, 2001.

Mooney, James. *Myths of the Cherokee and Sacred Formulas of the Cherokees*. Nashville, TN: Charles and Randy Elder, Booksellers, 1982.

Mooney, James. *The Sacred Formulas of the Cherokees*. Nashville, TN: Charles and Randy Elder, Booksellers, 1982.

Morgan, Jennifer L. *Reckoning with Slavery: Gender, Kinship, and Capitalism in Early Modern America*. Durham, NC: Duke University Press, 2021.

Morgan, Philip D. *Slave Counterpoint: Black Culture in the Eighteenth-Century Chesapeake and Lowcountry*. Chapel Hill: University of North Carolina Press, 1998.

Moses, Wilson J. *Black Messiahs and Uncle Toms: Social and Literary Manipulations of a Religious Myth*. University Park: Pennsylvania State University Press, 1982.

Moses, Wilson J., ed. *Classical Black Nationalism: From the American Revolution to Marcus Garvey*. New York: New York University Press, 1996.

Mullin, Michael. *Africa in America: Slave Acculturation and Resistance in the American South and the British Caribbean, 1736–1831*. Champaign: University of Illinois Press, 1995.

Mustakeem, Sowande. *Slavery at Sea: Terror, Sex, and Sickness in the Middle Passage*. Urbana: University of Illinois Press, 2016.

Myers, Amrita Chakrabarti. *Forging Freedom: Black Women and the Pursuit of Liberty in Antebellum Charleston*. Chapel Hill: University of North Carolina Press, 2011.

Nash, Gary B. *Forging Freedom: The Formation of Philadelphia's Black Community, 1720–1840*. Cambridge, MA: Harvard University Press, 1991.

Nash, Gary B. *The Forgotten Fifth: African Americans in the Age of Revolution*. Cambridge, MA: Harvard University Press, 2006.

New, Alfred Henry. *The Coronet and the Cross, or Memorials of the Right Honorable Selina, Countess of Huntingdon*. London: Partridge, 1858.

Nock, A. D. *Conversion: The Old and the New in Religion from Alexander the Great to Augustine of Hippo.* Baltimore: Johns Hopkins University Press, 1998.

Noel, James A. *Black Religion and the Imagination of Matter in the Atlantic World.* New York: Palgrave Macmillan, 2009.

Nora, Pierre. "Between Memory and History: Les Lieux de Memoire." In *History and Memory in African American Culture,* edited by Genevieve Fabre and Robert O'Meally, 284–300. New York: Oxford University Press, 1994.

Painter, Nell Irvin. *Sojourner Truth: A Life, a Symbol.* New York: W. W. Norton, 1996.

Parsons, Elsie Clews. "Folk-Lore of the Cherokee of Robeson County, North Carolina." *Journal of American Folklore* 32, no. 125 (1919): 384–93.

Patterson, Tiffany Ruby, and Robin D. G. Kelley. "Unfinished Migrations: Reflections on the African Diaspora and the Making of the Modern World." *African Studies Review* 43, no. 1 (2000): 11–45.

Perry, Seth. *Bible Culture and Authority in the Early United States.* Princeton, NJ: Princeton University Press, 2018.

Pierce, Yolanda. *Hell without Fires: Slavery, Christianity, and the Antebellum Slave Narrative.* Gainesville: University Press of Florida, 2005.

Piersen, William Dillon. *Black Yankees: The Development of an Afro-American Subculture in Eighteenth-Century New England.* Amherst: University of Massachusetts Press, 1988.

Porter, Joy. *Native American Freemasonry: Associationalism and Performance in America.* Lincoln: University of Nebraska Press, 2011.

Potkay, Adam, and Sandra Burr. "About John Marrant." In *Black Atlantic Writers of the Eighteenth Century: Living the New Exodus in England and the Americas,* edited by Adam Potkay and Sandra Burr, 67–74. New York: St. Martin's, 1995.

Pressly, Paul M. *On the Rim of the Caribbean: Colonial Georgia and the British Atlantic World.* Athens: University of Georgia Press, 2013.

Pulis, John W. *Moving On: Black Loyalists in the Afro-Atlantic World.* New York: Garland, 1999.

Quarles, Benjamin. *Black Abolitionists.* New York: Oxford University Press, 1969.

Quarles, Benjamin. *The Negro in the Making of America.* New York: Collier, 1969.

Raboteau, Albert J. *Slave Religion: The "Invisible Institution" in the Antebellum South.* New York: Oxford University Press, 2004.

Rael, Patrick. *Black Identity and Black Protest in the Antebellum North.* Chapel Hill: University of North Carolina Press, 2001.

Rawlyk, George A. *Ravished by the Spirit: Religious Revivals, Baptists, and Henry Alline.* Kingston: McGill–Queen's University Press, 1984.

Ray, Benjamin C. *African Religions: Symbol, Ritual, and Community.* Englewood Cliffs, NJ: Prentice Hall, 1976.

Rezek, Joseph. "Early Black Evangelical Writing and the Radical Limitations of Print." In *African American Literature in Transition, 1750–1800,* edited by Rhondda Thomas, 17–41. Cambridge: Cambridge University Press, 2022.

Richards, Phillip M. "Nationalist Themes in the Preaching of Jupiter Hammon." *Early American Literature* 25, no. 2 (1990): 123–38.

Roberts, John W. "African American Belief Narratives and the African Cultural Tradition." *Research in African Literatures* 40, no. 1 (2009): 112–26.

Roberts, John W. *From Trickster to Badman: The Black Folk Hero in Slavery and Freedom.* Philadelphia: University of Pennsylvania Press, 1990.

Roberts, Rita. *Evangelicalism and the Politics of Reform in Northern Black Thought, 1776–1863.* Baton Rouge: Louisiana State University Press, 2011.

Rucker, Walter. "Conjure, Magic, and Power: The Influence of Afro-Atlantic Religious Practices on Slave Resistance and Rebellion." *Journal of Black Studies* 32, no. 1 (2001): 84–103.

Rucker, Walter C. *Gold Coast Diasporas: Identity, Culture, and Power.* Bloomington: Indiana University Press, 2015.

Ruth Leslie, Annie. "Brer Rabbit, a Play of the Human Spirit: Recreating Black Culture through Brer Rabbit Stories." *International Journal of Sociology and Social Policy* 17, no. 6 (1997): 59–83. https://doi.org/10.1108/eb013312.

Saillant, John. "'Wipe Away All Tears from Their Eyes': John Marrant's Theology in the Black Atlantic, 1785–1808." *Journal of Millennial Studies* 1, no. 2 (Winter 1999): 18–41.

Schama, Simon. *Rough Crossings: Britain, the Slaves and the American Revolution.* London: BBC, 2005.

Schlenther, Boyd Stanley. *Queen of the Methodists: The Countess of Huntingdon and the Eighteenth-Century Crisis of Faith and Society.* Durham, UK: Durham Academic, 1997.

Sell, Alan P. F. *The Great Debate: Calvinism, Arminianism, and Salvation.* Grand Rapids, MI: Baker, 1983.

Sensbach, Jon F. *Rebecca's Revival: Creating Black Christianity in the Atlantic World.* Cambridge, MA: Harvard University Press, 2006.

Sesay, Chernoh M., Jr. "Emancipation and the Social Origins of Black Freemasonry, 1775–1800." In *All Men Free and Brethren: Essays on the History of African American Freemasonry*, edited by Peter P. Hinks and Stephen Kantrowitz, 21–39. Ithaca, NY: Cornell University Press, 2013.

Sesay, Chernoh M., Jr. "The Revolutionary Black Roots of Slavery's Abolition in Massachusetts." *New England Quarterly* 87, no. 1 (2014): 99–131.

Seymour, Aaron Crossley Hobart. *The Life and Times of Selina, Countess of Huntingdon.* Naples, 1859.

Shamala, Lucas Nandih. "Approaches to Peacemaking in Africa: *Obuntu* Perspectives from Western Kenya." In *African Traditions in the Study of Religion, Diaspora and Gendered Societies*, edited by Afe Adogame, Ezra Chitando, and Balaji Bateye, 13–24. Burlington, VT: Ashgate, 2012.

Shannon, David T., Sr., Julia Frazier White, and Deborah Van Broekhoven. *George Liele's Life and Legacy: An Unsung Hero.* Macon, GA: Mercer University Press, 2013.

Sidbury, James. *Becoming African in America: Race and Nation in the Early Black Atlantic.* Oxford: Oxford University Press, 2007.

Sidbury, James. "Plausible Stories and Varnished Truths." *William and Mary Quarterly* 58, no. 1 (2022): 179–84.

Smallwood, Stephanie E. *Saltwater Slavery: A Middle Passage from Africa to American Diaspora.* Cambridge, MA: Harvard University Press, 2008.

Smiley, Portia. "Folk-Lore from Virginia, South Carolina, Georgia, Alabama, and Florida." *Journal of American Folklore* 32, no. 125 (1919): 357–83.

Smith, Theophus H. *Conjuring Culture: Biblical Formations of Black America*. Facsimile. New York: Oxford University Press, 1994.

Sobel, Mechal. *Trabelin' On: The Slave Journey to an Afro-Baptist Faith*. Westport, CT: Greenwood, 1979.

Soyinka, Wole. *Myth, Literature and the African World*. Cambridge: Cambridge University Press, 1976.

Stein, Jordan Alexander, and Lara Langer Cohen, eds. *Early African American Print Culture*. Philadelphia: University of Pennsylvania Press, 2012.

Stewart, Dianne M. *Three Eyes for the Journey: African Dimensions of the Jamaican Religious Experience*. New York: Oxford University Press, 2005.

Stuckey, Sterling. *Slave Culture: Nationalist Theory and the Foundations of Black America*. New York: Oxford University Press, 1988.

Summers, Martin. "'Arguing for Our Race': The Politics of Non-Recognition and the Public Nature of the Black Masonic Archive." In *All Men Free and Brethren: Essays on the History of African American Freemasonry*, edited by Peter P. Hinks, 155–74. Ithaca, NY: Cornell University Press, 2013.

Sweet, James H. *Domingos Alvares, African Healing, and the Intellectual History of the Atlantic World*. Chapel Hill: University of North Carolina Press, 2011.

Sweet, James H. *Recreating Africa: Culture, Kinship, and Religion in the African-Portuguese World, 1441–1770*. Chapel Hill: University of North Carolina Press, 2003.

Thompson, Robert Farris. *Flash of the Spirit: African and Afro-American Art and Philosophy*. New York: Vintage, 1984.

Thornton, John K. *The Kongolese Saint Anthony: Dona Beatriz Kimpa Vita and the Antonian Movement, 1684–1706*. New York: Cambridge University Press, 1998.

Turner, Richard Brent. *Islam in the African-American Experience*. 2nd ed. Bloomington: Indiana University Press, 2003.

Turner, Sasha. "The Nameless and the Forgotten: Maternal Grief, Sacred Protection, and the Archive of Slavery." *Slavery and Abolition* 38, no. 2 (2017): 232–50.

Turner, Victor Witter. *The Forest of Symbols: Aspects of Ndembu Ritual*. Ithaca, NY: Cornell University Press, 1967.

Tyson, John R. *In the Midst of Early Methodism: Lady Huntingdon and Her Correspondence*. Lanham, MD: Scarecrow, 2006.

Tytler, Sarah. *The Countess of Huntingdon and Her Circle*. London: I. Pitman, 1907.

Vest, Jay Hansford C. "From Bobtail to Brer Rabbit: Native American Influences on Uncle Remus." *American Indian Quarterly* 24, no. 1 (2000): 19–43.

Von Frank, Albert J. *The Trials of Anthony Burns: Freedom and Slavery in Emerson's Boston*. Cambridge, MA: Harvard University Press, 1998.

Walker, Corey D. B. *A Noble Fight: African American Freemasonry and the Struggle for Democracy in America*. Champaign: University of Illinois Press, 2008.

Walker, James W. St. G. *The Black Loyalists: The Search for a Promised Land in Nova Scotia and Sierra Leone, 1783–1870*. London: Longman, 1976.

Walker, Sheila. *Ceremonial Spirit Possession in Africa and Afro-America: Forms, Meanings, and Functional Significance for Individuals and Social Groups*. Leiden: Brill, 1972.

Walkes, Joseph A., Jr. *Black Square and Compass: 200 Years of Prince Hall Freemasonry*. Richmond, VA: Macoy Publishers and Masonic Supply Company, 1994.

Wallace, Maurice. "'Are We Men?': Prince Hall, Martin Delany, and the Masculine Ideal in Black Freemasonry, 1775–1865." *American Literary History* 9, no. 3 (1997): 396–424.

Warner-Lewis, Maureen. *Central Africa in the Caribbean: Transcending Time, Transforming Cultures.* Kingston: University of West Indies Press, 2003.

Welch, Edwin. *Spiritual Pilgrim: A Reassessment of the Life of the Countess of Huntingdon.* Cardiff: University of Wales Press, 1995.

Wells-Oghoghomeh, Alexis. *The Souls of Womenfolk: The Religious Cultures of Enslaved Women in the Lower South.* Chapel Hill: University of North Carolina Press, 2021.

White, Shane. *Somewhat More Independent: The End of Slavery in New York City, 1770–1810.* Athens: University of Georgia Press, 2004.

Whitehead, Ruth. *Black Loyalists: Southern Settlers of Nova Scotia's First Free Black Communities.* Halifax: Nimbus, 2013.

Whiting, Gloria McCahon. "Emancipation without the Courts or Constitution: The Case of Revolutionary Massachusetts." *Slavery and Abolition* 41, no. 3 (2020): 458–78. https://doi.org/10.1080/0144039x.2019.1693484.

Whytock, Jack C. "The Huntingdonian Mission to Nova Scotia, 1782–1791: A Study in Calvinistic Methodism." *Historical Papers: Canadian Society of Church History* (2003): 149–70. https://doi.org/10.25071/0848-1563.39292.

Wilder, Craig Steven. *In the Company of Black Men: The African Influence on African American Culture in New York City.* New York: New York University Press, 2001.

Wilson, Ellen Gibson. *The Loyal Blacks.* New York: Capricorn, 1976.

Wimbush, Vincent L. *White Men's Magic: Scripturalization as Slavery.* New York: Oxford University Press, 2012.

Winch, Julie. *Philadelphia's Black Elite: Activism, Accommodation, and the Struggle for Autonomy, 1787–1848.* Philadelphia: Temple University Press, 1993.

Womack, Craig. "Baptists and Witches: Multiple Jurisdictions in a Muskogee Creek Story." *Southern Spaces,* July 17, 2007. http://southernspaces.org/2007/baptists-and-witches-multiple-jurisdictions-muskogee-creek-story.

Wood, Peter H. *Black Majority: Negroes in Colonial South Carolina from 1670 through the Stono Rebellion.* New York: W. W. Norton, 1975.

Young, Jason R. *Rituals of Resistance: African Atlantic Religion in Kongo and the Lowcountry South in the Era of Slavery.* Baton Rouge: Louisiana State University Press, 2011.

Young, Josiah Ulysses, III. "Dogged Strength within the Veil: African-American Spirituality as a Literary Tradition." *Journal of Religious Thought* 55–56 (1999): 87–107.

Young, Josiah Ulysses, III. *Pan-African Theology: Providence and the Legacies of the Ancestors.* Trenton, NJ: Africa World Press, 1992.

Ywahoo, Dhyani. *Voices of Our Ancestors: Cherokee Teachings from the Wisdom Fire.* Boston: Shambhala, 1987.

Zellar, Gary. *African Creeks: Estelvste and the Creek Nation.* Norman: University of Oklahoma Press, 2007.

Index

Clarkson, John, 143–45
Clay, Henry, 137
clothing, as symbolic of transformation, 55, 128
collective consciousness, Black, 5–6, 153n2
colonial Black religion, 13–34
Colored Methodist Society (Detroit), 138
communal values, Africana, 7, 42, 106–7, 164n41
communities, Black, 4, 8, 164n41; autonomy of, 11,
    15–16, 23–35, 87–88; conjure as operative framework
    in, 4; covenanted community, 140–41, 144; in
    between Indigenous people and white settlers, 24,
    45; Manhattan land grant, 24; mother-daughter
    relationship, 117; norms drawn from African Amer-
    ican mythic characters, 84; runaway communities,
    24–25; self-government, 18; spiritual and healing
    events in, 106–107. See also Fort Mose settlement
    (St. Augustine); Freemasonry, African American;
    Nova Scotia; Yamacraw neighborhood (Savannah)
community, reintegration into, 9, 36, 54–58, 64, 107,
    118, 164n43
Confessions of Nat Turner, The, 66–68, 158n9
conjure: of Africana initiatory rites, 47–48; of Africana
    nature spirits, 111; as agent of divine retribution, 62;
    Bible as conjure book, 4; of biblical genealogies,
    11, 120; of biblical narrative forms, 7, 41, 43, 52, 62,
    111–12, 148; of blood imagery, 110; centrality of in
    Marrant's texts, 5; disavowed by Black Christians,
    10, 62, 69; in early American religion, 53; of Exodus
    narrative, 62–64, 66, 70, 77, 81; and Freemasonry,
    7–8, 11–12; of High John narratives, 84–85; and
    literacy, 54, 57; Marrant's use of to denounce
    slavery, 10; mimetic principle, 6; Moses portrayed
    as conjure man, 62; pharmakon, variants of, 7–8;
    poison associated with, 75; rhetorical structure of
    narratives, 136–37; of ritual death and resurrection,
    52–53; as rituals of race, 7–8; and shout ritual, 89;
    suffering in narratives of, 69–70, 136; as theoretical
    lens, 148; used to interpret Marrant's texts, 10–12;
    witchcraft associated with by Europeans, 4, 10. See
    also Africana religious cultures; retaliation; West
    and West Central African religion and culture
Conjuring Culture: Biblical Formations of Black Amer-
    ica (Smith), 4
contemplative practice, 42, 58
conversion, rubric of, 59
Countess of Huntingdon. See Hastings, Selina
courage, 48
covenant, 9, 58–59
covenanted community, 140–41, 144
Covey, Edward, 69
creation myths, 129–30, 170n43, 172n88
Creek Indians, 3
Creek Nation, 46
Cushing, William, 122
cyclical nature of spiritual seasons, 42
Cyprian, 134

death: in biblical narratives, 49, 52–53, 63; fearlessness
    in face of, 47–48; representations of in earliest Black
    literary narratives, 48–49; ritual, in West and West
    Central Africa, 47–48; spirit possession as signifier
    of, 37; symbolic, 37, 42, 47–48
Declaration of Independence, 139
democracy, Birchtown settlement as experiment in,
    86–87
Diouf, Sylviane, 90, 91
disintegration-rejuvenation-reintegration pattern, 118
displacement, colonial, 3
Dogon cosmology, 130, 132–33
Douglass, Frederick, 10, 62, 69–70, 153n4
"drinking fetish," 74
drumming, 16, 37, 91
Du Bois, W. E. B., 162n21
Dunmore and Clinton proclamations, 104
Dutch Reformed Church, 17–18, 21, 23
Dutch settlers, 17–21
Dutch West India Company, 17, 24
Dutty, Boukman, 68

Earl, James, 118
Election Day celebrations, 18, 125–26, 127
Eliade, Mircea, 172n88
enslavement/slavery: biblical imagery used to con-
    demn, 4, 71–72; Black slavery among Cherokee,
    51–52; in Boston, 121; Catholic liberation of
    converts, 17; charter generation of enslaved people
    in New York, 20–21, 23–24; children kidnapped
    to lure mothers into, 117, 167n126; end of in Mas-
    sachusetts, 122, 169n11; in Exodus narrative, 10, 61,
    71–72, 139; freedom routes to Florida, 32; fugitives,
    32–33; as irreconcilable with Christian faith for
    African people, 70; Israelites associated with, 139;
    kidnapping of children, 48–49; New York imports
    of enslaved people, 16–17; in Nova Scotia, de facto,
    104; and sexual violence against women, 104
Equiano, Olaudah, 9, 48–49, 57, 82, 157n42, 161n57
Estelvste (Afro refugees among the Creek Indians), 46
ethnogenesis, racial, 11, 120
evangelicalism, 121, 149–50; Black, 8, 79, 87, 118, 144.
    See also Huntingdon Connexion; revivalism
Exodus narrative, 61–84; biblical versions of, 63–64;
    blood in, 63, 65, 110; call to prophecy in, 38–39,
    53; conjure of, 62–64, 66, 70, 77, 81; in Hurston's
    Moses, 61–62; in Margrett's retaliatory sermons,
    71–72; Marrant's interpretation of, 62–66; Moses,
    and bodies of water, 81–83; as pattern for retaliation
    narratives, 70–71; Red Sea crossing, 63, 71, 77, 81,
    82–83; slavery in, 10, 61, 71–72, 139; wilderness in, 1,
    5, 10, 38, 41, 43, 46, 62–63, 66, 112. See also biblical
    narratives; blood; retaliation; wilderness

"Face Zion Forward" (Brooks and Saillant), 3
Fairbank, Calvin, 137

Falconbridge, Alexander, 104

family, 7; rejection by linked with prophetic identity, 39–40, 57; and resurrection narrative, 57; West African preslavery customs, 145

fasting, 38

Fatokun, Samson, 67

feenda (forest), 41

Fifty-Fourth Massachusetts Regiment, 138

First African Baptist (Savannah, Georgia), 1

Florida, 9, 30–32; contested by Spanish and British Empires, 30–31; free Black societies permitted in, 31; St. Augustine, 2, 9, 14–15, 30–32

folklore, African American: Brer Rabbit, 89, 163n22; High John the Conqueror, 83–84

Foote, Thelma, 27, 153n6, 154n31

Fort George, 28

Fort Mose settlement (St. Augustine), 9, 15, 31, 32

Fortuyn (Dutch vessel), 26

Foster, Frances Smith, 6

free Blacks: family stability prioritized, 25; fear of enslavement, 76; in Florida, 31; impressment into military service, 76; in New York, 25–30; slave narratives written by, 6; widows, 30. *See also* Black Loyalists; Nova Scotia

freedom: beliefs of Black Freemasons, 122; found more in the south than north, 32; and "the jubilation period of ancient ritual," 6

Freedom's Journal (newspaper), 136

Freeman, Elizabeth "Mum Bett," 122

Freemasonry: Ancient and Accepted Order of Freemasons, 124; and biblical mythic history, 129; British forms of European, 120; and conjure, 7–8; English Modern Lodge, 125; European, 120, 126–127; Grand Lodge of Massachusetts, 125, 138; Irish, 124–25; Israelites associated with, 139; as holding society together, 120; and national politics, 138; racism within, 128–29, 135; rituals of race, 128–29; symbolic degrees, 139; Temple of Solomon in, 130–31, 140; universality of, 129, 135; West African initiation societies, similarities to, 11, 120; on west coast of Africa, 126–27; "Wisdom, Strength, Beauty" motto, 139

Freemasonry, African American, 2, 7–8, 11; in 1730s New York, 126; and abolition, 122; biblical lineage, 130, 132, 138–39, 170–71n56; and Black masculinity, 128, 131–32; and Cain's lineage, 130, 132, 170–71n56; at end of nineteenth century, 139; founding of Free Lodge, 122; Genesis as source of Masonic ancestors, 129–30; and masculine identity, 120, 131–32; militant, 137–39; official histories, 124–25; oration, tradition of, 7, 120, 128–33; passage from racial logic to community, 140; Pinkster and Election Day performances replaced by, 125–26; Prince Hall, 126, 128–29, 136; and racial prohibitions, 125, 128–29, 132, 172n81; Saint John the Baptist celebration, 2, 11, 120, 127–28, 133, 134; supranational citizenship,

135; temporal and geographic origins of, 11, 120, 127; work aesthetic of, 131–32. *See also* African Lodge of Free and Accepted Masons (Boston)

Freetown. *See* Sierra Leone

Furmage, William, 88, 162n15

Galphin, George, 1

Garretson, Freeborn, 99, 101–3, 107

genealogies, biblical, 11, 120, 129, 138–39

George, David, 11, 87, 144, 147; communal response to frostbite incident, 106; prevented from holding camp meetings, 91; white rage against, 96–97, 99, 145

Georgia: headright system, 32–33; planter emigres in colonial government, 33; poisoning legislation, 75; Savannah, 1, 9, 14–15, 32–34; slavery in, 2, 32–33

Gomez, Michael, 24

Gracia Real de Santa Teresa de Mose. *See* Fort Mose settlement (St. Augustine)

Gray, Thomas, 66, 158n9

Greenberg, Kenneth, 158n9

Griaule, Marcel, 130, 132–33

Gronniosaw, James Albert Ukawsaw, 9, 39–40, 49, 57

Gullah communities, 46–47, 75

Gullah Jack (Jack Pritchard), 75

Gullah Joe, 41

Gullah Society, 75

Haitian Revolution, 68

Halifax, Nova Scotia, 80, 86, 95, 144

Hall, Prince, 2, 11, 12, 120, 126–27, 133–36, 139; and abolitionism, 122; Marrant at residence of, 123–24

Harpers Ferry raid (Virginia), 138

Hart, Oliver, 37–38

Hastings, Selina (Countess of Huntingdon), 1, 10–11, 70, 78–80, 124, 162n15

Hayden, Esther Harvey, 137

Hayden, Harriet, 138–39

Hayden, Lewis, 12, 120, 137–39

Haynes, Lemuel, 151n2

healing, 106–7, 116–18

herbs, protective, 10, 45, 62, 69

hidden transcripts, 6; in Marrant's texts, 4–5

High John the Conqueror, 83–84

Hinds, Patrick, 71

Hodges, Graham Russell, 27

Holden, Vanessa, 158n9

Holmes, Barbara, 58–59

Horton, James, 171n67

Horton, Lois, 171n67

Huntingdon Connexion, 1, 4, 11, 62, 70–71, 78–79; and Arminian rivalry, 99–102; in Nova Scotia, 93, 133, 149; in Sierra Leone, 144, 174n23

Hurston, Zora Neale, 37, 61–62

Black worship, 91–92; poverty, famine, and plague in, 103–14; Preston community, 86, 144; Ragged Island, 104; schools in, 107, 166n93; self-emancipated Blacks in, 79–80; Shelburne, 86, 87, 91; smallpox outbreaks, 88, 108, 109–11, 115, 133. See also Black Loyalists

Nummo (twin spirits, Dogon cosmology), 133

oath-swearing rituals, 73–75, 160n33
objects, religious: at burial sites, 16; powders, 27; Sankofa bird, 16
Oglethorpe, James, 32
omusango ceremony, 68
oral cultures, Africana: historical memory preserved by, 7; and Neau's Sabbath school, 22; print culture linked with, 136–37; storytelling as didactic tool, 5–7. See also Africana religious cultures
oration, Masonic, 11–12, 120, 140; grand tradition of, 127–33; as ritual of race, 128. See also *Appeal to the Colored Citizens of the World* (Walker); *Charges* (Hall); *Sermon Preached on the 24th Day of June 1789, A* (Marrant)

Parr, John, 100
Peggy (ship), 80, 83, 88
Pentecost, 18
Perkins, Cato, 144, 147–48
Petersen, Lucas (enslaved man), 30
Peter the Doctor, 16
petitions for freedom, 24
Pharisees, biblical story of, 100, 102, 103
pharmakon, variants of, 7–8
physical impression, 47–54
Piercy, William, 71–72
Pinkster celebrations (New York), 9, 15, 18–20, 127; display of oratorical gifts, 53–54; Pinkster King, 18; replaced by Freemasonry, 125–26
plague, and blood imagery, 63–64, 66, 110
plantations: Jenkins plantation (Combahee, South Carolina), 1, 10, 64–65; maroon raids on, 31; Native Americans raids on, 3, 51–52
Pocahontas, 51
poison, 75
Poro societies, 42, 46–47, 48, 126
Portugal, 17, 20, 24
pottery, in Dogon cosmology, 130, 132–33
poverty, famine, and plague, in Nova Scotia, 103–14; abandoned woman's story, 104–7; communal responses to, 106–7; famine, 108–9; harsh weather, 105, 107–11; illness as manifestation of spiritual forces, 117; makeshift housing, 110–11; smallpox outbreaks, 88, 108, 109–11, 115, 133
Powhatan, Chief, 51
press gangs, British Navy, 2, 3, 76–78
Preston community (Halifax area, Nova Scotia), 86, 144

print, public function of, 136–37
Pritchard, Jack (Gullah Jack), 75
prophetic authority: Marrant's establishment of, 9–10, 19, 38–43, 52–54, 66, 80–83, 88–89, 93, 96, 98, 100, 112, 119, 141, 149
prophetic identity, 52, 160n31; in biblical narratives, 22, 38–41, 49, 52–54, 59, 81; blood symbolism, 62–63; concealed, 55–56; and family rejection, 39–40, 57; and oral symbolism, 53–54; and seclusion in wilderness, 39–41
Protestantism: American, 6; "Arminians," 78, 99–102, 165n62; Calvinism, 11, 78, 140, 165n62; dissenters, 78; Dutch, 17–18; Great Awakening, 121, 168n5; theological innovation, 78. See also Huntingdon Connexion; Methodism

quilombo communities (Brazil), 24, 31
quitrents, 146–48

Raboteau, Albert, 1, 151n1
racism, 5, 31, 87, 103, 128–29, 132, 135
recognition, biblical trope of, 55–57
reintegration, 54–58
resistance: ethnically diverse alliances, 24–25; and Manhattan land grant, 24; New York Conspiracy of 1741, 27–29, 31; New York rebellion of 1712, 26–27, 73–74; petitions for freedom, 24; *quilombo* communities (Brazil), 24, 31; runaway attempts, interethnic, 24–25; Southampton, Virginia, rebellion (1831), 66; Stono rebellion (1739), 28, 31–32; Vesey conspiracy of 1822, 74–75, 160n31. See also Exodus story
resurrection theme, 42, 52–58, 118
retaliation, 10–11, 61–84; conjure as agent of divine, 62; divine, for slavery, 62; in Douglass's narrative, 69–70; Exodus narrative as pattern for, 62, 70–71; in Genesis narratives, 72; in High John the Conqueror narratives, 83–84; linked with emotional injury, 70; and oath-swearing rituals, 73–75; as sanctioned by God, 62, 65, 70, 80; for slavery, biblically justified, 4, 71–72; standard narrative structure, 70; in Turner's narrative, 10, 62, 66–68; wilderness symbols in narratives, 10
revivalism, 2, 78–79; in Black Loyalist settlements, 87; Great Awakening, 121, 168n5
Rhode Island, 168n6
rituals of race, 7–8, 128–29
Rockaway Indians, 26
Rodrigues, Jan, 26
Rowe, John, 125

Sabbath schools, 22–23
Saillant, John, 3, 4, 139, 140
sailors, 23, 76; Black, 33–34, 121, 161n57; Black captains on Sierra Leone Company ships, 145–46
Saint John the Baptist celebration, 2, 11, 120, 127–28, 133, 134

salvation, 22, 58, 67, 68, 88–89; in High John narratives, 84; intergenerational, 115–18

Sambo (enslaved man, North Carolina), 75

Sande societies, 42, 46–47

Savannah, Georgia, 1, 9, 14–15, 32–34; Margrett in, 71; Yamarcraw neighborhood, 9, 15, 33–34

scarification and circumcision, 48

Schama, Simon, 167n106, 174n16

Scorpion (British sloop), 76–77, 83, 98

Scott, Mary, 115, 116

sea, allegories of, 76–77, 80

Sea Islands, 90–91, 94

seamen, Black, 15, 76, 81–82

seeking rituals, 38, 41–42

Senegambia, 90

Sermon Preached on the 24th Day of June 1789, A (Marrant), 2, 127–29, 168n1; biblical genealogies in, 11, 120, 129, 138–39; cosmos explained in, 130, 133, 141; egalitarian principles extolled in, 129; foundation of "anciency" in, 139; Genesis creation myth in, 129–33; *pharmakon* variants in, 7–8; racial ethnogenesis in, 11, 120. *See also* African Lodge of Free and Accepted Masons (Boston); Freemasonry, African American

Sesay, Chernoh, 169n11, 212

Seven Years' War, 168n9

Shamala, Lucas Nandih, 68

Sharpe, John, 23, 27

Shelburne, Nova Scotia, 86, 87, 91; emigrants to Sierra Leone, 145

shout ritual, 37, 88–92; African Islamic origins, 90–91; *sha'wt* (Arabic word), 90

Sidbury, James, 160n31

Sierra Leone, 48, 90; Black emigration to Freetown, 143–49, 173nn10, 14; Black political leadership in, 146–47; collective decisionmaking about emigration, 144; and family ties, 145; female voting in, 173n16; New Light meetinghouse, 147–48; quitrents, 146–48; self-governing legislature proposal, 147–48; Temne people, 173n14; "tithingmen" and "hundredors," 147–48; white opposition to emigration, 145

Sierra Leone Company, 143–48, 173nn10, 14, 174n23; Black captains, 145–46; independence from declared, 148

Silver Bluff Baptist (South Carolina), 1

simbi (nature spirits), 43, 82; and baptism, 97–98; establishment of in new places, 97–98, 112–13, 165n56

Simon ("Brer Rabbit in Red Hill Churchyard"), 89

sisters, 56–57, 63–64

slave narratives, 5–6, 9–10; of Douglass, 10, 62, 69–70, 153n4; of Equiano, 9, 48–49, 57, 82, 157n42, 161n57; of Gronniosaw, 9, 39–40, 49, 57

slavery. *See* enslavement/slavery

Smith, John, 51

Smith, Theophus, 4, 7

Society for the Propagation of the Gospel in Foreign Parts (SPG), 21–23, 27, 144

Society of Friends (Quakers), 20

Songhai of Upper Volta, 89

Southampton, Virginia rebellion (1831), 66

South Carolina, 1–2, 30, 32–33; Africana religious cultures in, 2, 9, 44–47, 94; concentration of ethnic Africans in, 90; Jenkins plantation, 1, 10, 64–65; poisoning legislation, 75. *See also* low country, Georgia and South Carolina

space, and cosmological narratives, 172n88

Spa Fields Chapel (Bath, England), 3

Spain, 9, 17, 24, 28, 30–31

"Spanish Negroes," in New York, 28–29, 31

Speain, Cato, 127

spirit possession, 37

spirituality: in Black oral traditions, 5

spiritual parents/leaders, 46–47, 54

spiritual transformation, as community event, 107

St. Augustine, Florida, 2; Afro-Catholic communities, 9, 15; Fort Mose settlement, 9, 15, 31, 32; oldest European city in North America, 14, 30

Stephens, Thomas, 32

Stillman, Rev. Dr., 119

Stono rebellion (1739), 28, 31–32

storytelling, African, 5–7

Stuckey, Sterling, 20, 89, 91

Summers, Martin, 172n81

supranational citizenship, 135

Suriname, 89

surveillance, 25, 91, 135

taverns, colonial, 25–26, 30

Taylor, Mrs. William, 108

Taylor, William, 108

Tertullian, 134

Thompson, Robert Farris, 114

tongues, speaking in, 19, 53–54, 87

Trevecca College (Wales), 71, 78, 88

Tucker, St. George, 135, 171

Turner, Nat, 10, 62; *The Confessions of Nat Turner*, 66–68, 158n9

Tybee Island, Georgia, 33

Underground Railroad, 138

urban centers: Africana religious cultures in, 15, 19; colonial Americas, 13–15; Spain and Portugal, 20

Vesey, Denmark, 74–75, 136, 160n31

Viets, Roger, 96

violin, in Africana religious traditions, 19, 89

Virginia, 33

Wale, 126

Walker, Corey, 125, 128–29, 135, 171n71

Walker, David, 12, 120, 136–37

Walker, James St. G., 161n48

Walker, Quok, 122

Wallace, Maurice, 131

Walter, William, 164n44

water: in Africana cosmologies, 81–82, 94; and baptism, 77, 94, 96–99, 164n43; as connection with ancestors, 81, 96–98; and Moses in Exodus, 81–83; natural bodies of used for baptism, 97–98; *n'langu, m'bu,* or *kalunga,* 96; rebirth and reemergence signaled by, 98; transformed to blood by Moses, 63, 65

Webster, Delia, 137–38

Wells-Oghoghomeh, Alexis, 72–73, 117

Wesley, Charles, 121

Wesley, John, 79, 101–2, 121, 123

West and West Central African religion and culture, 2–3, 5; brotherhood traditions, 20; Bundu societies, 126; burial practices in New York associated with, 16; creation myths, 130; disguised by biblical storytelling, 6; Dogon cosmology, 130, 132–33; expiatory sacrifices in, 67–68; granary, celestial, 130; initiation rites, 9; Kongo region, 42–43, 114; Mbundu region, 114; oath-swearing rituals, 74–75, 160n33; oral legacies of, 5; Poro and Sande societies, 42, 46–47, 48, 126; ritual death in initiatory rites, 47–48; Yoruba religious practices, 67. *See also* Africana religious cultures; conjure

West Indies, enslaved people imported from, 33

Wheatley, Phillis, 10, 124, 170–71n56

Whitchurch, Samuel, 151n2

Whitefield, George, 2, 11, 14, 49, 78, 121, 123, 150; and Bethesda Orphanage, 70–71

white Loyalists, 91

Whiting, Gloria McCahon, 169n11

wilderness, 36, 38, 40–43; and baptism, 97–98; in biblical narratives, 1, 5, 10, 38, 41, 43, 46, 62–63, 66, 112; death and resurrection narrative, 42; Douglass in, 69; forest as setting for teaching adolescents about natural world, 43–44; forty signifies ritual aspects of initiation, 38, 43; Kimpasi associations, 42, 66, 113; Marrant's bear encounter, 111–13; retaliation signified by, 62; sacred dimensions of physical landscape, 41; spiritual potency associated with, 47; Turner's consecration in, 66; in West and West Central African cultures, 36, 38, 40–47. *See also* initiation

Wilkerson, David, 11

Wilkinson, Moses, 87, 90, 99, 101, 144

witchcraft, European associations of conjure with, 4, 10

women, Black: autonomy in market settings, 15, 34; as cultural and linguistic liaisons, 72–73; sexual exploitation of, 30, 72–73, 104

women, Cherokee, 51

Yamarcraw neighborhood (Savannah), 9, 15, 33–34

Young, Jason, 107, 164n43

zo (spiritual leaders), 46–47

Zurara, Gomes Eanes de, 117